A Transport Strategy for London

The second in a series about Government action in London

London: HMSO

Contents

Part One: Defining the Strategy

Chapter 1: Introduction

The Transport Strategy for London: Background

1.1 In 1995 the London Pride Partnership published *'London's Action Programme for Transport: 1995-2010'*. This strategy has been developed as a response to that report. The Government agrees with the business community and local government that it is now appropriate to publish a transport strategy for London. We believe London has great transport strengths, and that it is important to communicate this message effectively, because the perception of a city's transport system is an important factor in determining whether or not internationally mobile businesses will choose to locate there. The strategy recognises that there are some tensions in attempting to reconcile all our environmental and economic goals, but it emphasises the need for greater account to be taken of environmental impacts in future transport decisions.

1.2 We want to set out what is already being done to improve London's transport systems and what is planned for the future. It would obviously help the boroughs, the transport operators and the business community at large to plan ahead if Government could dispel the uncertainties which exist about new road and railways; about likely future arrangements for the provision of bus and underground services; and about how the Government aims to balance the conflicts between economic and environmental goals. For reasons which are set out in paragraphs 1.18 - 1.20 below, we do not believe it is either possible or desirable for the Government to produce a fixed investment or legislative timetable for London. Nevertheless, we can set out the broad changes to transport in London we expect to see in the decade ahead and to indicate, where possible, an approximate timescale.

1.3 Much has changed since our publication of *Transport in London* in 1989. Changes include:

- significant public transport improvements, due to a combination of major investment funded by the Government; efficiency drives by operators; and a decline in commuter traffic;

- increased concern about environmental problems in general, and air pollution problems in particular; and recognition that these problems can have a material impact on the competitiveness of London;

- rapid growth of London's economy during the 1980s and rapid shrinkage during the early 1990s, raising questions about the robustness of the Capital's economy;

- intense pressures on public expenditure have made the Government look closely at its transport budget, which in 1996/97 will be £4.2 billion (£4.0 billion at 1994/95 prices), compared with £4.7 billion (£5.4 billion at 1994/95 prices) in 1990/91;

- the Private Finance Initiative has created opportunities for involving private sector finance and project management skills in public sector projects.

There have also been relevant developments in national policies, which need to be reflected in our transport strategy;

- the publication since 1990 of the Environment White Papers and in 1994 of the UK's Sustainable Development Strategy, which stresses the need to reconcile economic, environmental and social objectives;

- the publication since 1994 of the Competitiveness White Papers, with their emphasis on promoting sustained economic growth and higher living standards;

- the Secretary of State for Transport has recently been reviewing national transport policy following responses to the consultative document *'Transport: the Way Ahead'*. The response to this consultation exercise is contained in the Green Paper *'Transport: The Way Forward'*

In the light of such changes, we have had to review our transport plans for London, to ensure that they are addressing the right problems in the right manner, that they make the best use of scarce public funds and that they maximise the potential for harnessing private finance.

1.4 The debate we conducted on transport policy which has led to the publication of the Transport Green Paper centred on an increasing level of concern about the impacts of transport on the environment and how far forecast traffic growth is sustainable. In response we believe that there needs to be a greater emphasis on the environment, more emphasis on public transport and reduced dependence on the car, and on measures to reduce congestion without relying on road improvements. The Green Paper sets out an agenda for action, including proposals for further action at the national level in more than 20 specific areas of policy. Our view is that, without additional measures, currently forecast levels of traffic growth at a national level will not be sustainable indefinitely.

The aim, therefore, is to promote solutions which can reconcile our policy goals; we believe that a strong economy and a healthy environment will complement one another. This point is fundamental to the future success of London as a world class city.

1.5 This strategy aims to take forward and build on the challenges set by the Green Paper. London already has a good story to tell. It has one of the most extensive public transport systems in the world. Car usage and, therefore, per capita emissions from transport, are significantly less than in most other parts of the country. Planned infrastructure improvements reflect the continued importance of public transport as well as tackling congestion black spots. Strategies for cycling and walking will increase the attractiveness of these most environmentally-friendly modes. And the separate but complementary Strategic Guidance for London Planning Authorities will help to integrate land use and transport objectives so as to reduce dependence on the car.

1.6 We recognise that reconciling some of our environmental and economic objectives will not be easy. We also attach considerable weight to the freedoms which car ownership brings and the value of good quality transport to business. Some will feel that the strategy could go further, but as with the Green Paper this is not a prescription for all time. The strategy will continue to evolve; what is important now is that it should have a purpose and direction which meets the needs of this and future generations.

1.7 There have been repeated demands for a closer integration of London's transport systems and for the creation of a strategic transport authority for the Capital. We regard the former demand as a valid one, and have endeavoured to set out in this strategy document how we propose to ensure that it is delivered in practice. However, we believe that the creation of a strategic authority would be more likely to confuse and blur responsibilities than to deliver a better co-ordinated or better funded transport system for London. Hence, this strategy document aims to explain the Government's reasons for believing that a strategic planning authority for London is neither necessary nor desirable.

The Aim of the Transport Strategy for London

1.8 We have developed our transport strategy within the policy context referred to above, in particular bearing in mind the sustainable development strategy, the competitiveness White Papers and the transport Green Paper. These documents indicated

- the need to strike the right balance between the ability of transport to serve economic development and the ability of the environment to sustain future quality of life;

- the need for increased attention to the environmental impacts of transport; and

- that a high quality, efficient transport system is an important factor in determining regional competitiveness.

1.9 Bringing these principles together in the London context, we are seeking to enhance the competitiveness of London as a World City, to foster regeneration, to improve the environment, and to promote safety, mobility and freedom of choice. How these principles apply in practice to London's particular circumstances is highly complex. On both the economic and environmental fronts, the Capital has different strengths and weaknesses, and faces different opportunities and threats compared with other areas of the country. **Part One** of this strategy document endeavours to set transport issues in their London context. **Part Two** outlines the policies and initiatives that are proposed or in hand to implement our strategy. The rest of this chapter outlines both the key issues and the order in which this document addresses them.

1.10 **Chapter 2** looks at how the economy and demography of London have changed in the past and offers a view on how they might be expected to change over the next decade. Because forecasts based on extrapolations from past trends have become an increasingly unreliable guide to future developments, this chapter tries to probe beneath the statistics and consider both the structure of the London economy and the factors that govern the locational decisions of businesses and individuals. This is difficult territory, where subjective judgement can often be as important as objective fact. For example, most forecasters believe that 'quality of life' issues will be given increasing weight in business location decisions. However, 'quality of life' covers a host of issues, from crime and education (which are amenable to statistical analysis) through to friendliness and cuisine (which are not) - making it difficult to take a view on how such issues might combine to affect London's longer-term prosperity.

1.11 **Chapter 2** concludes that the most prudent assumptions that one can make about London are a healthy growth in output, coupled with modest growth in employment and population. It also concludes that, in relation to employment in the central business districts, there is a risk that London might experience an exodus of employment which could be damaging to both London and the nation. Minimising that risk is a key objective of the Government's transport strategy for London. That implies a need to concentrate particularly on the way in which transport can promote the competitiveness of London.

1.12 This issue is addressed in **Chapter 3**. In promoting London as a World City, the quality of the international transport links and of the public transport links to the central business districts are of vital importance. However, competitiveness also depends upon the pursuit of sound macroeconomic and environmental policies. Internationally mobile businesses are not going to locate in London if they believe that they will thereby expose themselves to steep and rising levels of inflation, interest rates and taxation; or expose their staff to unacceptable levels of air pollution. So, in promoting high-quality transport systems, we must also have regard to the economic and environmental costs. We must identify priorities in our transport investment programme; try to understand more clearly how different types of improvement to the transport system affect the competitive position of London; and ensure we are applying scarce financial resources to the projects which will most enhance the Capital's competitive position. Chapter 3 explores these issues more fully. It concludes that, whilst there is scope for further refinement, the existing cost;benefit analysis methodology gives a good measure of competitiveness benefit.

1.13 **Chapter 4** turns to the link between transport and regeneration. Since there are pockets of London which suffer from acute deprivation, it is vital that transport policies take regeneration issues properly into account. That has been done in framing this transport strategy. It is important that it continue to be done when new investment proposals come forward. **Chapter 4** makes proposals on how that goal should be delivered.

1.14 **Chapter 5** deals with the impact of transport on the environment. It identifies two broad categories of issue. First, there is the impact which transport has on London's own environment, particularly in relation to air pollution, noise and land-take. Second, there is the impact which transport has on global issues such as climatic change. There is a growing recognition that measures to improve air quality can be helpful for both economic and environmental goals, by making London a more attractive place in which to live and work. Nonetheless, there remains some conflict between environmental and other goals and these issues lie at the heart of the transport debate that the Government has sought to stimulate over the past year. The tension between economic and environmental concerns is perhaps most acute in the context of broader issues such as global-warming.

1.15 Considerations of safety, personal mobility and freedom of choice are touched on in **Chapter 6**. The last of these issues is probably the most difficult of the three. Although there are a few cases where the promotion of safety and mobility may come into conflict with the achievement of economic and environmental goals, they are very much the exception to the rule.

1.16 **Chapter 7** draws together the strands dealt with in the previous chapters and sets out the objectives which this transport strategy is intended to achieve.

Contribution of land use planning to transport objectives

1.17 This strategy does not look in depth at the contribution of the planning system to further transport objectives. These issues are dealt with in *Strategic Guidance for London Planning Authorities,* which encourages local authorities to develop land use patterns which reduce the overall need to travel, and promote the use of public transport, walking, and cycling as alternatives to the private car. Strategic Guidance also considers the part local authorities have to play in developing London's transport infrastructure, in partnership with operators and other agencies. The two documents are therefore complementary. The implementation of this transport strategy, which sets out the Government's priorities for transport in London, and the application of planning guidance, which is aimed at local authorities as they review and put into practice their Unitary Development Plans, need to be taken forward in tandem.

Flexibility and Certainty

1.18 In framing a transport strategy for London, it is necessary to strike a careful balance between two conflicting pressures. On the one hand, the strategy must give a clear enough description of the

Government's future intentions to allow businesses and local authorities to plan with a reasonable degree of confidence. Indeed, this is one of the main reasons for publishing this strategy document. On the other hand, history is littered with transport plans that have been over-prescriptive and over-detailed, with the result that they have been overtaken by events.

1.19 The difficulty of forecasting future trends for London (see Chapter 2) is particularly relevant here. We believe that a modest growth scenario is the most prudent assumption for transport planning purposes. We identify a risk that the economy of London in general, and of the central business districts in particular, might perform significantly worse than that. We have accorded the promotion of London's competitiveness the highest priority in framing this transport strategy. We must then plan on the assumption that our policies will be successful in stimulating economic growth and, hence, an upturn in transport demand which will need to be dealt with. We have also to reckon with the possibility that London's economy could surprise forecasters, as it did in the mid-1980s, by rallying very suddenly. It is, therefore, essential to recognise from the outset that the emphasis of the strategy may need to change over time for practical reasons, to take account of developments or changes in London. For example, some of the major rail projects were originally conceived in the 1980s as solutions to congestion problems at termini and on some hard-pressed sections of the Underground system. This motive for building them is no longer as strong, though other factors may make them still worth pursuing; and, if the economy (and hence transport demand) took a further turn upwards, congestion relief could then be a major issue once again, on both competitiveness and safety grounds. Similarly, on the roads side, Chapter 11 explains that congestion charging is not seen as a practical proposal at present; but we recognise that it could be a part of transport plans in the longer term.

1.20 There are other reasons why it is undesirable to promise too much and in too much detail. Governments have always been wary of entering into future expenditure commitments, because economic circumstances can change. Plans that seemed affordable when they were promulgated can become a serious burden on public expenditure, crowding out other investments which might deserve a higher priority, but which were not subject to the same prior commitment. For similar reasons, Governments do not commit themselves to introduce legislation in a specific Session of Parliament ahead of the Queen's Speech for that Session. And even when the Government does introduce Bills and when operators do seek powers to build new infrastructure, it does not follow automatically that the Bills will be enacted or the powers granted. Also, as we explain later, our strategy depends on other agencies to deliver many elements. These include local authorities, who are responsible for local transport plans and integrating them with land use plans, and are taking a keen interest in promoting sustainability through initiatives such as Agenda 21, and public transport operators who are responsible for meeting the needs of their passengers. Last but not least, a strategy needs to remain flexible because there are limits to the extent to which a democratic Government could or should bind its successors.

An Integrated Strategy

1.21 Few issues have generated more heat and less light than the debate about the need for an integrated transport strategy for London. The main problem is that different people mean different things by 'integration'. In the Government's view, the principal test of whether or not a transport system is properly integrated is its ability to meet the needs of users.

1.22 For example, users of public transport are not concerned about where responsibility for the provision of bus, rail or underground services rests. What matters to them is that the different services should connect with one another, that there should be proper interchange facilities and that reliable information about the best means of getting from A to B should be readily available. Equally, few road-users in London will know or care who is responsible for the provision of direction signs or the operation of traffic lights. They do, however, demand traffic signals whose timings are properly co-ordinated and direction signs that get them to their destinations, rather than petering out on moving from a trunk road to a local road.

1.23 Judged against such practical criteria, London's past performance has been patchy. For example, weaknesses in co-ordination have included inconsistent signing of routes between trunk and other roads and lack of cycle facilities at stations; and the relatively difficult access by public transport to London City Airport. Successes have included flexible ticketing arrangements across London and across modes; the balanced development of transport in the Docklands area; and good integration of services at specific sites such as Canning Town station. A key aim of this strategy is to secure better integration of transport provision.

1.24 The Government believes that integration has to be worked for by those who are directly responsible for transport services, rather than imposed from above. However, the Government believes that it can contribute to the process in three ways.

1.25 The first is by encouraging Boroughs to integrate land use and transport plans through co-operative working with other Boroughs and transport providers. Guidance to London authorities on their Transport Policy and Programme (TPP) submissions and on their Unitary Development Plans (UDPs) cover these issues.

1.26 The second is by fostering coordination between the different parties. This is an important task of Government, explored more fully in Chapter 15.

1.27 The third is by example. One of the obstacles to integration is the tendency to take a compartmentalised view of transport responsibilities. We have sought to counter that tendency by setting out clearly what the economic and environmental goals for the Capital are and how the different modes can contribute to their achievement.

Chapter 2: The Economic and Demographic Backdrop

Introduction

2.1 A transport strategy must take account of the transport movements it may have to accommodate, or may wish to promote. To identify these, this chapter looks at historical trends for relevant factors (population, households, employment and output), and notes where simple extrapolation of these trends may not be helpful. It attempts to look behind the figures at the way London's economy works, and at the factors which influence the location decisions of businesses and individuals. It then offers a view of how London's population and economy might change over the next ten years, and the implications of such changes for transport demand.

The Historic Trends: Population and Employment

2.2 Chart 2A shows the way in which London's population has changed since 1901 and how the number of people working in London has changed since 1951.

2.3 The long term trend has been for London to lose population to the rest of the South East, from the Second World War until the early 1980s. London's population started growing again in 1983. Growth between 1983 and 1994 was 3%, while the population of inner London grew by 4%. The latest Office for National Statistics (ONS) projections suggest further population growth between 1994 and 2011, particularly in inner London, which could see a further 10% rise. But we recognise the uncertainty of this figure, and do not rule out the possibility of a return to, or a move towards, the longer term downward trend.

2.4 The number of households in London has increased at a faster rate than population, from 2.64 million households in 1981 to 2.93 million in 1994. Over that period, the average size of a London household has fallen from 2.40 to 2.21 persons in inner London and from 2.63 to 2.43 in outer London (see table 2B). On the basis of this trend, and the population increases forecast above, the Department of the Environment suggests that the number of households in London could increase by 15% between 1994 and 2011, with inner London facing a 18% increase.

TABLE 2B: Average number of persons per household

	Inner London	Outer London
1981	2.40	2.63
1991	2.26	2.48
1994	2.21	2.43
Percentage change		
1981-91	-6	-6
1991-94	-2	-2

Source: Office for National Statistics

2.5 This is important, because household numbers are a key determinant of the total amount of personal travel and of the levels of car ownership and use. They have, in the past, proved valuable in projecting transport demand. Nevertheless, there are a number of reasons for treating these estimates with caution. First, they derive in part from the population projections, about which we are uncertain; and notably, they make the implicit assumption that the availability of dwellings will

Chart 2A: Population and employment in London 1901-1991

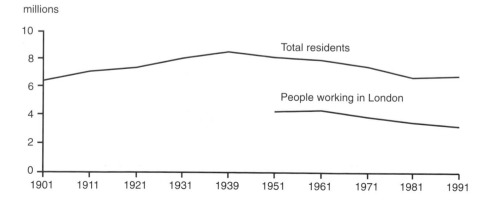

Source: Office for National Statistics

Notes: Population data are Census population present 1901-1951, and mid-year population estimates from 1961 onwards
Employment figures are estimates prepared by the GLC (1951/61) and Census of employment data from 1971

have no greater restraining effect on the formation of new households or on migration than it has done in the recent past. Since the projections imply an acceleration in the growth of households, this assumption must be subject to some doubt. The London Research Centre (LRC) has produced forecasts of households which take account of the expected availability of dwellings in 2001. Between 1994 and 2011 they forecast 7% growth in households London-wide, with 8% in inner London. However, the latest observed population growth has been stronger than the LRC projection would imply.

2.6 In the longer term, the employment trend has been similar to the population one, but employment in London has fluctuated considerably since the early 1980s. After falling until the early 1980s, total employment stabilised around 1982 and then increased by about 6% during the latter stage of the economic upturn of 1983-1988. Between 1988 and 1993, employment in London declined by 12%, roughly twice the national average. When the economy started recovering in 1994, employment in London began to increase again, but London has been slower to feel the effects of the recovery than many parts of the country.

2.7 Increased population and reduced number of jobs gives London a 1995 unemployment rate of 9.7% compared with a national average of 8.2%. Some inner London Boroughs have unemployment levels which are two or three times as high as the national rate. This reflects the fact that the inner and central areas have experienced higher population growth and

a steeper reduction in employment. Between 1987 and 1993, the number of employees in London fell by over 400,000. Inner and central London accounted for 70% of lost jobs, with the City and Westminster alone accounting for 40% of the total. There is Census evidence to suggest that the jobs that disappeared were, in general, those done by London residents, rather than non-residents.

2.8 Chart 2C compares the employment trend for London with that for the rest of the South East (ROSE). It shows that, throughout most of the period since 1981, ROSE has out-performed London in terms of generating and maintaining employment. There appears to a general pattern here of outward migration of employment from central and inner London through outer London and into ROSE.

2.9 The reduction in the number of payrolled employees may overstate the true level of job losses in London, because it was accompanied by a rapid growth in self-employment. The number of people working for themselves grew by 180,000 (65%) between 1981 and 1991 taking the share of the total number of people in work to 12%. Nevertheless, this increase was significantly smaller than the reduction in employment. Self-employment was 13% of the total in 1995.

2.10 Extrapolations of these trends would show a continuing decline in total levels of employment and a continuing migration of jobs out of central and inner London. Combining the employment and population

Chart 2C: Population and Employment in London and ROSE 1981-1994

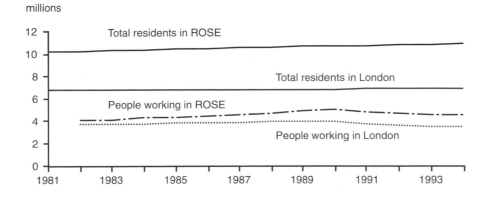

Source: Office for National Statistics

Notes: Data are June estimates

projections, this would imply a further steep rise in unemployment in the inner London boroughs. Apart from being highly undesirable, it also seems inherently implausible that people should continue to migrate into areas where the employment opportunities are so poor. So we would have some concerns about planning on the basis of such figures.

2.11 A number of organisations produce forecasts of employment levels in London. These are based on a combination of trend-extrapolation, modelling and the forecasters' judgement about the net impact of the sort of issues which have been discussed above. In view of the difficult and subjective judgements which are required, it is not surprising that their predictions span a very wide range. As Chart 2D shows, at least one

forecaster expects to see the number of jobs drift slowly downward over the next 20 years, whilst others foresee a resumption of modest growth.

2.12 Charts 2E and 2F analyse the sectoral composition of London's employment and output. The analysis needs to be treated with some caution, because the classification is determined by the activity of the organisation, rather than the activity of its London staff. For example, it has been estimated that about half the employment and output which is attributed to the manufacturing sectors relates to the presence of headquarters operations in London, rather than to manufacturing activity. Nevertheless, three trends emerge very clearly:

Chart 2D: Greater London employment 1981-2001

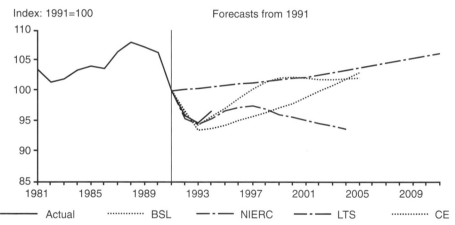

Source: Office for National Statistics

Forecasts for models by:

CE   Cambridge Econometrics
BSL   Business Strategies Limited
NIERC   Northern Ireland Economic Research Centre
LTS   London Transportation Studies

Table 2E: Output and employment structure of the London economy 1993

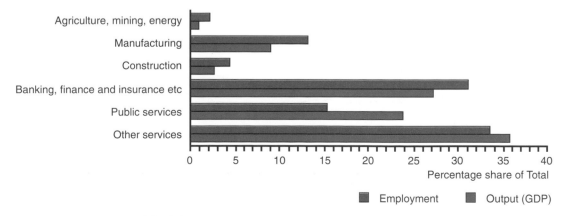

Source: Office for National Statistics

- The predominance of the service industries. These now account for 84% of jobs in London, compared with 73% of jobs across the UK as a whole.

- The extent to which employment growth in 1980s was delivered by the financial and business services sector. In this sector, employment increased by 182,000 between 1981 and 1991. In all other sectors combined, it declined by nearly 500,000.

- The rapid and accelerating decline in employment in manufacturing. This accounted for over half of London's jobs prior to World War II and for 20% in 1981. But it accounts for only 11% today, compared with just over 20% for the UK as a whole.

The Capital's prosperity is becoming steadily more dependent on the performance of a few key areas of its economy.

2.13 Chart 2G looks at the growth of GDP in London and ROSE between 1971 and 1993. Chart 2H looks at their share of UK GDP. The latter shows a long-term decline which was only partially arrested by the economic upturn of 1983-1988. Between 1971 and 1993, London's share of UK GDP declined from 16.6% to 14.9%, whilst ROSE's share increased from 18.6% to 20.6%. Even in the financial and business services sector, where London's greatest strength lies, the Capital's share of national output declined from 33% in 1971 to 26% in 1993.

Chart 2F: Change in sectorial composition of London's GDP 1982-93

£ millions (real prices: 1993 based)

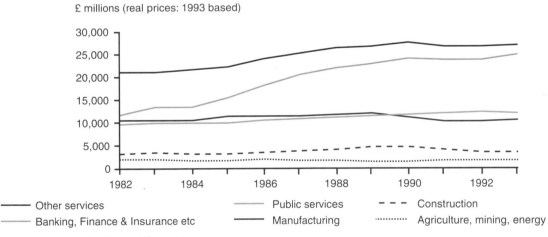

—— Other services
—— Banking, Finance & Insurance etc
Public services
Manufacturing
- - - Construction
·········· Agriculture, mining, energy

Source: Office for National Statistics

Chart 2G: London and ROSE GDP 1971-93

£ millions (real prices: 1993 based)

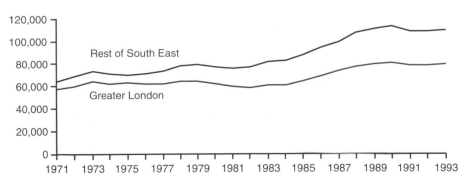

Source: Office for National Statistics

Summary of Trends/Forecasts

2.14 On balance the Government believes that, if market forces were left to their own devices, London would experience strong growth in output and modest growth in both employment and population.

2.15 However, this is subject to a high degree of uncertainty. The long term picture is one of decline in London's population, employment and share of UK GDP. On the output side, it appears that London's economy is volatile, growing more rapidly than the rest of the UK during the upturn of latter 1980s, but then declining more rapidly during the subsequent economic downturn. Productivity has increased rapidly in London, which means that growth in output has been accompanied by a decline in employment, which the rise in self-employment has not offset. There has been an outward migration of jobs and the job-losses have hit London residents harder than those who commute into London from ROSE. If these long-term trends in the labour market should continue it is difficult to avoid the conclusion that the upturn in population seen in the 1980s will prove short-lived.

The Structure of London's Economy

2.16 The economy of London is complex. To make sense of the linkages between transport and the economy of London, we put forward below a simplified picture which divides that economy into three broad categories of economic activity, each facing different issues in considering location decisions. These are as follows:

- central district business activities (eg corporate headquarters; stock, financial, commodity markets);

- other businesses which cater for regional, national or international markets (eg manufacturing and wholesaling); and,

- activities servicing resident population (eg shops, schools).

The rest of this chapter discusses the value of each category to London, and the extent to which transport might affect the location decisions of each category.

Central Business Activities

2.17 These activities generally cluster in the central business districts of major cities. They include the corporate headquarters functions of public and voluntary sector organisations and of national and international corporations, as well as the stock, financial, commodity and insurance markets. In London, they have traditionally been located in the City and West End, but are increasingly to be found also in Docklands and in the A4/M4 corridor. Their presence attracts suppliers of a wide range of other services, such as accountancy, merchant banking and legal advice, publicity and marketing, catering and security. Similarly, the ready availability of such support services attracts corporate organisations and internationally mobile financial services businesses. This mutually reinforcing effect is described by economists as the 'agglomeration benefit' and it is an important factor in the location decisions of the businesses concerned.

2.18 The fact that London and other major cities have continued to attract such activities, despite the high cost of doing business there, is evidence that the 'agglomeration effect is a powerful force. According to

Chart 2H: Contribution to UK GDP of London and ROSE 1971-93

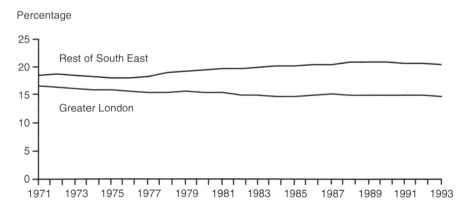

Source: Office for National Statistics

the London and South East Region (LASER) model, which has been developed to model the relationship between transport and land-use in London (discussed further in Chapter 10), the present concentration of employment in the central areas could indicate that the agglomeration benefit is equivalent to a reduction of about a quarter in the rental and travel costs of doing business there.

Businesses not tied to central areas

2.19 Businesses which have no particular connection with the central business districts include most manufacturing, warehousing, wholesaling and the operation of national or regional distribution centres, and many activities in the new information technology industries. Their location decisions are driven by considerations of cost and of access to labour, suppliers and customers. They may be influenced, to an extent, by the desire to cluster together to exchange ideas and to take advantage of pools of skilled labour. Such considerations are regarded as important in the fashion, media and IT sectors, for example. However, they have no particular need to locate close to the corporate headquarters or other functions which are found in the central business districts.

2.20 Paragraph 2.12 above demonstrated London's difficulties attracting and retaining such business, and its increasing dependence on a narrow segment of its economy. We would like to alter this trend to make London's position less vulnerable. In particular, the Government supports the London Manufacturing Initiative. The precise role that transport needs to play in meeting the objectives of this initiative cannot be determined centrally. As our discussions on manufacturing with local authorities and business have clearly shown, there is some debate on which types of manufacturing are suitable for different areas of London. Environmental concerns will play a large part in deciding this. We believe that local authorities, through their transport and planning functions, are well placed to form an accurate view of what activities will be acceptable where, when all the various strands, including the impact on transport networks, have been drawn together, considered and debated. This is particularly so in Outer London.

2.21 But there is a limit to what anyone can do to promote commercial activity. London's position at the hub of the nation's rail and trunk road networks and its rail, sea and air access to the principal markets of Europe are assets, but they are offset by cost. Property prices and rents are about one-third higher in London than in the rest of the UK. The gap between pay in London and the rest of the UK is widening: average earnings in London increased from 116% of the national figure in 1981 to 127% in 1991. This is partly because London has a higher and increasing proportion of workers in well-paid, high-value added jobs compared to the rest of the country, although earnings in London also tend to exceed those for similar jobs elsewhere in the country. And for the businesses referred to in paragraph 2.19, the agglomeration effect does not offer a counter-balance.

Service Provision

2.22 Third, there are activities which exist to meet the needs of the resident population. They include commercial businesses (such as shops, restaurants and banks), as well as public sector services (such as schools, hospitals and the police). Some of these organisations (particularly those in the retail sector) face difficult decisions about where to locate within London, but none of them faces a decision about whether to locate in London. The existence of a resident population, which generates the demand for their goods and services, requires them to have a London presence. London could not survive, let alone prosper, without the contribution made by such activities. However, the wealth upon which the existence of the Capital depends is ultimately created by activities within the first two categories.

Summary of scope to attract business to London

2.23 This analysis suggests that London's economic success over the next ten years is likely to turn primarily on its ability to attract and retain business in a few key areas of its economy. These are likely to be national and international businesses or others for whom the agglomeration effect satisfactorily balances out the higher costs associated with London. These are activities which are generally regarded as having strong growth potential, and are hence well worth attracting and retaining.

2.24 This should be made easier by the reversal of a long standing public policy of actively encouraging dispersal from London. As well as setting an example by relocating many of its own activities, the

Government previously promoted dispersal via the planning system and the work of the Location of Offices Bureau, by promoting new towns and by offering a variety of financial inducements. That policy no longer applies. In particular, planning guidance now requires local authorities to steer new developments towards existing settlements, where access by public by public transport is good, and to promote land use patterns which require less overall travel. This should benefit London as well as other established cities.

2.25 Other initiatives which bear upon the competitiveness of London are dealt with more fully in Chapter 3. They reflect a new recognition that London cannot allow unnecessary obstacles to get in the way of any business which wishes to locate there.

Risks to London's ability to attract business/jobs

2.26 We must recognise that there are risks, including the possible impact of information technology. This will probably raise productivity, reducing the number of jobs required in existing organisations. It may also reduce the advantage of operating from a single headquarters site and, importantly, may eliminate some of the benefits of agglomeration. As the quality of IT links improves, the need for face-to-face contact may reduce and with it, the case for physical co-location. Our discussions with business suggests that opinion on this varies from sector to sector and changes with experience. Face-to-face contact with clients is still regarded as important in most parts of the business services sector, and as vital in advertising and marketing, but in publishing, where face-to-face contact was recently seen as vital, contact via IT links is now regarded as a good substitute.

2.27 Some forecasters predict that 'quality of life' issues will exert an increasing influence on the location decisions of the most mobile businesses, such as the Henley Centre Report commissioned by London First Centre in 1994. This covers a diverse package of factors - everything from air quality, culture and sporting amenities to personal security. On many of the relevant counts, London scores very well. On a few, notably air quality, it scores less well. How far the 'quality of life' issues work to London's advantage or disadvantage will depend on the weight attached to the individual factors and on London's success in improving its performance in areas where it is held in relatively low regard.

2.28 There are also reasons for concern about the extent to which attracting business will serve to stem the further loss of London jobs. In particular:

- The size of corporate headquarters will be affected by the drive to raise productivity by 'delayering' and by the current trend towards more federal structures within national and international corporations. This in turn has an impact on the level of business services required by such headquarters teams. For example, Takeda, a Japanese pharmaceutical company, and Allnet, a US telephone service provider, have recently located their headquarters in London. Such operations typically employ a relatively small number of staff, but can be a first step towards establishing a larger operation.

- There is a well established pattern of seeking to relocate the more labour-intensive 'back-office' functions away from London. Examples include the relocation of claims-processing work by insurance companies during the 1970s and 1980s.

- Just as many businesses are becoming more internationally mobile, so are some of their key personnel. When a company in the financial or business services sector relocates into London, it will, typically, bring many of its existing staff with it, offering little net employment gain to London.

Location decisions of People

2.29 So far we have concentrated on the location decisions of businesses. However, the locational decisions of people are also important. In London, as in most European cities, the central area is regarded as an attractive area to live in, as well as to work in. Although the City is almost exclusively a business enclave, there are substantial residential populations, representing a mix of socio-economic groups, in Westminster and in the inner areas of Kensington & Chelsea, Camden, Islington, Tower Hamlets, Southwark and Lambeth. This is in contrast with some American cities, where the central areas are either deserted after nightfall or have become enclaves for the poorest members of the community.

2.30 London also has enormous attractions as a tourist destination. In part, this reflects its status as a Capital city and the quality of its international and UK transport links, but it also reflects the fact that London has a unique historical and architectural heritage. The decision to base the Millennium Exhibition in London will boost London further as a tourist destination.

The Implications for Transport in London

2.31 The above analysis has two main implications for transport in London and for this strategy.

2.32 First, it reinforces the Government's determination to tackle some of the downside risks identified above by promoting the competitiveness of London as a World City. This is discussed in Chapter 3.

2.33 Second, it permits us to draw up a base-case for transport demand, which will be employed for investment appraisal and modelling purposes and which informs the policies which are mapped out in Part Two of this strategy.

Transport Demand

2.34 London has a database on transport demand and travel patterns spanning the last 25 years. The most significant trends that emerge from this are:

- increasing car ownership and usage
- falling average road traffic speeds
- the declining mode share of public transport

2.35 Over the last two decades traffic levels have continued to grow in London in common with most other major cities. Between 1971 and 1992 the number of vehicles crossing the London boundary cordon each day grew by 64%. However, the growth in traffic levels shows significant variation across the Capital. All day radial traffic volumes crossing the Inner

London cordon grew by just 11% between 1972 and 1993 while volumes crossing the central London cordon changed very little over the same period.

2.36 A consequence of the increase in traffic volumes on London's roads has been a reduction in average speeds, as Chart 2I shows. Between 1968-70 and 1990-94 speeds in central London during the morning peak declined from an average of 12.7 miles per hour to just over 10 miles per hour. In the rest of inner London average speeds fell from 15.1 miles per hour to 13.3 miles per hour over the same period. The largest reduction was in outer London where the average speed fell by 3 miles per hour to 17.5 miles per hour in 1990/94. Off-peak and evening peak speeds displayed similar declines. However, since 1994 there is some evidence that speeds have begun to level out.

2.37 Car trips continue to dominate London's travel patterns. Chart 2J shows that between 1971 and 1991 the share of trips by mechanised modes undertaken by London residents by car in the capital increased by 10 percentage points to just under 70%. This growth has been at the expense of public transport. The modal share for BR train dropped back from 7% in 1971 to a 5% in 1981, but stabilised at that level in 1991. Underground modal share remained broadly constant between 1971 and 1991 at 9%. The modal share of bus trips by London residents exhibited a steady decline over the period from 23% in 1971 to 15% in 1991.

2.38 These long running changes are not the result of a steady trend nor have they applied to all parts of London. The last 10 years has witnessed rapid growth

Chart 2I: Traffic speeds in the morning peak period 1968 –1995

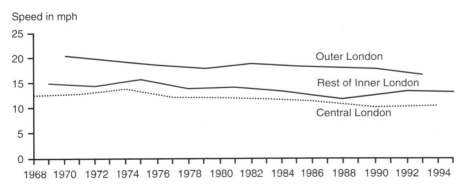

Source: Department of Transport

followed by rapid decline in commuting to central London - see Chart 2K. Over the period 1984 to 1994 the number of people entering central London in the morning peak for work and other purposes first increased from 1.06 million to just under 1.16 million in 1988, before falling to 989,000 in 1994. The proportion of people entering by public transport increased from 74% to 80% over the same period. The increase in travel by public transport into central London in the mid 1980s occurred during a period of significant growth in the London economy.

2.39 Chart 2L shows that in 1994 about three quarters of people working in central London used public transport to travel to work. The corresponding proportion was 45% in the rest of inner London and just 17% in outer London where there is less opportunity for travel by bus or rail services for many journeys than in other areas of London.

2.40 The dominant patterns of movement can be seen from Charts 2M and 2N. These show public transport trips and road vehicle trips for the morning peak period within and between the central, inner and outer areas. The radial nature of public transport movement contrasts with the more diffuse pattern of private and commercial vehicle trips.

2.41 The Department's strategic multi-modal transport model, known as 'LTS', is used to produce forecasts of the demand for transport in London into the next century. The main focus of the forecasts is the weekday morning peak period between 7.00 a.m. and 10.00 am when travel demand is at its highest, although forecasts for other times of day are also produced. Forecasts include vehicle kilometres and traffic speeds in different parts of London and public transport patronage for bus, rail and Underground, including DLR. Walk and cycle trips are not included in the model.

Chart 2J: Trends in modal trip share in London 1971-91

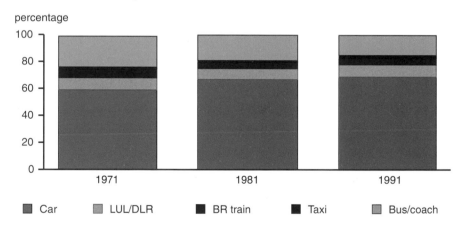

Source: Department of Transport

Chart 2K: People entering central London in the morning peak 1975 - 94

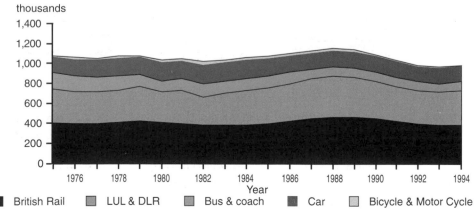

Source: London Transport

2.42 The key inputs which LTS uses to derive its forecasts are:

projections of employment, demographic trends and car ownership;

information about the expected future movements of motoring costs and public transport fares;

details of anticipated changes to the highway and public transport networks;

All these inputs are determined outside the model and so are not influenced by the forecasts of travel demand it produces. In other words, LTS forecasts transport demand for a predetermined, fixed pattern of land use.

2.43 Two scenarios involving different assumptions about the key inputs have been prepared to illustrate potential travel patterns and demand in 2011, as compared to 1991, the base year for the model. They clearly show the significance of the economic and demographic backdrop in determining transport demand, as well as the importance of the other, or 'supply side' factors.

2.44 The first scenario, called the 'base case', uses the assumptions about population and jobs which have been used in LTS since 1993. These allow for continued moderate growth in employment and population between 1991 and 2011 of 6% and 3% respectively. Because average household size is falling, the number of households increases at a faster rate than the population, by 7%. Road fuel prices reflect the Government's strategy of increasing fuel duties by at least 5% in real terms each year to reduce carbon emissions. The scenario has been prepared using the assumption that the strategy continues to the year 2000. Average public transport fares rise in line with economic growth, an annual 2.5%. The highway network and enhancement to it is broadly in line with that before 'Managing the trunk road programme' was published by the Department in November 1995. All major planned and proposed public transport schemes expected to be operational by 2011 are also included.

2.45 The transport forecasts from this scenario suggest traffic volumes in the morning peak period will be 20% higher by 2011 in inner and outer London, and about 10% higher in the central area. A corollary of the projected increases in traffic is a reduction in vehicle speeds. Central London fares worst, with speeds estimated to fall one-fifth below their 1991 levels. The reduction forecast for inner London is less marked, at around 5%, while in outer London little change is expected on average despite the increase in traffic volume. Speeds hold up better in inner and outer London due to the improvements in the highway network which are assumed to take place, offsetting the effects of higher volumes.

2.46 Despite the assumed real fare increases, rail patronage, in terms of people entering London in the morning peak is predicted to increase by more than one-quarter between 1991 and 2011. This is partly due to continued growth in central London employment and also reflects the major improvements to the rail network such as Crossrail, Thameslink 2000 and the Channel Tunnel Rail Link, which are all assumed to be operational by 2011. Underground patronage also increases, but by a more modest 5%. Use of buses for commuting to central London declines by nearly one-fifth.

Chart 2L: Main mode of travel to work in London 1994

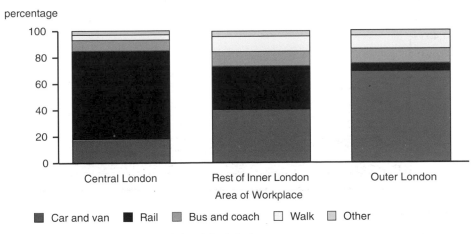

Source: Labour Force Survey (Office for National Statistics)

Chart 2M: Rail, Underground and bus passenger trips: morning peak period 07.00 - 10.00
London Area Transport Survey 1991

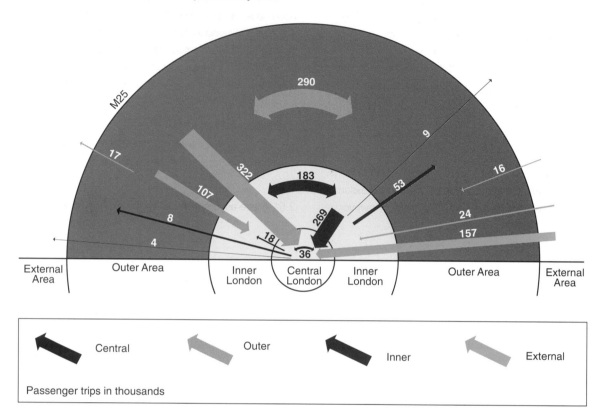

Passenger trips in thousands

Chart 2N: Vehicle trips: morning peak period 07.00 - 10.00
London Area Transport Survey 1991

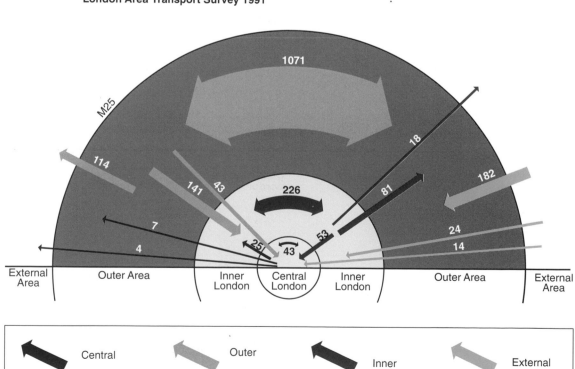

Vehicle trips in thousands (scheduled buses not included)

2.47 The alternative scenario developed is indicative of the 'downside' view of the potential performance of London's economy mentioned above. Another key feature is that it incorporates recent policy developments on regulating commuter rail fares in London. It has been labelled the 'low demand' scenario for the sake of convenience. The scenario takes a more pessimistic outlook on prospects for employment in London, with no net increase in the total number of jobs between 1991 and 2011, although within London, areas such as Docklands experience an increase in employment at the expense of other parts of the capital. Greater London's population is assumed to be virtually unchanged on 1991 levels. However, household size is still assumed to fall as in the base case scenario, resulting in a 4% increase in the number of households.

2.48 On the supply side, the 5% annual increase in fuel duties is assumed to be extended to 2011. And to represent the policy of regulating certain rail fares, including commuter fares in London, all public transport fares (rail, Underground and bus) are assumed to be held at their 1995 level in real terms to 2011. Improvements to the highway network are limited to only those schemes which were already committed as of December 1995 so a number of major proposals included in the base case scenario are omitted. A similar approach is adopted with the public transport network.

2.49 Despite the significant difference in public transport fares relative to motoring costs, the growth in rail commuting to central London in the morning peak between 1991 and 2011 is only one-half that in the base case, around 15%. This reflects the lower employment levels in central London and the absence of the major rail schemes mentioned in paragraph 2.44. However, Underground patronage increases more and bus patronage decreases less than in the base case scenario.

2.50 The effects of the two scenarios on public transport patronage are considered in more detail in Chapter 10, as are the car ownership assumptions used.

2.51 These assumptions halve the expected increases in traffic volumes expected in inner and outer London by comparison with the base case scenario. Traffic growth in central London is reduced by one-quarter. With the lower traffic growth, speeds are forecast to change very little in inner and outer London between 1991 and 2011, but central London still sees a fall of about 15%.

2.52 Table 2P sets out observed and forecast average annual growth rates for the number of vehicles crossing the Greater London boundary and the inner and central London traffic cordons in the morning peak period between 7.00 am and 10.00 am. Figures in the chart are not strictly comparable with those in paragraph 2.35 above, which are for all day traffic flows. This measure is used for comparison of actual and forecast traffic demand as time series data for observed vehicle miles are not available over a long period.

Table 2P: Average annual rates of traffic growth in London: observed and forecast, morning peak, early 1970s to 2011 (%)

	Greater London boundary	Inner London cordon	Central London cordon
Observed Early 1970s-1991[1]	2.2	0.5	0.6
Forecast 1991 - 2011[1]			
Base Case	0.9	0.9	0.7
Low demand	0.5	0.4	0.4

Note

[1] Periods differ due to data availability: Greater London boundary, 1971 to 1991; inner cordon 1972 to 1991; central cordon 1974 to 1991.

All vehicles, in and out bound

Source: Department of Transport

Chapter 3: Transport and Competitiveness

The Concept of Competitiveness

3.1 This chapter discusses the role of government in promoting the competitive position of London within the UK; the transport issues involved; the extent to which investment decisions take account of competitive benefits; and the extent to which the existing transport systems help London's competitive position.

3.2 In competition with other national economies, the UK's success or failure turns largely upon the performance of British businesses, and their ability to satisfy consumers on product quality, price, delivery and after-sales care. However, the Government also has a part to play by creating an environment which fosters competition within the domestic market and helps business compete successfully in international markets. There are delicate balances to be struck here - such as between the need to provide business with access to good infrastructure and to a well-educated workforce and the need to avoid adding unnecessarily to their costs by imposing an excessive tax burden. Such issues are explored more fully in the two White Papers - *Competitiveness: Helping Business Win* and *Competitiveness: Forging Ahead.*

3.3 Just as businesses and nations compete, there is a sense in which regions and cities within the UK are in competition with one another to attract businesses. In general, this not a form of competition which the Government is keen to encourage. There is the risk that it engenders wasteful and potentially counterproductive effort on the promotion of inward investment or, indeed, on encouraging businesses to relocate within the UK without regard to whether such relocation can be justified on regeneration grounds.

3.4 Promoting the competitive position of London as a World City is a partial exception to this rule, reflecting the fact that there are some activities for which London is either the only or much the most plausible UK location. In order to attract these businesses, we must continue to be able to offer a network of business services and must therefore defend the 'critical mass' of London's central business districts, as discussed in Chapter 2. This decision reflects the fact that the health of these key sectors is a matter of importance to the UK as a whole, and not just to London. The contribution of the City's financial services to UK invisible earnings is the principal case in point.

3.5 The same argument does not apply to other activities. So if less crucial businesses see commercial advantage in relocating into the rest of the South East or elsewhere in the UK, there is no good argument on competitiveness grounds for incurring public expenditure, either directly via grant or indirectly via investment in transport infrastructure, to encourage them to remain in London.

Transport and Competitiveness

3.6 In the context of promoting London's competitive position as a World City, we are concerned primarily with four issues: access to work in the central business districts; ease of movement within and between business districts; access to suppliers/customers in the UK and abroad; and transport's adverse impact on 'quality of life', the environment, and air pollution in particular. These are summarised below.

Cost and convenience of travel to work in the central business districts.

3.7 About 1 million people travel into central London each morning. The extent of the transport network feeding London allows firms in the central business districts to attract skilled staff from a wide catchment area across London and the South East. An increase in the time and cost of travel to and from London would have to be absorbed partly by the employer and partly by the employee. For the employer, it would feed through into higher pay levels, thereby increasing the cost of doing business in London and making the Capital a less attractive base. To the extent that is absorbed by employees, it would tend to reduce the labour market catchment area of London organisations as workers in the South East sought employment nearer to their homes. Firms in London might then respond by relocating their operations elswhere in the South East, nearer to those workers they are attempting to attract, thereby sacrificing the benefits of a London location.

Movement within and between business districts

3.8 The rationale for physical collocation within business districts is to facilitate face-to-face contact with customers, suppliers and, in some cases, with competitors, too. This purpose is frustrated if movement within the Capital is excessively costly or time-consuming.

Access to UK and international suppliers and customers

3.9 The international dimension is particularly important to the sort of businesses which we are keenest to attract to London. London is one of the three financial capitals of the World, along with Tokyo and New York, each city dominating its own time-zone, thereby permitting 24-hour dealing around the globe.

Adverse impact on quality of life and the environment

3.10 As noted at paragraph 2.27, some forecasters expect the 'quality of life' issues to become an increasingly important determinant of business location, and international businessmen regard air quality as one of the less attractive features of London. However, whilst air quality and noise are seen as important facets of 'quality of life', so too is freedom of movement and, for many people, the freedom to own and use their car. Like other major cities around the world, London faces the challenge of improving its environment without imposing levels of restraint on car use which erode people's quality of life and which would place us at a competitive disadvantage.

3.11 As well as seeking an improvement in air quality, there is concern about the longer term environmental and health impacts of transport, and particularly that existing levels of road traffic are not sustainable. While we accept there are benefits in mitigating these impacts, the extent and rate of change depends on the costs involved. For the longer term more sustainable land use patterns and the location of complementary activities nearer each other, in line with planning guidance, offer a solution which can encompass both economic and environmental aspirations.

3.12 However, in dealing with the particular requirements of a Capital City which depends on good international and national, as well as local, links, we must have regard to competitive benefits and disbenefits in framing our policies and investment programmes. The practical measures which we are taking and which bear upon the competitiveness of London as a World City are dealt with elsewhere in this strategy. However, there are two further general points about competitiveness which need to be dealt with here. One is the question of whether existing investment appraisal systems take proper account of competitiveness benefit. The other is the question of how well London's existing transport systems further its competitiveness.

Competitiveness and Investment Appraisal

3.13 The whole question of investment appraisal is one properly considered at national level as part of the national transport debate; and it is addressed in the Government's Transport Green Paper. But London has particular problems in moving people around, primarily to facilitate travel to work, and we therefore discuss here some of the issues linking transport and competitiveness in the capital, and the extent to which they are dealt with already in our investment criteria.

3.14 The criteria which are used to appraise London Underground investments require that, where the investment is to maintain the safe operation of an existing service, London Underground must demonstrate that they have adopted the most cost-effective solution. Where the investment is to provide a new service or enhance the quality of an existing service, they must carry out a cost:benefit analysis and demonstrate that the project earns the required 8% real rate of return. The use of cost:benefit analysis to appraise transport infrastructure investment is intended to ensure that resources are used in an economically efficient manner. The benefits which count in calculating the return comprise:

- reductions in journey;time,

- increases in revenue;

- service improvements for which users are demonstrably willing to pay, even though it may not be practicable to recover the cost via the farebox; and

- benefits to road-users resulting from decongestion.

Road schemes are appraised using similar cost-benefit techniques. Our reason for concentrating on the appraisal methods used by London Underground is that public transport accounts for the vast majority of commuter journeys into central London, and therefore furthers most directly our goal of promoting London's competitiveness as a World City.

3.15 We believe that the existing investment appraisal criteria already take account of the benefits to London's competitive position as far as these effects can be identified and measured. Our arguments are set out below. Moreover, there is no shortage of public transport projects in London which satisfy these criteria. In determining which projects should be accorded priority for scarce financial resources, the level of the benefit:cost ratio is only one of a number of factors which are taken into account. For example, engineering considerations may require one project to be completed before another is begun; or a road improvement may be required first to provide site access for a rail project, as in the case of the A13 and the CTRL works; or the availability of private finance for a particular project may affect timing. So a narrow focus on the investment appraisal criteria may not reflect the full basis on which decisions are taken. That said, some detailed points on the criteria are discussed below.

3.16 The argument on criteria suggests that because employers pay enough effectively to reimburse employees for the time they spend travelling to work as well as the time they spend at work, reductions in journey time should feed through into a reduced pay bill. The Government accepts that changes in travel-to-work time impact upon competitiveness and that investment which cuts public transport journey times in London will benefit the competitive position of employers in the central areas by exerting downward pressure on labour costs. We also consider that this benefit is fully taken into account in the existing investment appraisal criteria for both road and rail schemes. We cannot accept that the same journey time saving should score twice - once as a benefit to the user (as is counted now) and separately as a benefit to the employer. It might be more accurate to describe it as a benefit which is shared between the user and (for travel-to-work journeys) the employer, but the important point about the saving is that it is counted now.

3.17 Second, it is argued that improvements in reliability can be as important as a reduction in average journey time. There is some evidence that people value reductions in the variability of their journey times. Obvious examples are the employees who must be at work by a particular time, eg to open up shop or to attend a meeting. To be confident of reaching work by the due time, they will have to leave home sufficiently early to allow for all but the slowest of trips, which means that they will normally arrive earlier than they need to. The wider the variance around the mean journey time, the earlier they have to leave home and the more time they spend unproductively. Narrowing the variance around the mean journey time is, therefore, a benefit in its own right. It is, as before, a

benefit which is shared between user and employer. Research is currently being undertaken by the Department of Transport to establish how improvements in journey time reliability might be measured and valued as an additional benefit in the appraisal of new transport investment.

3.18 Third, it is suggested that an improvement in the speed, reliability or quality of the journey to work has a beneficial impact on output at work, staff turnover and attitudes to working overtime. Staff turnover is of particular concern to employers in London. Such benefits - including quality improvements such as reducing overcrowding, improving comfort and providing better information - are taken into account via the test of users' willingness to pay. Although there may well be an additional indirect benefit to the employer from such service improvements, which is not currently scored in the investment appraisal, we have no means of isolating it or setting a value on it. And, even if we could isolate it and value it, there is no reason to suppose that this would lead to more or different projects being taken forward.

3.19 The Government considers that the question of competitiveness is relevant in determining the overall level and shape of the transport investment programme for London and in determining which schemes to tackle first. These issues are considered alongside environmental impacts too, as each scheme in the programme is subject to rigorous environmental assessment, the results of which are weighed up against the results of cost:benefit analysis. Ensuring that the cost:benefit analysis takes account of all the relevant benefits and disbenefits is important to the Government - hence the research on reliability. Increasing the value set upon benefits which are already brought fully into the reckoning (such as reductions in journey time and improvement in journey quality) is a lower priority, because it is unlikely to have as much influence on which schemes are tackled first.

The Adequacy of London's Existing Transport Systems

3.20 The whole of this strategy is about the adequacy of London's existing transport systems. However, there is a particular issue here in relation to competitiveness which needs to be aired. It relates to the gap between the way in which transport in London is perceived by international businessmen and the way in which it is perceived by businesses which are already located here. The *Healey & Baker* annual survey of European executives showed that in 1995 they ranked London first out of 29 major European cities in terms of 'ease of access to markets, customers and clients', 'transport links with other cities' and 'ease of travelling around the city'.

3.21 Businesses considering relocating to London might be reassured to know that a survey of ordinary Londoners undertaken for the *Evening Standard* in October 1995 found that 70% of Londoners thought that public transport met London's needs 'fairly well' or 'very well'. Similarly, customer satisfaction indices compiled by London Transport show an increasing majority of bus and Underground users are satisfied with the service. But the surveys also highlight the concern which both businesses and individuals feel about issues such as pollution, congestion and quality of life. And a survey by London First in June 1995 showed that businesses are concerned about the problems their staff experience in getting to work, the high cost of delivering goods and services due to traffic congestion, under-investment in infrastructure, and difficulties in getting to and from Heathrow.

3.22 The statistics show how London's public transport systems have improved and highlight the more patchy performance of the road network. The new point-to-point journey-time survey will offer us an overall measure of ease of movement within London. These surveys consist of a rolling cycle of three annual recordings of set 'door to door' journeys in different parts of London by different modes. The second survey in the current cycle was conducted in 1994 and published in April 1995. Comparison over time will be possible when the 1993 surveys are repeated in 1996. However, the problem of making valid comparisons between the transport statistics published by the major cities across Europe remains formidable. The '*World Study of Urban Transport Systems*' being undertaken by the London Research Centre, and partly funded by the Government Office for London (GOL), will look at existing sources of data in an attempt to make more meaningful comparisons of the physical extent, size and usage of the transport systems in London, Paris, Tokyo and New York.

3.23 For the time being, however, the perception of London (as monitored by *Healey & Baker* and others) is probably the best evidence we have. It is also important in its own right, because perception can be as important as reality in terms of attracting businesses to London. Accordingly, we take *Healey & Baker* to provide evidence that London is well placed to attract international business, and we take the concerns voiced to London First as evidence that retaining businesses may raise different issues.

3.24 In particular, there are two aspects of London's transport systems targeted by London First which may be more obvious to businesses based in London than they are to visitors. One is the problem of travel to work, which does not feature in the *Healey & Baker* survey and may not be an important factor in determining whether a business locates in London, but could be much more important in determining whether it remains there. The other is the fact that the recent improvements in transport in London may be more fragile than they appear. For instance, both the road and public transport systems are vulnerable to an upturn in congestion as the economy expands.

3.25 In December 1992, the Department of the Environment published its findings on business relocation involving the South East region between 1985 and 1990. Over this period London was a major net loser of some 600 companies both to ROSE and to other regions. In a survey of 234 organisations that had relocated, 28% suggested that traffic congestion at their old locations was an important factor. The issue appeared to be of equal importance to both service providers and the larger manufacturing firms in the sample. Similar numbers of respondents cited improved access to labour, better surroundings or environment, and being in an improved position for distribution as their reasons for leaving London. However, the overriding reason for relocation was the need for business expansion on more suitable sites and premises. In choosing a new location, 13% of the sample suggested access to the transport network was a major deciding factor. Only 11% reported relative freedom from traffic congestion was important, with 8% and 7% stating that locations near to customers and an airport scored highly. This suggests that, even during a period when London's transport systems were under acute pressure, transport issues did not constitute the major reason for relocating outside London.

Conclusions

3.26 First, much of London's prosperity derives from economic activity in the central areas, covering the whole of the City, most of Westminster and parts of the surrounding boroughs. Around 28% of all jobs in London are in the central business districts, as are about a quarter of London's residents' jobs. The incomes earned by these London residents support jobs in retailing, leisure, education, health and local government in the Boroughs where they live. Additionally, the companies based in the central areas purchase a variety of goods and services from businesses located in other areas of London. Although no precise estimate has ever been made of the extent of London's dependence on its central business districts, it is clearly very considerable.

3.27 Second, London's success in attracting internationally mobile business raises issues of regional and national competitiveness. At the regional level, the ranks of Londoners working in the central business districts are swelled by the quarter of a million people who commute in daily from the rest of the South East. At the national level, London remains the major contributor to the UK's invisible earnings. In seeking to attract and retain businesses in the financial services sector and the corporate headquarters of multinational companies, London is competing with other major European cities and with New York and Tokyo. London's success in that competition is a matter of vital importance to the country as a whole.

3.28 Third, the concentration of businesses in the central areas creates a pattern of demand which the existing transport network, with its strong emphasis on radial roads and railways, is well placed to accommodate.

3.29 We believe that promoting the competitive position of London as a World City is the top priority for this transport strategy, because the future of London depends upon it and because of the importance of London's invisible earnings to the economy of the UK as a whole. Our assessment of the existing investment appraisal criteria suggests that they give due credit to competitiveness benefits, although we are ready to modify them subject to appropriate research. The more important issue is the priority given to investment to maintain and enhance the speed, reliability and quality of service of public transport in general and of the commuter services by rail and Underground in particular.

Chapter 4: Transport and Regeneration

Introduction

4.1 In Chapter 3, we concluded that the traditional cost:benefit analysis provides a reasonably good measure of the extent to which a transport project contributes to the competitiveness of London as a World City. The improvements to the speed, reliability and quality of a journey have traditionally been regarded as user benefits, but they can more accurately be viewed as benefits shared between employers and employees.

4.2 Regeneration raises a different and more difficult set of issues. The aim of regeneration policy is to breathe new life into areas which have fallen into serious decline. This may well bring economic and social gains with it. For example, the creation of jobs in a deprived area represents an economic gain if those jobs would otherwise have been located overseas. Even if the jobs concerned would otherwise have been located in a more affluent area of the UK, the creation of employment in a depressed area may alleviate social problems which would otherwise be extremely costly to deal with. Nevertheless, regeneration policy is, ultimately, justified primarily on equity grounds, rather than on considerations of narrow economic benefit. It is often possible to derive from a cost:benefit analysis an indication of which groups benefit and who bears the costs by making certain assumptions about the incidence of costs and benefits. But cost:benefit analysis gives no guidance about the relative importance to be attributed to each of the groups concerned. There is also the problem that regeneration benefits are difficult to assess *ex ante* because there is limited evidence on which to base forecasts of the impact of new transport links on business location decisions. In many cases it is not even clear whether improved transport, either on its own or in conjunction with other policies, will give rise to regeneration.

4.3 Squaring this circle is a high priority for the Capital, because London's regeneration needs are pressing and there is a general recognition that transport can - and ought - to play an important part in meeting them. Deciding on transport priorities which properly reflect regeneration needs also requires an analysis of the specific social, economic and geographical considerations which pertain within a region. *Strategic Guidance for London Planning Authorities* sets out the broad structural framework within which both central government and local authorities work.

4.4 The Government's proposed approach is also set out more fully in the Transport Green Paper. A major issue is the timing of investment in transport infrastructure relative to development. There are three options - transport infrastructure can be provided in advance as a direct stimulus to economic regeneration (as has happened with the DLR to Beckton and the Royal Docks), it can take place at the same time as the increase in economic activity (and in this case might be partly developer-funded), or it can follow the lead set by development activities. The first case entails a real risk element - will the development follow the investment? The second can too easily tend to rely on developer contributions although this ought not to be an overwhelming factor. The third option can discourage increasing levels of economic activity if transport infrastructure is perceived as inadequate to a potential inward investor.

4.5 A further issue arising from the identification of areas of need within London is the prospect of growth in demand for transport it creates. Realistically some of this growth will be met by increased travel by road. Nevertheless we are seeking to encourage these new demands to be met by less polluting modes as far as possible, in line with our sustainability objectives. This is an objective both of planning guidance and our regeneration programmes with their emphasis on sustainable land use patterns and sustainable economic growth.

London's Regeneration Need

4.6 We have discussed in Chapter 2 the problems which London has experienced in retaining businesses which are not tied to the central business districts. As in the rest of the country, the traditional manufacturing areas have been exposed to overseas competition from countries with lower labour costs and better access to raw materials. In addition, London's docks have closed and with them went their satellite processing industries. Gas and electricity production has all but ceased and major railway marshalling yards and engineering facilities have closed leading to vast tracts of derelict land. Key industries - such as electronics, food processing and machine engineering - have dispersed to locations outside London, for a mixture of cost, environmental and access reasons. They have left behind them industrial buildings and estates throughout London which are often obsolescent, sometimes polluted and generally ill-served in terms of access by both public and private transport. They have also left behind them a population which does not always possess the skills needed to attract employment in those sectors where London's economy is faring better.

4.7 The relocation within London of service provision activities has also caused problems. In particular, the movement of retail activities towards new hypermarkets and out-of-town centres has tended to undermine the more traditional shopping areas. This leaves town centres under-utilised and in search of new roles.

4.8 The Capital's success in retaining central business activities means that there is an increasingly wide gap opening up between those in employment (where London pay levels now stand at 32% above the national average) and those who are unemployed. The general outward migration of employment has left pockets of acute deprivation - particularly, but not exclusively, in inner London. Table 4A illustrates this. It shows how the ten poorest Boroughs in London rank amongst the 366 enumeration districts in England on the basis of the deprivation index which is employed by the Department of the Environment.

4.9 Many factors are responsible for these indices of deprivation. In Newham for example, high unemployment is rife including a high proportion of long-term unemployment. Linked to this is an especially marked prevalence of those on income support. Children in the Borough have a comparatively low level of educational attainment, partly due to a poor level of participation in education. A high proportion of households have no car and health appears less good than elsewhere. In addition there are a whole series of indicators pointing to problematical housing conditions - overcrowding, too high a proportion of unsuitable accommodation and a lack of proper amenities. Derelict land blights the Borough also. By contrast Bromley, London's least deprived Borough, tends to avoid most, but not all, of these problems - unemployment is low, with relatively few long-term unemployed and housing is neither crowded nor lacking in amenities. With comparatively high income levels, the biggest blot on the landscape in Bromley is the relatively high amount of derelict land.

4.10 This index is constructed by measuring and quantifying such indicators as housing quality, unemployment and car ownership. Other indicators highlight specific housing issues such as overcrowding, high proportions of unsuitable accommodation and lack of proper amenities, as well as levels of educational achievement.

4.11 Ten of the most deprived authorities in England fall within London, including the top four. Although the problems are most acute in the inner London area,

TABLE 4A

Borough	Overall Ranking	Enumeration District %	Deprived Rank	Rank of Worst wards
Newham	1	56.0	5	9
Southwark	2	62.2	3	5
Hackney	3	82.1	1	4
Islington	4	60.8	4	11
Tower Hamlets	7	78.0	2	1
Lambeth	8	49.8	6	3
Haringey	10	44.4	7	16
Lewisham	11	31.0	12	8
Greenwich	14	21.9	15	20
Camden	15	40.4	8	13

Note: ranks are out of 366 districts in England.

there is not a single London Borough which does not contain a major focus of such problems - examples include Harold Hill in Havering, the Cray Estate in Bromley, the Hayes/West Drayton area in Hillingdon and the Roundshaw Estate in Sutton.

Fostering Regeneration

4.12 The key ways in which the Government is seeking to foster regeneration are spelled out in the objectives of the Single Regeneration Budget (SRB). These are to:

- enhance the employment prospects, education and skills of local people, particularly the young and those at a disadvantage, and promote equality of opportunity;

- encourage sustainable economic growth and wealth creation by improving the competitiveness of the local economy, including support for new and existing businesses;

- protect and improve the environment and infrastructure and promote good design;

- improve housing and housing conditions for local people through physical improvement, better maintenance, improved management and greater choice and diversity;

- promote initiatives of benefit to ethnic minorities;

- tackle crime and improve community safety; and

- enhance the quality of life of local people, including their health and cultural and sports opportunities.

4.13 This wide range of objectives reflects the fact that, since the causes and symptoms of deprivation are complex, remedies have to be pursued on a broad front. They are about removing the different obstacles that discourage people from living and working in these areas and which discourage businesses from locating there.

4.14 There are two main ways in which improved transport links can contribute to the achievement of regeneration goals:

- by helping exploit development potential within the area;

- by providing residents with improved access to jobs outside the area.

Exploiting Development Potential

4.15 To make sense of the role that the transport networks can play in encouraging businesses to relocate into deprived areas, a spatial interpretation of London's changing geography is essential. London tended to expand along radial lines. Commercial and industrial activities tended to concentrate in corridors which fanned out from the central area, with residential developments infilling the gaps between. The four main corridors are: the Lea Valley to the north, the Thames Gateway to the east, the Wandle Valley to the south and the west London road and rail corridor. Two distinct outliers are the Belvedere/Cray Valley area in the south east and Eastern Avenue. These sectors form part of the structural framework of London, which is contained within the Government's *Strategic Guidance for London Planning Authorities*. Setting out these sectors within planning guidance is intended to promote the integration between the decisions that individual local authorities make on their land use plans for these areas and the development of transport programmes for which both the local authorities and other transport providers are responsible.

4.16 The exodus of manufacturing and other activities has left vacant sites in these areas which have development potential. Developable land is a scarce commodity in London, hence the fact that the DOE survey (see paragraph 3.25) found that the main reason for relocating from London to the South East was the need for business expansion on more suitable sites and premises. Most of London is built on already. Much of the land that is not built on is protected by Metropolitan Open Land status. The Green Belt, as a deliberate matter of policy, inhibits the outward expansion of London. The developable sites in these four corridors are, therefore, one of London's most important assets.

4.17 In some cases, businesses have been quick to exploit this potential. For example, the West London corridor now accounts for some 7% of national GDP and, as noted in Chapter 2, has in effect become an extension of London's central business district. This was undoubtedly encouraged by the fact that the existing road and rail networks were good and by the proximity of Heathrow.

4.18 In most cases, however, the development potential will be difficult to exploit without improvements in transport infrastructure. For much of industry, this means access by road. However, following the public response to the four major assessment studies undertaken in the late 1980's, the Government ruled out major new road building across large areas of the capital. The LDDC has had considerable success in stimulating the redevelopment of London's Docklands within the inner sector of the eastern corridor. However, achieving this required *inter alia* significant investment in new transport infrastructure, because the area had relied heavily on transport by sea for freight movements and was not particularly well served by the public transport system. The dramatic improvement in accessibility and regeneration potential has been secured by the construction of the Jubilee Line Extension and the Docklands Light Railway, by the construction of the Docklands road network, by the provision of new bus services and by the new London City Airport. The combined effect has been to open up the area in ways that have made it much more attractive as a place to live in or to do business in.

4.19 The Lea Valley, the Wandle Valley and the outer sector of the Thames Gateway area continue to combine development potential with high levels of deprivation. Even within the Western Corridor, there are areas such as Park Royal which are in urgent need of regeneration.

4.20 Park Royal is a good example of ways in which national, sub-regional and local transport initiatives can, when properly co-ordinated, foster the regeneration of a depressed area. Improvements to the North Circular Road (which are national trunk road schemes) and the related construction of the Twyford Abbey link and the Hayes Bypass (which are local authority schemes supported by Government grant) have been important in helping attract inward investment. Such inward investment also requires that employees are able to access new and existing jobs. This 1930s trading estate was built at a time when car ownership amongst industrial employees was minimal and public transport dependency high. In the subsequent half-century, modal splits have reversed and travel by car now predominates. Even though the typical journey to work is relatively short (no more than 3-5 miles), these trips are not achieved easily by public transport. Hence, the availability of a car has translated into car-dependency. In an area where parking facilities are inadequate, this leads to excessive on-street parking, which in turn causes congestion and hampers bus operation. This in turn reduces the attractiveness of bus services,

leading to the perceived benefits of car commuting. It demonstrates a progressive downward spiral common to many of the areas in the four main development corridors. Harlesden City Challenge is funding local bus routes that have increased access to new and existing jobs for those without access to private transport. By linking the estate with Willesden Junction and Ealing Broadway, these bus services give the area access to the rail and tube networks which it would otherwise lack.

4.21 Three more generally relevant lessons can be drawn from the Park Royal example.

4.22 The first is the importance of partnerships. Transport responsibilities in London rest with a number of different bodies, who will need to work together to ensure that transport makes a proper contribution to regeneration goals. The Boroughs have a key role to play via their planning responsibilities and as providers of local services. The TECs need to be involved to ensure that the area can meet the skills requirements of existing and new employers. The sites also need to be marketed, which is where the London First Centre comes in.

4.23 Second, the partners need to have a properly thought-out regeneration plan and to be clear how they see transport contributing to its delivery. Where transport links are poor, their improvement is likely to be a necessary precondition for attracting new business. However, it does not follow that the provision of new links or enhancement of existing links will, in itself, deliver regeneration. Partners need to be clear what businesses they are seeking to attract, based on a sober assessment of their area's comparative advantages and disadvantages, and how the transport requirements of such businesses can best be met. They also need to focus on cost. The regeneration budget is relatively small and the transport budgets are hard-pressed. One reason why the Park Royal programme is a good one is that it works with the grain of the trunk road investment programme, has sought to match that to local transport funding, and has harnessed that to other funding regimes, including a relatively low-cost bus-based solution that eases the transport access problem.

4.24 Third, the provision of additional road connections or capacity and more parking will often be an essential element in the regeneration package. Certainly, additional road capacity will be expensive both in economic and environmental terms, as may additional parking provision. Improved connections between development sites and the existing road network need not be that expensive, however, and will frequently be funded in whole or part by developers as part of their site marketing. We also want to see improvements made in access to development by alternative modes, to ensure that increases in traffic as a result of new development are minimised.

Facilitating Access to Jobs

4.25 As noted in paragraph 4.14, transport links are not only about encouraging business to relocate into an area, they are also about providing residents with better access to jobs outside the area. Ideally, mixed use development and developments in locations accessible by public transport would allow places of work and residential areas to be situated close to one another, allowing economic activity, even during periods of growth, to take place without increasing demand for car travel. But we need to recognise that existing land use patterns and the location of London's labour force at some distance from the workplace make meeting that longer term objective difficult.

4.26 Some of the most deprived areas of inner London are essentially residential. They have relatively little scope for attracting new businesses in and no scope for attracting those which require access to developable sites. They could not easily accommodate an increase in road traffic. Nor would it be in the overall interests of London for them to do so - partly because it would aggravate the air pollution problem and partly because it would compound the problems which we face in promoting access to the central business districts. To the extent that transport can make a contribution to the regeneration of such areas, it is likely to be via improved public transport links to more prosperous areas or to areas with greater development potential.

4.27 However, it is important that regeneration plans take a realistic view of the contribution that such improvements can make. Journey times between most inner and central London locations, by existing routes, are not long. And the reduction in journey time which new or improved public transport services can deliver is typically small. It is, therefore, difficult to believe that the difficulty of the journey to work is a major obstacle to securing employment, which transport investment is capable of remedying. There are conspicuous exceptions to this, particularly in the

Thames Gateway area. Cases must be looked at on their merits. As a general rule, the simple availability of public transport is unlikely to be an obstacle to the efforts of inner London residents to secure employment. Cost, however, may be a factor that deters people from taking up low-paid employment.

Regeneration in the Transport Strategy

4.28 In framing this transport strategy, we have had regard to the contribution which specific transport infrastructure projects can make to the regeneration of the Thames Gateway, Lea Valley, Wandle Valley and to Park Royal. The wider economic, social and planning priorities for these areas are covered in *Strategic Guidance for London Planning Authorities*. One of the key themes of this document is that transport improvements and the promotion of new development in these areas must be taken forward in an integrated manner. Chapter 2 of *Strategic Guidance for London Planning Authorities* brings out the major development opportunities that are created by the transport networks of these areas. Making the most out of the existing infrastructure and planned improvements is a central plank in promoting sustainable economic activity.

4.29 The **Thames Gateway** area has already seen significant investment in transport and this programme is set to continue with improvements completed or in hand to the road networks on both sides of the River Thames and modernisation of the passenger train service in north Kent. The construction of the Channel Tunnel Rail Link, with its domestic and international stations at Ebbsfleet and Stratford, will be a focus for investment. The latter may well also encourage developments at Rainham Riverside and Barking Reach with their close proximity to planned improvements to the A13. The A13 schemes have been accorded a high priority within the trunk roads review. Potential development sites run along both banks of the river from Beckton to Rainham/Thurrock on the north side and Greenwich to Dartford/North West Kent on the south, all of which will be dependent on improvements in their transport provision and cross-river links to be wholly successful. We have taken this into account in proposing the package of new river crossings in the East Thames Corridor.

4.30 Like the Thames Gateway, the southern end of the **Lea Valley** corridor will benefit from the completion of the Jubilee Line and from the new regional and international interchange stations at Stratford. The Hackney-M11 link facilitates access to the M25. The proposed third Blackwall crossing would facilitate access to the Channel ports and tunnel. European Regional Development Fund (ERDF) funds are also supporting infrastructure projects at Stratford, Seven Sisters and Tottenham Hale, the latter being a major development and transportation node at the heart of the Lea Valley. Developer contribution is expected to fund the provision of an improved linkage to the M25 at the northern end of the area.

4.31 The **Wandle Valley** is more problematical. The construction of Croydon Tramlink will be an impetus to investment in the Purley Way and Waddon areas. It will also enhance Croydon's linkage to other population centres. More importantly, transport interchanges at Croydon and Wimbledon will encourage the attraction of new employment to the southern part of the Valley. Encouraging new businesses to locate in the northern end of the valley is more problematical, given the limited scope for upgrading either the A23 or A205.

4.32 The **West London Corridors** start with good transport links. The Park Royal area, in particular, will benefit from the further improvements planned for the A406 and A40. There is to be SRB support for infrastructure improvements to Willesden Junction, a key public transport hub for the area, and road improvements at Stockley Park. Further in, additional services are to be run on the West London Line.

4.33 In focusing on the four corridors, we recognise that the true position is more complex. Each of the corridors has its own inventory of development areas. There are, in addition, designated development areas within the central area and around its margins. Across the Capital as a whole there are 75 in total, to which one might add significant free-standing sites such as Crystal Palace and Alexandra Palace, as well as hospital sites at Cane Hill, Claybury and Tooting Bec. Given the complexity of this picture, there are limits to the extent that a high level strategy can focus on regeneration issues, although they will be taken into account in appraising individual schemes.

4.34 Accordingly, our overall emphasis is on the provision of networks, into which local transport connections can plug. The trunk road network is the most important of these. London has a significantly higher mileage of motorway and trunk road than most other major conurbations. For a combination of

economic and environmental reasons, the scope for expanding and enhancing that network is limited, although there will remain a number of locations where planned improvements will help encourage economic regeneration - the A13 corridor improvements and schemes on the A40 come into this category.

4.35 Because the scope for improvements to the trunk road network is so limited it is important not just to ensure that the schemes that are undertaken are concentrated at locations or on corridors where they will have the greatest regeneration impact, but that they are designed to encourage the marketing of those locations to potential inward investors. It will then be for the partnerships and others directing the regeneration activity to maximise the impact that improved access to the trunk road network provides - in London's case, that means access to other parts of London as well as the remainder of the national road network. The 'ring-and-spoke' approach, which is explained more fully in Chapter 11, was designed with regeneration requirements and opportunities very much in mind.

4.36 The Red Route network, also discussed in Chapter 11, covers some 315 miles of road, running from the Greater London boundary to the outer fringes of the central area. Red Routes have a particular contribution to make in improving access to areas where enhancement of existing roads is not an option - the northern sector of the Wandle Valley is an obvious case in point. The improved mobility offered by Red Routes, as well as other traffic management initiatives or local improvements schemes, will similarly improve the attractiveness of sites and offer improved access for goods deliveries and the export of finished products.

4.37 The quality of the London-wide public transport networks is, likewise, of importance to local-level regeneration initiatives. There are many types of movement for which public transport, particularly the bus, will be the natural choice for some people - whether it is a question of bringing shoppers into a town centre, getting staff to an office development or science park, or facilitating travel to work from deprived residential areas. The better the London-wide networks, the easier it will be to enhance local-level access. In putting particular stress upon access by road, we do not mean to downplay the importance of rail. Rather, we seek to counter the mistaken belief that it is possible to bring new business into an area without making proper provision for access for goods and service vehicles, for cars and for buses.

Conclusion

4.38 Although we have accorded top priority to promoting London's competitive position as a World City, we regard the regeneration of the deprived areas of the Capital as an important issue, to which transport has a significant contribution to make. We believe it is possible, even operating within tight constraints on public expenditure, to make progress on both fronts simultaneously. Our existing investment programme demonstrates this. So does the longer-term programme which is mapped out in Chapter 14.

4.39 Although there are difficulties about bringing regeneration benefits into the reckoning in a cost:benefit analysis, the practical importance of this should not be over-stated. In the Thames Gateway area, for example, regeneration considerations played an important part in the decisions to provide new access roads, to build the Docklands Light Railway and to extend the Jubilee Line. Equally, much of the new investment proposed for the area, such as the upgrading of the A13 and the provision of a mix of new road and rail crossings, represents schemes which perform well in terms of both their regeneration impact and their economic benefit.

Chapter 5: The Environment

Introduction

5.1 The environmental impact of transport in London, particularly road transport, is widely recognised as one of the major concerns of residents, businesses and visitors alike. We believe that future transport policy will need to attach greater emphasis on reducing the environmental impacts of transport. This strategy addresses each of the key areas where transport has an adverse impact: air quality, climate change, land take noise and visual intrusiveness. In each case we need to consider:

- what is the scale of the problem in London?

- what can be done to improve the environment?

- how far can such measures further the achievement of other policy goals?

5.2 However, before proceeding to an analysis of the individual areas, it is worth making some more general points. The Government accepts the desirability of minimising transport's environmental impacts in all four of the above areas. This underlines the policies contained within the Government's *Sustainable Development Strategy, PPG13 - Transport,* and *Strategic Guidance for London Planning Authorities.* These documents stress that it is as important in the environmental field to set priorities as it is in any other field. These priorities need to take account of local circumstances. For example, the question of air pollution is a much more serious problem for London than the question of land-take, in particular because plans for new road construction are limited; the opposite would probably be true in most rural areas. For a combination of economic and environmental reasons, there has long been a strong presumption against transport schemes in London which demand significant land-take. The priorities also need to take account of the environmental goals and the other policy goals - hence the particular importance which we attach to the last of the three questions posed in paragraph 5.1.

5.3 The need for this is most obvious in relation to the relationship between economic and environmental goals, where two broad generalisations are commonly made, both of which are potentially highly misleading. At the national level, it is argued that there is an inherent conflict between the pursuit of economic growth and the preservation of the environment, because growth has always implied increased transport activity and because all forms of transport have, in the last analysis, an adverse impact on the environment. At the London level, in contrast, it is increasingly being argued that the pursuit of economic growth necessarily implies the pursuit of environmental improvements, because of the increasing importance that environmental issues will have in determining business location. Both arguments oversimplify the issues.

5.4 The relationship between economic and environmental goals is an important one, at the heart of The Government's Sustainable Development Strategy and the national transport debate. However, it is important to note that the relationship between environmental goals and some of the other transport goals is not straightforward either.

5.5 Broadly speaking, there is an environmental gain whenever people substitute one of the more environmentally friendly modes for one of the less environmentally friendly ones. In some cases, such as travelling by rail rather than car, this modal shift also has safety benefits. In other cases, it does not, for example travelling by cycle rather than bus would involve substituting a relatively dangerous mode for one of the safest.

Air Quality

5.6 We have identified in earlier chapters the fact that air quality is an area of major concern to Londoners and is also one of the few areas where the Capital is held in low esteem by those who take business location decisions. Tackling London's air quality problems is therefore a high priority on environmental, health and competitiveness grounds.

5.7 We already know a great deal about air quality in London. All the major pollutants are subject of co-ordinated monitoring and assessment by the Department of the Environment, local authorities and other bodies. The broad picture which emerges is that the pattern of air quality in London is very similar to that in other urban areas of the UK. The traffic-related pollutants likely to be of continuing concern are nitrogen dioxide (NO_2), fine particles (PM_{10}) and ozone. Lead is also traditionally a pollutant which has needed careful attention. Charts 5A, 5B and 5C look at the central London trends in relation to three of the most important pollutants: airborne lead, NO_2 concentrations and ozone concentrations. They illustrate very different trends:

- Annual mean airborne lead concentrations in London have reduced dramatically, mainly as a result of the increased use of unleaded petrol. Lead concentrations in London in 1993 were less than 4% of the EC Directive limit value (2,000 nanograms/m^3).

- Traffic emissions modelling suggests that since 1990 nitrogen dioxide emissions have been falling. This has translated into a modest reduction in the monthly average concentrations of NO$_2$ over the last five years, but there is no clear downward trend in the number of days when air quality is classed as poor (ie where NO$_2$ concentrations in excess of 100 parts per billion are recorded).

Chart 5A: Airborne lead: central London site 1976/7 to 1993/4

Nanograms per cubic metre

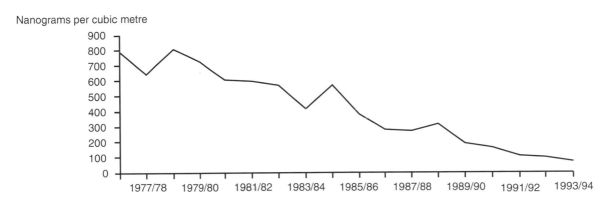

Chart 5B: Mean and maximum hourly nitrogen dioxide concentration: central London

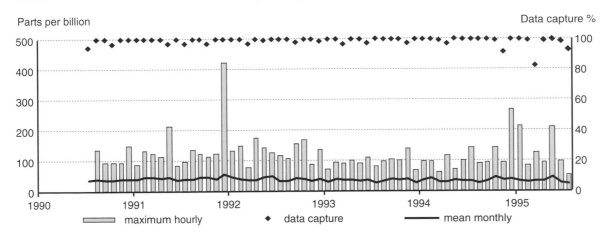

Chart 5C: Mean and maximum hourly ozone concentration: central London site

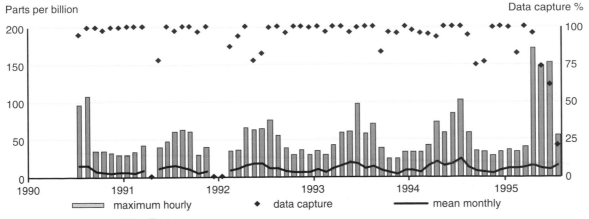

Source: Department of the Enviroment

- Ozone formation is heavily influenced by weather conditions, tending to peak on hot, still days. Although ozone concentration in central London is lower than in rural areas, it still represents a problem. The most we can say, on the evidence of Chart 5C, is that is difficult to discern any improvement.

5.8 Chart 5D indicates the extent to which road transport contributes to different categories of emission in London and across the UK as a whole. It confirms the fact that, in London, traffic is by far the most significant source of air pollution. There are three main reasons for the disparities between the London and the national figures. The first is that London is a busy and congested city. The second is that London has seen the demise of traditional manufacturing and power-generating industries which continue to contribute to atmospheric pollution in some other areas of the country. The third is that London imposes tight restrictions on the fuels that can be burned in households. What is clear from Chart 5D is that delivering the air quality improvements which business and the public demand, and which domestic and EU legislation will increasingly require, is going to have to be achieved, in London, primarily by reducing the level of emissions from road vehicles in London and the South East.

5.9 The general framework for policies to improve air quality both nationally and in London will be set in the Government's national air quality strategy. A consultation draft of this strategy is due to be published in Summer 1996. According to the Environment Act 1995, the Strategy must include:

- standards and objectives relating to air quality;

- measures for the achievement of those objectives.

5.10 The Environment Act also requires local authorities to review and assess air quality in their area. Where air quality standards and objectives are not being or are not likely to be met, the authority is obliged to create a local air quality management area, and to draw up an action plan aimed at improving the situation in that area. The Government will be issuing guidance to local authorities on the assessment of air quality and in the development of air quality action plans. In order to ensure that the guidance genuinely reflects the needs of local authorities in this respect, the Government is co-ordinating a first phase of assessment and reviews in conjunction with a selected number of local authority groupings. This developmental stage includes all the London local authorities.

5.11 Clearly, where road traffic is the principal source of pollution for areas in which ambient air quality needs improvement, the measures of greatest relevance will be those which reduce vehicle emissions. The air quality strategy will address all the options for emissions abatement. These options generally include:

Chart 5D: Contribution of transport to total air pollution

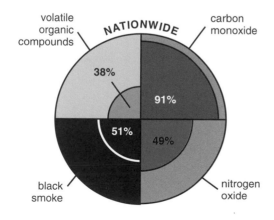

Source: Digest of Enviroment Statistics
           No. 17 1995 HMSO

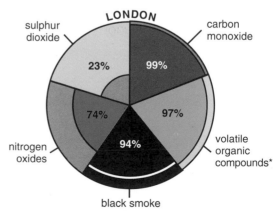

Source: London Research Centre (1993)
           London Energy Study, Energy Use and
           Enviroment (M. Chell and D. Hutchinson, eds.)

           * In the case of VOCs, non-energy sources
           comprise a large fraction of total emissions

at the national level:

- the regulatory approach, designed to improve vehicle technology and fuel quality;

- the fiscal approach, which can be used to encourage the use of cleaner fuels and vehicles.

at the local level:

- the demand management approach, based on containing or reducing the total level of vehicle movements in an area such as London as a whole or central London in particular;

- the traffic management approach, based on improving the flow of traffic so as to reduce the emissions caused by stop-start driving in congested areas;

- use of the land use system, to reduce the overall need to travel and to promote alternative modes of transport to the car.

5.12 The broad picture for the UK and London on national measures is readily identifiable. The current regulatory framework includes:

- the continued penetration of cars fitted with catalytic convertors into the national car fleet, as a result of European vehicle standards applied since 1993;

- the tightening of MOT standards for petrol-engined vehicles without catalysts and diesel engined vehicles introduced in September 1995;

- the introduction of new MOT limits for cars with catalysts in January 1996;

- the tightening of standards for new heavy diesel vehicles from October 1996;

- the tightening of the limits for new cars from January 1997 and for light commercial vehicles from October 1997.

5.13 The projected impact of these measures is illustrated below. Charts 5E to 5H show projections of

Chart 5E: UK and London PM$_{10}$ emission forecasts 1991-2011

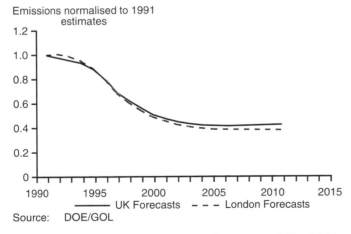

Source: DOE/GOL

Chart 5F: UK and London VOC emission forecasts 1991-2011

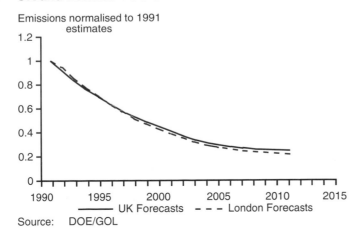

Source: DOE/GOL

major emissions for the UK and London. The broad picture is that at a national level, total emissions will continue to decline until at least 2010, when the increase in traffic growth begins to erode this advance. The initial modelling work we have done based on London traffic projections seems to confirm a similar picture for the Capital. However, these projections do not include the effect of further vehicle emission and fuel quality standards due to be proposed by the European Commission for the year 2000 and beyond.

5.14 As regards fiscal measures, we have already used the tax system to encourage environmental improvements by making fuels which are less damaging either to health or the environment relatively less expensive. Paragraph 5.7 above shows the impact that the duty differential applying to unleaded petrol has had. In the 1995 Budget the Chancellor reduced the duty on liquefied petroleum gas and compressed natural gas by 15% so that their retail price is in line with petrol and diesel. For the future the Government is keeping under review, through its own research and by monitoring the research of others, the tax treatment of road fuels and technologies, so that we can take on board new ideas as they come forward. As our understanding of relevant health and environmental effects improves, we will consider whatever options are appropriate to create the right fiscal and regulatory framework which ensures the natural emergence of the most cost effective fuels and technologies to meet environmental objectives. Very careful analysis of the impacts of particular changes, including an analysis of the costs and benefits, needs to be carried out.

5.15 This transport strategy is also concerned with demand management and traffic management, since they directly impinge on programmes which must be taken forward across London as a whole. The promotion of less polluting modes in particular is central to how the national air quality strategy will be implemented in London. These are considered further in chapters 10 and 11 below. Close liaison between Boroughs, the Traffic Director, TCSU and central Government will be necessary to ensure effective co-ordination of local and London-wide initiatives. Land use planning is also key, and is considered in further depth in *Strategic Guidance for London Planning Authorities.*

5.16 It is clear that the Air Quality strategy, this

transport strategy, and the implementation by Boroughs of *Strategic Guidance for London Planning Authorities* need to be taken forward together. The Departments of Environment and Transport and the Government Office for London are already consulting with local authorities and other agencies with an interest in transport policy on ensuring effective co-ordination of programmes.

5.17 In London it will be necessary for all concerned, particularly local authorities, to be clear about the progress being made towards achieving the objectives set out in the light of the national air quality strategy. To help achieve this we will publish in our Annual report on this transport strategy both the results of monitoring of air pollution in London and our best estimate of future trends, particularly as they relate to forecast traffic patterns.

5.18 As noted, the net effect of the additional national measures would be to deliver further reductions in pollution and therefore to push back beyond 2010 the point at which traffic growth starts to offset pollution improvements. These significant improvements will provide the backdrop for decisions taken at the London or Borough level. It is clear that improvements in air quality in London, as in the rest of the UK, will need to be made, and it is this task which both this transport strategy (including our consideration of traffic management programmes) and the air quality strategy need to address. Both strategies will be subject to regular review, in order to take into account changes in knowledge and understanding of the issues. For example;

- Research may alter our understanding of the relationship between congestion and pollution. For example, Government Office for London traffic simulation work has shown that, where links and junctions are operating at close to capacity, a 10% increase in traffic can turn into an increase of emissions by 30%-70%.

- Transport demand and car ownership forecasts for London are subject to a degree of uncertainty;

- The pattern of car use varies significantly between central, inner and outer London, which is an important consideration because the research undertaken to date suggests strongly that the majority of pollution problems are locally generated;

• The interaction between pollutants is complex and not fully understood - for example increases in nitrogen oxides emissions can actually, under certain conditions, inhibit ozone formation.

5.19 These uncertainties underline the importance of the national air quality strategy, so that we do not rely on improvements already planned. The whole issue of air quality is one where attitudes and policy are bound to change as more research is done. We have referred above to other research into vehicle and fuel technologies, and the monitoring that is carried out of the actual levels of air pollution. Through these mechanisms and the air quality strategy, the Government will be able continually to improve its understanding of the extent of the problem.

5.20 Although the programme of research and policy development is ongoing, the broad message to Londoners and potential inward investors is a reassuring one. There is a clear downward trend forecast for vehicle emissions, which entail

improvements in air quality. Furthermore, the framework established by the Environment Act and the air quality strategy will provide the mechanisms for progressive movement towards our air quality objectives. London is therefore set to become a cleaner and healthier place to live and work in.

5.21 Against this background, the priorities for traffic and demand management are:

• to accelerate the downward trend in pollutants and to eliminate the post-2010 upward trend by encouraging a shift towards less polluting modes of transport and through better traffic management; Chapter 10 deals with our proposals designed to achieve this.

• to ensure that the development of traffic management and parking policies in London takes into account their impact on both local and regional levels of pollution. Chapter 11 deals with our strategies for traffic management and parking, including work seeking to identify a solution to the

Chart 5G: UK and London NO$_X$ emission forecasts 1991-2011

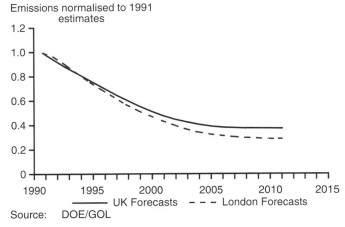

Source: DOE/GOL

Chart 5H: UK and London CO emission forecasts 1991-2011

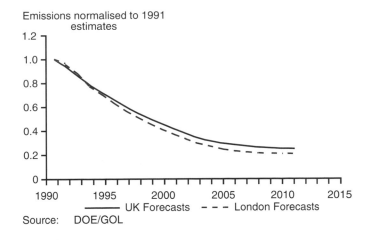

Source: DOE/GOL

problem of the pollution peaks on days when weather conditions cause sharp upturns in the concentrations of certain pollutants.

Climate Change

5.22 In their Second Assessment Report the Intergovernmental Panel on Climate Change (IPCC) reported that the balance of evidence now suggests a discernible human influence on climate change. Unless urgent action is taken the global temperature is projected to rise by 2∞C by 2100. Climate change will have adverse effects on human health, terrestrial and aquatic ecological systems and on socio-economic systems.

5.23 In 1993, the road transport sector accounted for 22% of UK emissions of carbon dioxide, the main greenhouse gas. The Government's projections suggest that this may rise to 25% by the year 2000 and 29% by 2010, reflecting traffic growth over this period. Transport is the fastest growing sector contributing to carbon dioxide emissions.

5.24 To help reduce carbon dioxide emissions from the transport sector, the Government announced in 1993 its long term intention is to raise road fuel duties on average by at least 5% a year in real terms. Higher fuel costs will encourage manufacturers to improve the fuel efficiency of vehicles and encourage road users to consider fuel efficiency when buying vehicles, when planning journeys and when driving. This should lead to reduced fuel consumption and therefore moderate the increase of CO_2 emissions.

5.25 Other measures complement the fuel duty strategy, such as planning guidance to local authorities to reduce the need to travel, traffic calming schemes, and action on speed limits and their enforcement. Many of these are primarily concerned with another purpose, such as reducing congestion, but nevertheless can make a small but significant contribution to the reduction of carbon dioxide emissions.

5.26 In the longer term, the United Kingdom is calling on all developed countries to agree to aim to reduce total greenhouse gas emissions to a figure between 5 and 10% below 1990 levels by the year 2010. In advance of international negotiations it is impossible to identify which measures should be implemented. Along with the rest of the UK, London will be expected to contribute to reductions in carbon dioxide emissions in all sectors, including transport.

Land Take

5.27 London has more open space than any European city other than Berlin and is particularly fortunate in having preserved the fine Royal Parks within the central area. Nevertheless, those who visit or live in the capital cannot fail to be aware of the large areas taken up by road infrastructure. In fact, the total proportion of London's surface area given over to transport is around 17%, most of which is local roads, compared with the 10% which is park or other open land. It is worth noting that this figure, an estimate made in the late 1960's, has not increased as a result of road construction since then, because land released by the closure of railway yards and related areas has been devoted to other, non-transport uses. Although the programmes of trunk and local authority road improvement schemes in London have been modest in scope and have focused on upgrading existing roads rather than building new ones, the tension between road space and open space has been acute in recent years. This reflects the fact that both represent finite resources, which are under pressure. In the case of the Hackney-M11 Link Road, the Government concluded that the claims of road space had to come first. In the case of the East London River Crossing, we concluded that the claims of the open space had to come first. These reflect judgements on the importance of the respective roads (in both transport and regeneration terms) and on the value of the respective stretches of open land.

5.28 Our forward infrastructure plans are spelled out in Chapters 9 and 12. On the rail side, they rely primarily upon the use of existing railway lines and on tunnelling. On the roads side, they consist mainly of schemes to widen existing roads and to improve junctions, which will have minimal land-take implications and will not impact on open land. The only significant exception to the foregoing is the proposal to construct new river crossings in the Thames Gateway. Taking all the road and rail schemes in Chapters 9 and 12 together, the total land-take requirement is estimated at around 0.33% of London's total surface area. Only one trunk road scheme, the A13 west of Heathway to Wennington scheme, will encroach on an area of special scientific interest. The only schemes which we know involve encroachments upon Metropolitan Open Land are those listed in Table 5I. The loss associated with public transport schemes is minimal. Those trunk road schemes which involve the loss of more than 250 square metres provide exchange land to compensate for this loss.

Table 5I - Schemes encroaching on Metropolitan Open Land

Channel Tunnel Rail Link
Croydon Tramlink
Docklands Light Railway Lewisham Extension
A12 Hackney M11 Link road
A13 Prince Regent Lane - A112 Junction
A13 Beckton - A117 Junction
A13 Movers Lane
A406 Golders Green Road/Brent Street Junction
A406 Hanger Lane - Harrow Road
A406/A1/A598 Regents Park Road
A406 Silver Street - Fore Street

5.29 We cannot rule out further land take associated with transport improvements. While the focus of local transport programmes is currently on the development of local strategies aiming to promote public transport and better intermodal exchange, local authorities may in future decide to promote local road schemes, particularly in outer London where the environmental relief provided by a local bypass scheme could justify its construction. There may also be land take associated with public transport schemes which London Transport are also considering, for example covering intermediate modes in outer London. Rigorous appraisal will ensure that any direct environmental damage which such schemes bring will only take place where it can be justified on wider grounds.

Noise and Visual Intrusiveness

5.30 The noise created by transport movements and the visual intrusiveness of transport infrastructure is often highlighted as one of Londoners' major concerns. Surveys carried out on behalf of DoE in 1990 and 1991 found that road traffic noise was the most common type of outside noise heard in the home, and annoyed more people in total than other external noises.

5.31 Significant changes for the better have already taken place. Improvements in their design mean that modern cars make one third of the noise of cars in the 1970s. Lorries are also quieter; it is estimated that ten of today's lorries make the same amount of noise as one lorry did in the seventies. New standards for aircraft mean that they are much quieter than previously. For example, the number of people around Heathrow affected by aircraft noise more than halved between 1979 and 1992, despite the growth in aircraft movements.

5.32 Improvements across all modes have been secured at a cost to travellers which the economy has been ready to bear, in view of their importance. Possible future improvements need to be considered with a view to striking the right balance between providing for transport demands and the desirability of environmental protection which has already been highlighted. As with other environmental effects, the mitigation of noise and visual intrusiveness will come about from a range of different responses. In the longer term policies which reduce the overall need to travel, particularly by car, will improve urban quality. As *Strategic Guidance for London Planning Authorities* makes clear, the planning system has a central part to play in this process, through better integration of transport and development policies, allowing developments to be served by public transport, walking and cycling, rather than the private car.

5.33 In the short to medium term, there are a number of other measures which are being taken to reduce these impacts. Noise regulations provide for compensation to those affected by new road schemes. The Noise Insulation Regulations (1975) and Amendment (1988) detail which properties qualify for compensation by highway authorities promoting individual road schemes. Similar regulations govern noise pollution which results from new rail infrastructure. The current legal framework is provided by the Noise Insulation (Railways and Other Guided Transport Systems) Regulations 1996. The Government also recognises that noise from the increased use of existing rail lines is a source of pollution which affects London residents. Over the last two years the Department of Transport has provided over £1.5 million towards local authority schemes, which are being pursued with the railway industry, to mitigate the noise from increased use of rail lines to the Channel Tunnel. There have been a number of statutory sound insulation schemes at Heathrow and Gatwick, and a voluntary scheme at Stansted.

5.34 The Highways Agency's landscape strategy, launched in November 1995, provides for a comprehensive approach to improving the visual appearance of the trunk road network. The strategy sets a high standard for improving the appearance of London's major road traffic routes, establishes priorities for action, and forms a basis for joint initiatives with local authorities, businesses and residents. The Government is also promoting the 'Green Corridors' concept, through strategic planning guidance, and by encouraging co-operation between transport agencies and highway authorities responsible for road and rail networks. This initiative aims to improve the visual appearance of the major transport corridors into London, particularly through tree planting strategies. And the Government is working with the London Boroughs and the Freight Transport Association to devise ways of making the ban more effective, extending it to cover all Boroughs and reducing the need for night movements through residential areas.

5.35 It is clearly not realistic to expect the complete abatement of noise and visual pollution. For example the costs of noise barriers to protect all Londoners from road and rail noise would be extremely high. Extensive noise barriers would also themselves be regarded as visually intrusive, and as such environmentally controversial. Some forms of protection against noise or visual pollution could only be achieved at the expense of road safety. The measures described above should however make some contribution towards alleviating noise and visual pollution which results from transport use. As noted in the Transport Green Paper, the Government has undertaken as an objective to promote measures to reduce the proportion of the UK population experiencing excessive noise levels from all sources, including transport. Aircraft noise, which we deal with in more detail in Chapter 8, is also a difficult issue.

The use of targets

5.36 Many have suggested that, in order to balance the achievement of environmental and economic objectives in London, we need to adopt targets, as we did for accident reduction. As described above we have set national targets for reductions in CO_2, although not specifically for the transport sector, and we are developing standards and objectives for air quality and an objective for noise. We believe there may be a case for some form of target-based approach for traffic, and note the work that the London local authorities have begun in this area. There do remain questions about how such targets might operate, and at what level. The Royal Commission on Environmental Pollution (RCEP) in their 18th Report on Transport and the Environment suggested that the Government should set itself the target of reducing the proportion of urban journeys undertaken by car in the London area from the present 50% to 45% by 2000 and 35% by 2020. The London Planning Advisory

Committee (LPAC) proposed in their 1994 *Advice on Strategic Planning Guidance for London* that Government should establish targets for traffic levels to reduce the levels of CO_2 emissions from cars in London.

5.37 We believe that these particular recommendations would be difficult to achieve. As can be seen from the statistics in Table 5J below, Londoners travel less overall, taking into account all modes, car ownership is lower and fewer journeys are made by car. The advantages brought by effective public transport provision and availability of local facilities have already been extensively exploited. Whilst this strategy aims to build on these advantages further, it becomes increasingly difficult to achieve modal switch without excessive restraint. This does not make target setting impossible, but it may limit the possibilities of achieving tougher targets than in other urban areas.

Table 5J

Londoners' Travel Behaviour

- London residents travel about 5,000 miles each year, less than the national average of 6,000 miles and a ROSE average of 8,000 miles. In addition, the amount of travel undertaken by Londoners appears to be declining.

- Car ownership in London is below the national average; in 1993, 62% of London households owned one or more cars, compared to 69% nationally.

- Londoners undertake fewer journeys by road (48% of total journeys) than the national average (59%) or the ROSE average (68%).

- Londoners undertake more journeys by public transport than residents in any other part of the UK. Public transport accounts for 85% of commuter journeys into central London.

5.38 It is also suggested that meeting such targets would require reductions in road capacity. Such a blanket approach would be inappropriate. In view of the evidence of Chapter 3 on London's competitiveness, the Government believes that providing for strategic traffic movements remains a high priority, and so would not wish to introduce a presumption against the policy of making limited improvements to road capacity, where these can be justified in both economic and environmental terms.

This approach does not entail major new road construction, but making better use of the existing network, as we explain later. Nor does it preclude measures to restrain traffic. In the context of the Government's commitment to environmental sustainability, the fact that London starts from a position ahead of the rest of the UK cannot justify exempting it from the requirement to make a contribution to the overall environmental objectives.

5.39 One important reason for facilitating movements of through-traffic on the **strategic** road network is to take it away from unsuitable **local** roads, in particular those serving residential areas. Allowing through traffic to bypass such areas can allow local authorities to pursue calming policies which reduce the impact of the car locally. Since 65% of car journeys in London are of less than 5 miles and 42% are of less than 3 miles, the achievement of CO_2 targets - as well as other local air quality targets - will benefit from reductions in these local trips. This leads us to the conclusion that central Government programmes need to **facilitate** strategic traffic movement, in order to sustain the economy while respecting global environmental considerations. At the local level the same objectives can be achieved through programmes which **restrict** traffic movements. It is in this context that we believe local traffic targets may have a role to play, but we would not seek to impose them. Our approach to the difficult question of preserving access to central and inner London and facilitating orbital movements, whilst discouraging traffic from entering the centre unnecessarily, is pursued in Chapter 11.

5.40 It may be that Boroughs want to pursue some form of restrictions on car use, such as higher parking charges, traffic calming, restricted access, or pedestrianisation. Local authorities will need to reach a balanced view, based on local consultations with residents, businesses, and other interested parties. The Road Traffic Regulation Act 1984 gives local authorities extensive powers to make Traffic Regulation Orders prohibiting, restricting or regulating vehicular traffic or particular types of vehicular traffic. The Environment Act 1995 extended the purposes for which TROs can be made to cover explicitly pursuit of air quality objectives.

5.41 But the exercise of such powers is something that local authorities need to consider carefully, bearing in mind the balance between maintaining traffic flow whilst improving the quality of the environment. Some traffic calming and pedestrianisation schemes can be implemented successfully, without causing congestion by diverting traffic. Other traffic management schemes may have positive benefits for air quality, but at the same time increase the risk of personal injury accidents. Conditions for success generally involve a combination of:

- good alternative routes for traffic to bypass the calmed area;

- effective demand management strategies, including local authority parking controls; and

- good access by public transport, as an alternative to car use.

5.42 We need to strike a balance in meeting the needs of all road users. In many areas of London, such as town centres and shopping streets where many people come by foot, this may involve direct restrictions on traffic. In other areas, it is sensible to give priority to road transport, because of the wider benefits of so doing. In cases where these needs conflict (and this is inevitable in a built up area such as London) interested parties should work together in order to attempt to find constructive solutions or compromises. This underlines the importance of the Local Agenda 21 process, established at the Rio Summit, which brings in the views of communities, with local authorities in the lead.

Conclusion

5.43 The Government's primary environmental objective in London is to improve air quality. While this is a complex area, it is essential to secure improvements, because the health both of Londoners and of the London economy depends on the atmosphere being as pleasant as it can be in one of the busiest metropolitan areas in the world. Existing policies will provide many of these improvements, while transport and environmental agencies in London will need to work closely in partnership to build upon these in the longer term.

5.44 It would be unrealistic of the Government to suggest that the visual and noise impacts of existing transport activity can be mitigated much further. Such environmental intrusion, while it should be minimised where feasible, is an inevitable consequence of our economic aspirations. Nevertheless, there are measures which can be taken. Technology has played a part in reducing noise levels, and will continue to do so. At a local level management of traffic can allow the separation of people and traffic, without stymieing the local economy.

5.45 We also believe promoting modal shift forms part of this longer term programme, but the Government does not believe particular targets can be set at this stage covering all of London. There cannot be a central view on the right levels of road traffic in London, and imposing one, with the significant constraints for residents, businesses and visitors arbitrary targets would entail, could only risk putting in jeopardy the prospects for economic growth. Nevertheless, more work needs to be done into the possibilities of restraining traffic more sensitively, in conjunction with the local authorities. These issues are discussed in more depth at Chapter 11.

5.46 As far as possible demands for transport arising from economic growth should depend on public transport, walking and cycling, such that these modes will take a relatively greater burden of London's transport needs. But we need to recognise that existing levels of transport activity of whatever sort cannot readily be reduced. We are committed to ensuring that as far as possible attempts are made to resolve conflicts between the economic and environmental objectives which are inherent in any modern economy, by a process of discussion with as wide a number of interests as possible, both at a local and at a London-wide level.

Chapter 6: Safety, Mobility and Freedom of Choice

Safety

6.1 Safety is an essential feature of any transport system. No matter how rapid, reliable and comfortable a transport system may be and no matter how effectively it contributes to our economic and environmental objectives, nobody can be satisfied with a transport system which results in an unacceptably high toll of deaths and injuries.

6.2 From the safety perspective, London starts with some strengths and some weaknesses. The principal strength is that London is more heavily dependent on public transport than any other part of the country, and the statistics demonstrate conclusively that public transport (by bus, train or Underground) is inherently safer than private transport (by car, bicycle or on foot). The principal weakness is that London is an urban area, and the statistics demonstrate just as conclusively that urban roads are inherently less safe than motorways or trunk roads, because they bring the most vulnerable users, particularly, cyclists and child pedestrians, into closer proximity with heavy traffic.

6.3 London has secured significant reductions in road casualties, as Chart 6A shows. The Government has set itself the objective of reducing the number of deaths and injuries on Britain's roads by one-third by the year 2000, using the 1981-85 average as the baseline. In 1994, London was 15% below the baseline, in terms of total numbers of casualties, and it had secured a welcome and impressive reduction of 50% in the number of people killed on London's roads.

6.4 In framing this transport strategy, we have constantly borne in mind the importance of safety issues. In the rare cases where safety conflicts with other goals, safety considerations prevail. However, such cases are exceptional. The most significant of

these is the conflict between safety objectives and the promotion of some of the more environmentally friendly modes (see paragraph 5.5). In their 18th report, the Royal Commission on Environmental Pollution recommended that the Government set the objective that, by 2010, 10% of all journeys be undertaken by cycle. In looking at how far London can go in this area, we have been forced to conclude that the safety objections are very serious ones.

6.5 In general, however, there is no particular conflict between safety concerns and our competitiveness, regeneration and freedom-of-choice goals, whilst many of the measures taken in pursuit of environmental goals (the promotion of public transport and traffic calming measures) have significant safety benefit. Safety considerations bite more at the detailed level than at the strategic level. They bear more, for example, on how a railway is designed or operated than on the question of whether it should be built in the first place. The key constraints on our ability to secure further improvements in transport safety are partly financial and partly behavioural.

6.6 The financial constraint is an obvious one. It bites on all aspects of transport expenditure, and is explored more fully in Chapter 14. The behavioural constraint is, in a sense, the opposite side of the same coin. On the roads, in particular, the greatest scope for making London a safer place to live and work in lies with the ordinary road-user - the driver, the cyclist and the pedestrian. If we could persuade them to modify their behaviour patterns, much of the investment programme would be unnecessary. To take an obvious example, the use of road-humps, chicanes and other means of slowing traffic in residential areas achieves by cost and coercion something that we have failed to achieve by persuasion - namely, getting motorists to accept that a speed which is appropriate on a through-

Chart 6A: London road casualties by type 1981 - 94

Index of road casualties (1981-1985 average=100)

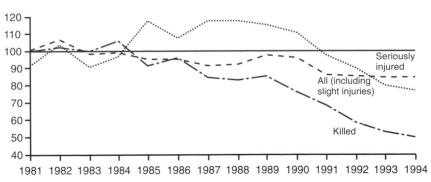

Source: Department of Transport

road is inappropriate on a back-street.

6.7 Personal safety is also a key issue. Many public transport users are concerned about their personal safety, for example, using public transport at night. This has a disproportionate effect on women, elderly people, disabled people and those on lower incomes, who are major users of public transport. Although overall levels of reported crime are falling, violent crime is still increasing and there is doubt that the overall downward trend will continue. The perception of crime and the risk that it brings is increasing, particularly among women. This, in turn, is leading many women to restrict or change their personal travel patterns and to be more likely to be car or taxi dependent. How people feel, rather than their actual experience of crime, may be the deciding factor in whether to make a journey or how they will make it.

6.8 While there are clearly expenditure implications for operators in improving levels of safety, for example through better lighting, higher levels of staffing, presence of closed circuit television and so on, there are also potential gains in terms of increased patronage if levels of confidence in the public transport systems can be restored. Further research is needed and greater emphasis on understanding the perception of personal risk, as well as the reality of it. The Department of Transport will be conducting further research into this area later this year, to investigate to what extent fear of crime is discouraging the use of public transport, and what it will take to counter this.

Mobility

6.9 The personal mobility and freedom of choice issues overlap, but it is worth stressing that the Government is committed to achieving fully accessible public transport systems which are responsive to the needs of those with mobility problems. We are not thinking only of those with physical disabilities. We are also thinking of elderly people, travellers with heavy baggage, shoppers with children and so forth. For all these people, the 'easy' solution is transport by car or by taxi. In the absence of suitable public transport or fully accessible taxis there is often no alternative to the private car and for some disabled people the car will always be the only suitable transport mode. However, there are two very obvious problems with this approach. The first is that not everyone can afford to use cars or taxis. The second is that, in environmental and sustainability

terms, London cannot afford it either. Hence, promotion of access to bus, taxi, rail and Tube services is important. Indeed, under the terms of the Disability Discrimination Act 1995, regulations will be brought forward setting standards for full accessibility to all new public transport vehicles.

6.10 The timetable for implementation of these requirements is likely to be staggered over a number of years and will depend upon the availability of technically and operationally sustainable solutions. It may, for example, be many years before significant improvements to access in the London Underground can be achieved because of the enormous cost involved in improving stations as well as rolling stock. Where it is economically viable Underground stations will be made more accessible, but there are no plans to require accessibility at existing stations. On the other hand, relatively rapid progress can be made with improved access to bus services. There is already a significant number of fully accessible low floor buses running in the outer London area and they are likely to provide the most effective access solution for the wide range of people described above who have mobility difficulties. All licenced taxis in London will be wheelchair accessible by the turn of the century.

6.11 It must be recognised that even with the requirements of the Disability Discrimination Act, it will be many years before we have achieved a fully accessible transport network in London. This involves not only tackling transport vehicles and infrastructure, but also removing barriers from the pedestrian environment so that people, for example, who use wheelchairs, can move unimpeded between their homes and the bus stop or railway station, or their final destination. There will, therefore, remain for the foreseeable future a need for the more specialised door-to-door transport service, particularly for the most severely disabled people, provided by Dial-a-Ride or by the growing number of wheelchair accessible taxis. Increasingly, these services should, however, become a complement to - rather than a substitute for - accessible public transport. Within the next 20 to 25 years, it should be possible to ensure that all the surface transport systems running in London have achieved full accessibility.

Freedom of Choice : Why It Matters

6.12 As a matter of general principle, the Government believes that the freedom of individuals to travel, and to do so by the mode of their choice, is of vital importance and needs to be preserved to the maximum possible extent. The same goes for the freedom of companies to locate where they wish and to use the mode of their choice for business trips and for the movement of goods and services. The caveat that we need to preserve such freedoms 'to the maximum possible extent' is a necessary one, to which we shall revert. However, before doing so, we should set out briefly the three main reasons why we regard these freedoms as important ones.

6.13 The first reflects our broader concern to preserve civil liberties. Freedom of movement is an important characteristic of an open society, and not one that should be infringed lightly.

6.14 The second relates to economic efficiency and thereby has an impact on competitiveness. The risks associated with constraining the locational or transport decisions are obvious. Any such constraint inhibits the ability of UK-based companies to reduce their costs and/or improve the quality of their output and has a detrimental effect on their and the nation's competitive position. However, the concern extends to the travel of individuals. Londoners, like anyone else, want access to job opportunities, to shops, to leisure activities, to schools and to other people. Access to ever-widening opportunities lies at the root of economic growth and development. If we impose constraints on such access, we impose additional costs on individuals and thereby drive up pay levels, we undermine a stimulus to economic growth and we make London a less attractive place to live and work in. The last of these concerns is particularly important, given what is said in Chapter 2 about London's economic vulnerability. Promotion of individuals' freedom of choice also promotes competition, leading to lower costs and higher standards.

6.15 The third relates to the complexity of the transport system and to the risk that measures to restrain freedom of choice will have perverse effects. Any intervention by Government in the workings of markets carries such risks. For example, we referred at paragraph 2.24 to the dispersal policies which were pursued by Governments throughout the post-War period and which have contributed to the regeneration problems which London now faces. Measures which restrain freedom of choice are particularly likely to have perverse effects, because the way in which modal choices are made is not as well understood as we

would like. They are also likely to be more difficult to unpick or reverse.

6.16 In debating transport policy, there is a natural tendency to refer to people as motorists or bus users or cyclists. It should be recognised, however, that this is merely a convenient form of shorthand. Most people use different modes for different trips and often use more than one mode for a single trip. That is particularly true in London. There is no such thing as a single 'best' mode of transport for getting round London. It depends critically on where and when one is travelling.

6.17 Indeed, the use of the word 'best' begs a number of questions in itself, because people want a number of different things from a transport system. We know that the two key determinants of modal choice are journey time and cost. Our transport models concentrate on these two variables and have a good track record of forecasting modal split. However, they are not the only issues.

6.18 Reliability, convenience and comfort are also factors which people clearly take into account. Paragraph 3.17 referred to the fact that an improvement in reliability may be as important for some people as a reduction in average journey time. The impact that Travelcard has had on public transport demand is evidence of the value which people set on convenience. Comfort may well be one reason why so few people cycle to work, despite the fact that it is a quicker means of getting round inner London than the car or public transport. The evidence does not suggest that either safety or environmental concerns have much impact on the travel decisions of most Londoners. However, the influence of environmental concerns may grow and it is, indeed, an important task for Government to foster an informed understanding of the environmental issues - a point which we have dealt with more fully in Chapter 5. Equally, we have an educational role to discharge on the safety front, where the actual safety of the different modes has little impact on transport choices, but perceptions of safety and security do exert some influence, even though they bear little relation to the facts.

Freedom of Choice : The Limitations

6.19 Freedom for the resident and visitor alike to choose where, when and how to travel in the Capital does, however, raise some difficult issues, given people's clear preference for using their private cars.

Road space in London is a finite resource. Across London as a whole, there is very little scope for increasing it and, in some areas, there is no scope at all. The importance of sustaining and enhancing London's economic performance within these constraints underlines the objectives of reducing the need to travel and promoting less polluting modes of transport. Additionally more effective use of the existing road network has long been - and will remain - an important objective of central and local Government alike. Central London has the benefit of one of the most sophisticated traffic control systems in the world, and this is being extended progressively into the outer areas. The Red Routes initiative, the London Bus Priority Network, parking enforcement and other approaches are being pursued, and are described more fully in Chapter 11. However, the Government harbours no illusions that all these initiatives can make more than a modest impact on traffic flows. Moreover, to the extent that they create additional capacity, the private car does not have the first claim upon it.

6.20 As noted elsewhere, about a million people commute into central London each day. Chart 2K (see Chapter 2) shows the modal split and the change in each mode's share of the market over the period 1975 to 1994. Rail (including London Underground and the DLR) accounts for nearly three-quarters of the market, and its market share has strengthened over the last decade. All forms of road transport - bus, coach, car, cycle and motorcycle - have declined. There is a variety of factors at work here and some of the trends are more welcome than others. These points are discussed more fully in Chapter 11. The points that we are concerned to make here relate to the nature of the freedom of choice that we can provide in London and to the way in which that freedom is, in practice, exercised.

6.21 Viewed individually, each of these one million people has the freedom to choose where they live and how they travel to work. Viewed collectively, they are subject to serious constraints: they cannot all live in central London and they cannot all commute by car. It is in the former sense, therefore, that we regard freedom of choice as something which can and should be preserved. We do not view it as creating a requirement to criss-cross London with new roads or railways until every conceivable demand for transport is satisfied.

6.22 In exercising their freedom of choice, individuals

devise solutions to their transport problems which meet their personal requirements and result in a reasonably efficient use of the available infrastructure. Since the supply of transport capacity is fixed in the short term, demand adjusts accordingly. People experiment with modes and routes until they find the one that best satisfies their requirements, in terms of the balance which they strike between the different factors discussed at paragraphs 6.13 and 6.18. The result is that transport demand is in a permanent state of unstable equilibrium, in which people find solutions which work, but which may not be optimal viewed from a broader economic or environmental perspective.

6.23 For the reasons discussed in Chapters 3 and 5, a combination of economic and environmental concerns cause us to be particularly concerned about congestion and pollution problems in central London. The extent to which pollution is a central area problem is graphically illustrated by Map 6B. The environmental concerns also drive us in the direction of promoting modal shift. The key question, therefore, is how we maintain and enhance freedom of choice, whilst furthering these other goals.

Freedom of Choice : The Balance

6.24 The answer turns principally upon the choice of policy instrument. There are four possible instruments, which we rank in the following order.

6.25 Our first preference is for the price mechanism. In inducing modal shift, the most efficient mechanism is to change the relative cost of public and private transport. Similarly, in order to discourage traffic from entering the central area, the most efficient mechanism is to levy a charge for doing so. The attraction of the price mechanism is that it achieves the environmental goal in an economically efficient manner. Ensuring that users pay the full environmental costs of their transport decisions improves the efficiency of those decisions for the economy as a whole, and also brings with it environmental benefits. There are limitations on the short term contribution of the price mechanism, which are discussed more fully in Chapter 11, but this remains an important area for transport policy, and is covered in more detail in the Transport Green Paper.

6.26 Our second preference is for approaches which harness speed and quality signals and which involve 'levelling up', rather than 'levelling down'. For example, an attractive approach (from the freedom of choice perspective) to discouraging traffic from entering either central London or the town-centres of outer London is to provide good alternative routes around the centre or to offer public transport alternatives for those who do need to get the centre. Similarly, one of the most effective ways of promoting greater use of buses, in particular, is to tackle some of the competitive disadvantages - their comparative slowness and unreliability - under which they currently labour. Again, however, there are limitations, on environmental and cost grounds, to what can be done in this way.

6.27 Our third preference is for measures which restrict the use of the car, for example by limiting the availability of parking or by reassigning road space to higher-priority traffic. Such measures may be necessary. . They do not eliminate freedom of choice, but they begin to encroach upon it. They also risk having the sort of perverse effects referred to above. For example, eliminating capacity for cars on the through-routes risks diverting them into residential areas, where they risk doing more harm in both safety and environmental terms.

6.28 The option of denying individuals the ability to travel by car, by the use of bans or road closures, is one that we are extremely reluctant to contemplate. It is a possible solution to local problems. It is not an acceptable solution to London-wide problems.

Competition and Privatisation

6.29 Competition is the opposite side of the 'freedom of choice' coin.

6.30 Like the Underground, the railways are the choice of several hundred thousand commuters every morning. For many parts of London, especially in the South, they are the main link into the central area of the capital. Until now, the services have all been provided by British Rail, a monolithic nationalised industry, which has often seemed remote from the day-to-day needs of its passengers.

6.31 For many users, the railway has such a significant competitive advantage over other modes that it is the virtually inevitable choice. This should not mean that the rail service need not be attractive or efficient, for there is a wider choice, perhaps not at individual level, but at the level of companies and businesses. If transport is not attractive companies increasingly have the choice of moving to other cities in the UK or in Europe, or of moving to greenfield sites on the edge of the urban area, where car transport is the only option. For London to prosper, therefore, the rail choice has to be one that travellers are happy about making. This is a prime aim of the privatisation of the railways.

6.32 Through rail privatisation, it is the Government's intention to ensure that each part of the railway is operated by groups specialising in delivering efficient and effective services in their own area of expertise. This means that the owners of the infrastructure concentrate on making sure it operates effectively, that the train operators concentrate on providing the services that their customers want and that the other specialist elements in the railway - rolling stock providers, maintenance facilities, etc - operate on a similar basis. The key to making the rail option more

Map 6B: Distribution of carbon monoxide

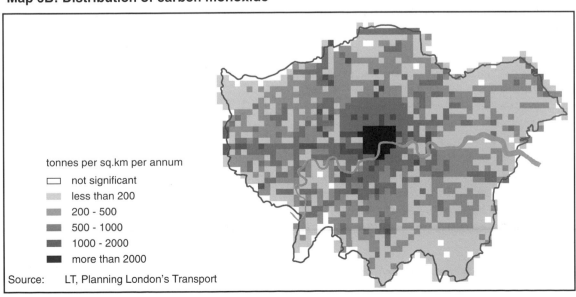

tonnes per sq.km per annum

☐ not significant

less than 200

200 - 500

500 - 1000

1000 - 2000

more than 2000

Source: LT, Planning London's Transport

attractive to people is giving the operators an incentive to deliver the best service possible and empowering them to take the decisions they need to take to achieve this. Making rail more attractive will in turn help to promote modal shift and the achievement of our wider environmental objectives.

6.33 The priority for London Underground is to improve the quality of the existing network through investment, and to make the business more efficient by harnessing private finance and by improved management of the operation of the railway, including the contracting out of activities where this offers better value for money.

6.34 Bus services in London were, until 1994, carried out mainly by wholly-owned subsidiary companies of LT. These were privatised in 1994/5, either being sold to the existing management teams and staff, or to other major bus companies. The pricing and routing of bus services remains the responsibility of LT. In an urban area as large and complex as London, and one that relies so heavily on the bus as one of the main modes of transport, it is necessary for passengers to be able to obtain coherent information and have the use of a unified service. Privatisation is enabling private sector expertise to find the maximum in efficiency savings and make commercial decisions about investment in new vehicles.

6.35 As contracts with the private bus operators are renewed, a further incentive to improve efficiency and attract passengers is being implemented in the shape of 'net cost' tendering. This involves operators bidding for the minimum amount of subsidy from LT they need to run a service and allows the operator to keep the fare revenue. This gives them a direct incentive to make their services as attractive and user-friendly as possible.

6.36 In the rest of the country, privatisation of bus services has been accompanied by deregulation. The Government believes that the overall effect of deregulation has been very successful, with more operators running more services, at lower cost and at much lower levels of subsidy. Detailed refinements to the operation of the system are now being taken forward by the Government in co-operation with operators and local authorities, and should further improve its effectiveness in delivering better bus services.

6.37 In London, the prospect of deregulation has

however, posed particular concerns, given the potential impact of short-term fluctuations in the level of bus competition on traffic congestion in parts of the Capital, and given the greater complexity of the interactions between and within the public transport modes, for instance in terms of ticketing arrangements. However, the Government believes that these difficulties are not insuperable, and remains committed to the extension of deregulation to London, although it has made clear that this will not be pursued in the course of the present Parliament.

6.38 The London black cab is one of the Capital's great institutions, but its importance goes far deeper than being a symbol of the city that is recognised around the world. It is an important transport choice and a transport option of great importance to people that live in London and visitors alike - a fast way of getting to where you want to go without knowing more than the address. It is a choice that most people cannot afford to make use of every day, but there are few people who cannot say that they have been very glad to make that choice once or twice. The private hire car or minicab also offers an important service, mostly away from the central area and for lower income groups. The Government has outlined proposals for primary legislation to licence minicabs.

Chapter 7: Transport Objectives

Introduction

7.1 So far in Part One of this document, we have looked at London's economic and demographic prospects. In the light of those, we have looked at how transport can help to promote competitiveness, foster regeneration and improve the quality of London's environment. We have also looked at how considerations of safety, mobility and freedom of choice affect transport decisions.

7.2 We have stressed the fact that London has an extensive and complex transport system, serving a large and complex economy. We have noted the dangers of oversimplifying the picture, particularly in dealing with the relationship between economic and environmental goals, where there are tensions in some areas and synergies in others.

7.3 In this Chapter, we attempt to draw the strands together and translate the underlying transport aim set out at paragraph 1.9 into transport objectives for London. Part Two of the document deals with the specific initiatives that can be taken in pursuit of these objectives, and the implementation of the strategy - by which we mean the funding, the forward investment programme and the allocation of responsibilities.

7.4 This is therefore a key chapter. It is an attempt to address one of the valid criticisms of our approach to transport in London - that we have not spelled out clearly enough what we are doing, what we plan to do, and why.

The Conclusions of Chapters 2-6

7.5 We conclude that the Capital retains significant competitive advantages in key sectors, and that it is likely to experience modest growth in output and employment, but that there are significant risks. This prompts us to aim first to promote the **competitiveness** of London as a World City. This means focusing on the quality of international transport links (London's principal competitive strength), tackling air pollution problems (London's principal competitive weakness) and facilitating access to, and ease of movement within, the central business districts.

7.6 The promotion of **safety** must always take priority. This also points in the direction of promoting modal shift to public transport, which in general terms is safer than motorcycling, cycling and walking. However, as noted in Chapter 6, safety bites more on how things are done than on the question of whether they should be done.

7.7 In framing the rest of our objectives, we have sought to pursue our environmental and regeneration goals without being too restrictive on the scope for individual mobility and freedom of choice; and to give priority to initiatives which further the regeneration or environmental goals, but which also contribute materially to promoting competitiveness and safety.

7.8 On the **environmental** side, therefore, tackling the air pollution problem has a high priority, because of its synergy with the competitiveness goal. It points towards encouraging modal shift and managing access to the central area. We also wish to seek further environmental improvements in other areas. But the competitiveness and regeneration considerations impose constraints on how far and how fast we move; and freedom of choice considerations guide our choice of policy instruments, creating a strong preference for 'levelling up', by which we mean trying to promote modal shift by making services more attractive rather than by restricting access or seeking to force particular options on people.

7.9 The **regeneration** goal requires the promotion of access. It also imparts a geographical emphasis to the strategy, by identifying areas of London where the access problems need to be tackled urgently and underlining the need to look at transport and development issues together. To the extent that there is a London-wide dimension to the regeneration problem, it is the need for a good strategic network of trunk roads and Red Routes, into which local access roads can feed.

7.10 In both the regeneration and the environmental areas, we have also stressed the importance of local plans and partnerships. The focus of this strategy is on what can and should be done at the London-wide level. Thus, we have a lot to say about the management of access to the central areas, because that means looking at how we use the London-wide road and rail networks. We have much less to say about access to local centres of population, not because they are unimportant, but because (a point reverted to in Chapter 15) we believe strongly that the lead in resolving these problems must rest firmly with the Boroughs.

The Objectives

7.11 On this basis, we have identified five key objectives.

7.12 **Objective 1** is *to maintain and enhance the quality of London's international transport links.* These are London's main competitive strength in the transport field. It makes sense to give a high priority in this strategy to initiatives which build upon our strengths. The pursuit of this objective is dealt with in Chapter 8.

7.13 **Objective 2** is *to enhance the quality of commuter services by rail and underground.* Chapter 9 deals with the pursuit of this objective. Enhancing the speed, reliability and quality of rail and Underground services makes a contribution to London's competitiveness. Rail travel is safer than travel by car, and more environmentally friendly.

7.14 **Objective 3** is *to promote greater use of less polluting forms of transport, subject to the need to maintain competitiveness and safety.* Although it is sometimes viewed narrowly as an environmental issue, the sensible pursuit of modal shift promotes competitiveness (by improving quality of life) and safety (by moving people onto inherently safer modes). Chapter 10 spells out the measures that are being and will be taken in this area. Encouraging the use of the bus is one of the most effective means of achieving the modal shift objective.

7.15 **Objective 4** is *to facilitate access to the central business districts and ease of movement within them.* These two aims address a closely linked set of competitiveness and environmental concerns. The requirement to improve air quality and promote ease of movement within the central area (which is not coterminous with the central business districts) points to the need to keep traffic volumes down and to facilitate traffic flow. However, this has to be achieved whilst preserving and enhancing the access which businesses require. It also has to be achieved without aggravating the regeneration or environmental problems of inner and outer London. The simultaneous achievement of these objectives is a formidable challenge, discussed further in Chapter 11.

7.16 **Objective 5** is *to plug major gaps in the road and rail network.* This furthers the regeneration goal and needs to be pursued in a manner consistent with our environmental goals. Its impact on competitiveness and modal shift is helpful, but relatively modest. It is dealt with in Chapter 12.

7.17 These are our London-wide objectives. The focus of this strategy is, quite deliberately, on how we can facilitate the international links and access to the central business districts and key regeneration areas, whilst trying to protect London's environment. Our objectives generally have a London-wide focus, rather than a local focus. However, it will be obvious from Chapter 3 that some of the steepest increases in transport demand are likely to be felt in outer London. The question of facilitating or controlling access to the outer London town centres, some of which already suffer from serious congestion, is a particularly difficult one. Much of this strategy focuses on inner and central London, not because we underestimate the importance of the outer London problems, but because we believe the responsibility for finding solutions must rest primarily with local authorities, rather than with central Government.

7.18 We set these five transport objectives alongside the Government's objectives for land use planning in *Strategic Guidance for London Planning Authorities*, in particular:

- to encourage a pattern of land uses and provision of transport which minimises harm to the environment and reduces the need to travel by car, consistent with the principles of sustainable development;

- to facilitate the development of transport systems which are safe, efficient and which contribute to the achievement of competitiveness, regeneration and environmental quality.

7.19 We have ranked our five objectives in a logical order, rather than in order of priority. However, all five objectives are subject to the general and overriding requirement to ensure that public expenditure on transport in London represents good value for money, is affordable, and does not represent (through the tax burden) a drag on the competitiveness of not only the London but also the UK economy. Chapters 13 and 14 deal with the funding of transport in London, including the forward expenditure programme. When we turn to the question of 'affordability', we conclude that it is possible to make good progress across the board in pursuing **Objective 1** and **Objectives 2-4**. Accordingly, it is not necessary to assign priorities to these objectives and it would be unhelpful to do so in the case of **Objectives 2-4**, which are closely interrelated. However, it will take significantly longer to make progress on **Objective 5**, given the high cost of new infrastructure. Chapter 15 then deals with allocation of responsibility for taking the strategy forward. In doing so, it addresses the question of a transport authority for London, explaining why the Government does not think it either necessary or desirable.

Part Two: Implementing the Strategy

Chapter 8: Promoting International Transport Links

8.1 This chapter identifies key transport links supporting London's existing position as an international centre; summarises current policies and initiatives to improve these links in the future; and discusses briefly the Government's reasons for continuing its current policy rather than making any radical shifts.

Competitiveness : Making the Best Better

8.2 One of the main reasons why businesses are attracted to London is the quality of the transport links. These links can be grouped broadly as follows:

- **Air Services and Airports** - There are five London airports (Heathrow, Gatwick, Stansted, London City and London Luton). These give London-based businesses an unparalleled range of connections, making London more easily accessible for overseas tourists, business traffic and air freight than any other city in the world, and allowing London to act as a hub for services all over the world.

- **Channel Tunnel** - The Channel Tunnel passenger and goods services operating out of Waterloo and the freight terminal at Willesden, offer direct services to and from Europe. Access to these is better from London than from elsewhere in the UK.

- **Road and rail access** - London is in the South East corner of the UK, at the hub of the national road and rail systems. This gives it a pivotal position between domestic and European markets with easy access both to the UK regions and continental Europe. This makes it attractive as a focal point, whether for a corporate headquarters, a goods distribution point, or a tourist visit.

- **Port Traffic** - 90% of Britain's international freight travels by sea. The Port of London is Britain's busiest port. The geographical links, both with the UK road, rail and sea routes, as well as the City of London, give the Capital a level of sea access unmatched by any other in Europe.

8.3 Chapters 2 and 3 make the case for bolstering London's competitive position, and explain why we have made this our top priority. Our existing strategy has been to support the maximum possible transfer of responsibility for service provision and investment to the private sector; maintain a sensible approach to regulation; and demonstrate a willingness to commit substantial public sector funds to infrastructure improvements where appropriate. London's success to date supports the Government's view that this policy works. There are no compelling competitiveness arguments for a radical departure from existing policy. This chapter accordingly sets out policies and initiatives which should maintain and enhance the quality of London's transport and hence consolidate its competitive advantages.

The following sections look separately at air, access to air services, international rail, and UK road/rail and ports issues; though we would hope they would play complementary roles.

Air Services and Airports

8.4 London's current position as the prime international aviation hub is the envy of other European cities.

- 139 international destinations are served daily from London's airports, putting businesses in London within 24 hours reach of 80% of the World's GDP;

- weekly direct scheduled flights to 251 international destinations;

- 9 of the 11 busiest European air routes run to and from London;

- 80 million passengers a year travel through London's airports, more than 50 million of them through Heathrow alone.

- Freight worth £35 billion a year passes through the two major airports, with around three quarters of this being handled by Heathrow.

- Heathrow is the largest airport in the world in terms of numbers of international passengers, and Gatwick ranks eighth.

The Government's strategy is to encourage this successful industry by providing an economic and regulatory environment that allows and encourages airlines and airport operators to meet the needs of their customers and thereby to contribute to the economy of the capital. This policy is supported by public sector funding for investment in surface access where there are clear benefits for the wider community.

8.5 The UK's membership of the European Union has provided a regulatory framework that promotes competition, leading to new market entrants, reduced fares and higher passenger numbers on the busiest routes. The Government's strategy has been to press hard for a liberal regime within Europe and the resulting removal of restrictions is continuing. From 1997, EU airlines will be able to fly between any two airports in the Union. The Government has also pressed hard to ensure that UK airlines enjoy the same degree of freedom to operate in other countries that airlines from other EU states enjoy here.

8.6 The three main London airports are subject to detailed economic regulation under the system set out in the 1986 Airports Act. This has successfully focused the operators' attention on cost control and efficiency. Airlines, and thereby passengers, have benefitted from airport charges which are very competitive in the European context. The three BAA airports are also subject to statutory requirements on noise mitigation.

8.7 Privatisation has played an important part in the development of London's aviation links. The move of both British Airways and BAA plc into the private sector during the 1980's led to dramatic improvements in the quality of service, the transport infrastructure and the level of competition - all bringing considerable benefits for the air passenger and reinforcing London's preeminent position.

8.8 Since privatisation in 1987, BAA plc, formerly the British Airports Authority, has transformed itself into the World's foremost airport operator. Milestones in that time include:

- a new £400 million terminal at Stansted with a dedicated rail service to Liverpool Street station;

- the modernisation and redevelopment of Heathrow's Terminals 1 and 3;

- a new Flight Connections Centre at Heathrow;

- the new North Terminal at Gatwick, and

- the 'Fast Track' priority scheme for business travellers.

8.9 Investment has not been limited to BAA-owned airports. London City Airport was opened in 1987. Traffic figures have increased dramatically in recent years. This reflects improved access following the completion of the Docklands road network, giving travel times of around 15 minutes to the City. It also reflects the greater range of destinations made possible by the decision in 1992 to allow smaller and quieter jet aircraft to use it. Passenger numbers reached 554,000 in 1995, a 17% rise over the previous year, and the upward trend seems likely to continue.

8.10 Traffic at London Luton airport has been around the 2 million mark for some years. Major improvements to the airport are planned, including the construction of a terminal with a new railway station offering direct Thameslink services across London.

8.11 Air freight and business aviation are also important to the competitiveness of London business. Over the last ten years, the amount of freight handled by London's airports has increased by nearly 80%. At £35 billion, the value of the cargo passing through the two major airports is approximately equal to that of the top five sea ports - although, naturally it is very much smaller in volume; the top items in terms of value are cut and uncut diamonds. Around three quarters of the total is handled by Heathrow, with Gatwick accounting for most of the remainder.

8.12 There are currently over 65,000 business aviation movements a year in the South East, most servicing businesses in the London area. This is expected to grow by at least 2% a year. Users increasingly need to find alternatives to the limited facilities at Heathrow and Gatwick. Other sites, particularly Biggin Hill, Farnborough, Northolt, Luton and Stansted, will therefore have an important role to play. The Government suggests that the benefits of business aviation should be taken into account by Boroughs alongside environmental impact when considering planning proposals on the future of individual airfields.

Airport Capacity

8.13 The Government is committed to enabling the development of additional airport capacity where this makes economic, social and environmental sense. Against this background, airports operate on a commercial basis. It is for operators to come forward with specific proposals for development and take them through the planning processes. The question of terminal capacity is currently being examined by the Public Inquiry into BAA's proposal to build a fifth terminal at Heathrow. The proposed fifth terminal would extend Heathrow's capacity from 50 million to 80 million passengers a year.

8.14 In recognition of the continuing strong demand for air travel in the South East, the Government established a working group on Runway Capacity to serve the South East (RUCATSE) in 1990. RUCATSE examined a number of options for additional runway capacity, but did not make specific recommendations. Following a period of consultation the Government responded to the group's report in February 1995, stating no further work should be undertaken on the RUCATSE options for Heathrow and Gatwick, but announcing additional studies to take forward the work of the group. This work will assess the implications of making better use of the existing runway infrastructure at Heathrow, the possibility of less environmentally damaging options for development, such as a close parallel runway at Gatwick, and also surface access issues (see below). Proposals will be subject to environmental assessment as appropriate.

Access to Airports

8.15 Most investment in aviation facilities will continue to be provided by the private sector, but the Government is mindful of the need to contribute towards infrastructure developments where a wider interest is to be served - notably surface connections between London's airports, central London and the rest of the region. The existing links compare reasonably well with those of other major cities as Map 8A shows.

8.16 With the completion of the Heathrow Express project in 1997/98, all three major airports will be connected to central London by dedicated express rail services. The Heathrow Express is a joint public/private sector venture with a total cost of around £400 million. The majority of the investment is being provided by BAA which is funding the underground spur between the Great Western Main Line and the Heathrow terminals, with Railtrack carrying out the electrification and upgrading of the existing rail lines into Paddington. The Heathrow Express will allow a journey time of 16 minutes between the central terminal area at Heathrow and Paddington station. The service will run every 15 minutes.

8.17 The Government and BAA are committed to looking at further ways of accommodating the projected increases in the numbers arriving at and departing from the airports. Local authorities have been closely involved in this work, given their responsibilities for local transport and traffic and the scope for improving access to airports by bus and coach. BAA has targets for increasing the percentage of passengers and employees arriving at Heathrow by public transport. Improved public transport access needs to be addressed whether or not Heathrow Terminal 5 goes ahead.

Map 8A: Comparison of major international cities' accessibility to their main airports

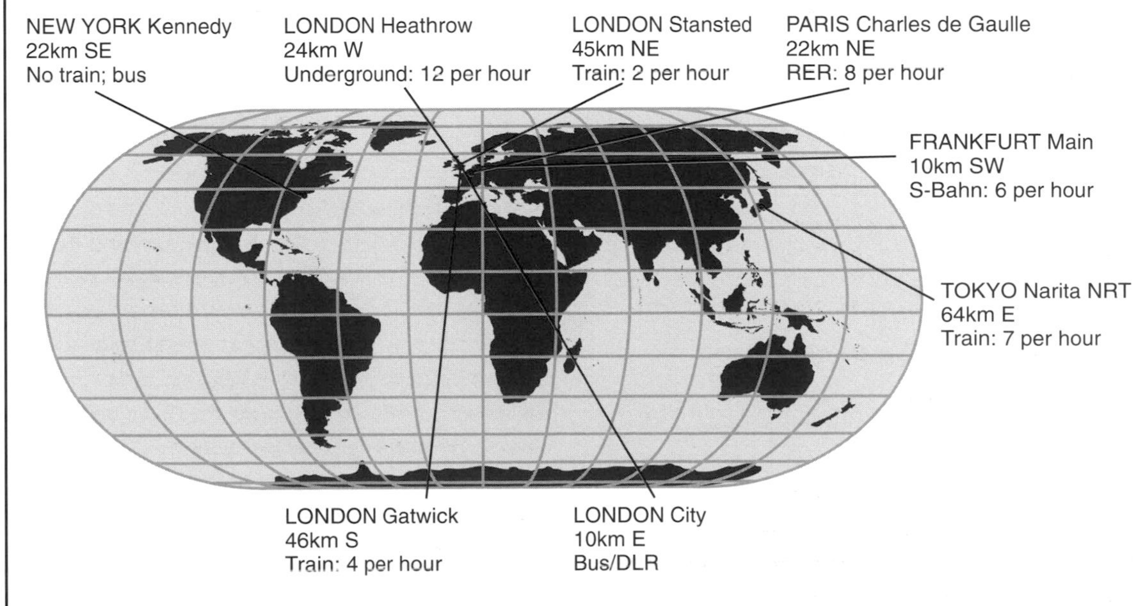

NEW YORK Kennedy
22km SE
No train; bus

LONDON Heathrow
24km W
Underground: 12 per hour

LONDON Stansted
45km NE
Train: 2 per hour

PARIS Charles de Gaulle
22km NE
RER: 8 per hour

FRANKFURT Main
10km SW
S-Bahn: 6 per hour

TOKYO Narita NRT
64km E
Train: 7 per hour

LONDON Gatwick
46km S
Train: 4 per hour

LONDON City
10km E
Bus/DLR

Source: LT, Planning London's Transport; Railway Gazette International, December 1995

8.18 In this context the Government has initiated the London Airports Surface Access Study (LASAS) which is due to report in summer 1996. Its remit is to investigate ways of improving surface links and, in particular, increasing the modal share of public transport, to and from all the London airports. The steering group, under the chairmanship of the Minister for Transport for London, brings together transport providers and Government representatives. Possibilities being addressed include new or improved rail links to and between airports, better bus and coach services, improved traffic management on the road network, and better interchange between modes. The study will examine how far improved rail links between the airports and from the airports to other destinations could help to maximise the use of existing airport capacity, and promote the use of public transport.

8.19 The study is also considering work already begun by local authorities through the South West London Transport Conference (SWELTRAC). This is a consortium of twelve local authorities, led by the London Borough of Richmond, and includes London Transport, Railtrack, and South West Trains. Working closely with BAA, it is evaluating an integrated programme of rail, bus priority and traffic management proposals aimed at improving access to Heathrow and traffic conditions in the South West of London. The Government has allocated resources towards bus priority measures in Richmond and Merton for 1996/97 and the further evaluation of bus measures in Kingston and a Southern Rail Link into Heathrow airport.

8.20 Privatisation of airports provision and the commercialisation of railways has allowed operators to work together to offer their passengers the types of services they expect. The Gatwick Express from Victoria, with check-in facilities at the London terminus, offers a good example of this. Progressive privatisation of the railway industry will increase the opportunities for such integration.

Environmental Problems

8.21 Whatever is achieved by regulation, investment and the efforts of airport operators and airlines, a major international airport such as Heathrow will continue to have adverse environmental impacts. The two main ones are noise and road traffic using the airport. These concerns have to be balanced against the benefits from meeting the competitive demands outlined above. So this section explains some of the efforts being made to address environmental concerns, and discusses the Government's reasons for not wishing to suppress or redirect air traffic. At Heathrow, Gatwick and Stansted the Government has implemented a range of measures to control and mitigate noise, including noise preferential departure routes, noise limits for departing aircraft and night restrictions. There have been noise insulation schemes, statutory for Heathrow and Gatwick, voluntary for Stansted. At other airports, noise mitigation measures are the responsibility of the airport operator.

Aircraft Noise

8.22 A great deal has already been done to reduce noise impact. As Chapter 5 noted, there was a reduction of more than 75% in the number of people adversely affected by aircraft noise from Heathrow between 1979 and 1992. This was despite a 40% increase in aircraft movements and the trend towards larger, heavier planes. Developments in technology have allowed operators to reduce the noise made by new aircraft. To accelerate the benefits of these advances, the older (noisier) aircraft are being phased out before the end of their operational lives. The first generation of subsonic jets, like the Trident and the Boeing 707, had to be phased out by 1988 or modified to meet internationally agreed standards. The second generation of subsonic jets ('Chapter 2' types) must be progressively phased out by 2002, or modified to meet tougher 'Chapter 3' standards. Already some 90% of aircraft using Heathrow meet 'Chapter 3' standards or better. The airport has encouraged this by setting higher landing charges for 'Chapter 2' aircraft, in line with the 'polluter pays' principle.

Road Traffic around Airports

8.23 Similarly, much has been done to minimise the adverse impact of road traffic using the airport and facilitate use of public transport. At Heathrow, for example, 34% of passengers and 11% of employees travel to the airport by public transport. Similar levels of passengers travel by public transport to Gatwick and Stansted. On completion of the Heathrow Express Rail Link, the proportion of air passengers using public transport there is forecast to rise to 38%. BAA's target is then further to increase the proportion of non-transfer air passengers arriving by public transport to 50% for the next century. The initiatives described at paragraphs 8.15 to 8.19 above will assist in meeting this target and promoting public transport access to London's other airports.

Regeneration

8.24 Further pressure to restrict activity at Heathrow derives from the regeneration argument. There is an imbalance between the economies of the eastern and western halves of London. Although there are pockets of deprivation in west London (eg at Park Royal - see paragraph 4.20), the west is more affluent than the east, as Chart 8B illustrates. The affluence of west London owes something to its road and rail links, but much is due to the proximity of Heathrow. Other causes lie behind the economic situation in the east, particularly the decline of the ports and its industrial base. The ALG *Airport Strategy for London* suggests restricting the use of Heathrow and encouraging the greater use of Stansted. They suggest this might meet both regeneration and environmental aims.

8.25 The Government's efforts in relation to noise and traffic show its acceptance of the need to strike a balance with environmental concerns around Heathrow. But it also believes that there are strong economic arguments for allowing the facilities at Heathrow to be used to their full potential, as far as that balance allows. It does not believe that a policy of capping Heathrow's movements, or seeking to use Traffic Distribution Rules to encourage traffic to use the other London airports, represents a good way of striking this balance. The scope for using pricing mechanisms to try to achieve the same end is limited by international agreements and the UK's regulatory regime.

8.26 There is already a significant differential between average airport charges at Heathrow and Stansted. In order to force traffic to switch from Heathrow charges would need to be raised above market clearing levels and there is no economic justification for such intervention.

8.27 Furthermore, whatever mechanism was used to reduce access to Heathrow, there is no guarantee that traffic would obligingly switch as desired to alternative UK airports. On the contrary, if airlines switched to mainland European airports (which are already competing with Heathrow) the UK might suffer a net reduction or loss of services, and the resulting reduction in choice and flexibility for passengers, particularly important for business passengers, might undermine London's attractiveness to business and tourists.

8.28 The Government is nevertheless keen to provide the opportunity for other airports in the South East to develop. There may be substantial scope for increasing the contribution from Gatwick, Stansted, and Luton in particular. This multi-airport structure provides valuable flexibility when it comes to considering options for development and in maximising the accessibility of air services to the region as a whole.

8.29 The Government has concluded that the demand for air transport to and from London is one that should be accommodated as far as possible. Environmental concerns mean that it is not possible to accommodate demand fully at particular sites, but there is not a general policy to divert or deter traffic to or from London.

Chart 8B: Average gross weekly earnings 1995; male full time (£)

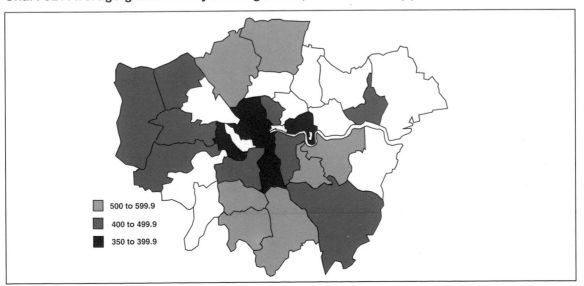

- 500 to 599.9
- 400 to 499.9
- 350 to 399.9

8.30 Roads in the Heathrow area are covered in Chapters 11 and 12. Road access will clearly remain important and there are plans for some further enhancement of road capacity. But the fact that the existing capacity of the strategically important roads in the area, the M4/A4 and M25, is severely stretched by the volume of traffic generated by Heathrow indicates that the emphasis does need to be placed on increasing the share of public transport.

Heliports

8.31 Many similar considerations apply to heliport development as to airport development, with the economic benefits set against the often severe local environmental impacts. London is presently served by a single commercial heliport at Battersea, and we recognise that there is demand for further provision. The environmental sensitivity of meeting that demand was reflected in the Environment Secretary's decision to reject a proposal for a heliport at Cannon Street, in 1991. The Department of Transport set up a study following that decision, to make a comparative evaluation of possible sites, without making particular

recommendations about the siting of a new development. As with airport development, we look to the private sector to come forward with proposals. The report of the London Heliport Study, published in March 1995 did however identify a number of technical issues which would need to be addressed at any future inquiry, and also developed an effective method for measuring the impact of helicopter noise.

Channel Tunnel

8.32 The opening of the Channel Tunnel in 1994 was an historic development in Britain's and in London's international links. The Government's strategy has been to invest to ensure that London, and the UK as a whole, enjoys the full benefits of this new link with France and Belgium.

8.33 To prepare for the Tunnel, improvements were made to the existing railway lines between London and the Tunnel, and the new international terminal was built at Waterloo - one of the most highly acclaimed modern buildings in London. Passenger services started in 1994 with a journey time from London of 3 hours to

Map 8C: Eurostar rail services

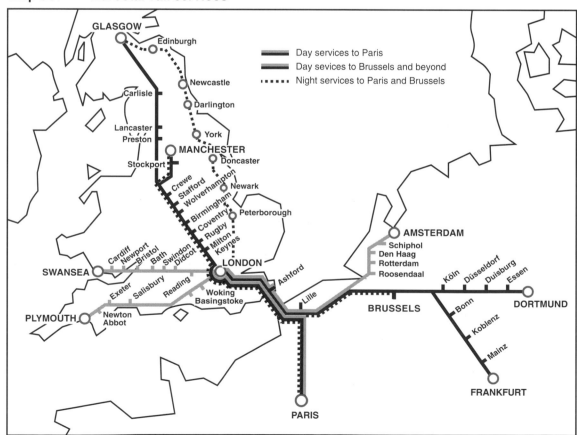

Source: European Passenger Services

Paris and 3 hours 15 minutes to Brussels. This will reduce to 2 hours 45 minutes with a new section of high speed line between Lille and Brussels, expected to open in 1998. Eurostar services are operated jointly by the British company European Passenger Services (EPS) with the French and Belgian state railways. EPS is due to be privatised shortly. By April 1996, over 4 million passengers will have travelled on Eurostar. Night services between London and the Netherlands and Germany are due to start in 1997. Map 8C shows the route map of day and night services.

8.34 BR has invested around £400 million in works and rolling stock for the freight service. The existing rail lines from the regions converge on Wembley, where there is a marshalling and operating centre, and then run south to the Tunnel. Around fifteen trains a day each way currently run from the North West, Midlands and London through to Europe. This is projected to rise to 27 trains a day each way during 1996.

Channel Tunnel Rail Link

8.35 Looking ahead, the aim is to facilitate the construction and operation by the private sector of a new high-speed railway line between London and the Channel Tunnel entrance at Cheriton along the route shown in Map 8D.

8.36 The Government recognises that new capacity will be needed through Kent to accommodate the traffic generated by the Channel Tunnel. The new Channel

Tunnel Rail Link will increase capacity for international rail services between London and the Continent, and reduce journey times by half an hour. Furthermore, the domestic rail services which will operate on the rail link will bring benefits for Kent commuters into London, including reduced journey times, new rolling stock and new infrastructure; and it will relieve congestion on the existing routes. The rail link will further benefit towns and cities beyond London. A fast connection is proposed between the rail link and the West Coast Main Line for use by through freight and passenger services, which will put Birmingham four hours from Paris by train.

8.37 On 29 February 1996 the Secretary of State announced the choice of London and Continental Railways as the private sector consortium that will construct and operate the high-speed link. As part of the contract, the consortium will take over both European Passenger Services and Union Railways, the Government-owned company that has so far taken forward the design work on the link. In view of the substantial benefits to the UK - worth around £6 billion - the Government will make a contribution with a present value of £1.4 billion towards the construction of the link. Part of this will be in the form of a payment for train paths to be used by the new commuter services.

8.38 The Government also announced, in the light of the bidders' proposals, that a combined international and domestic station would be provided at Stratford.

Map 8D: Channel Tunnel Rail Link route

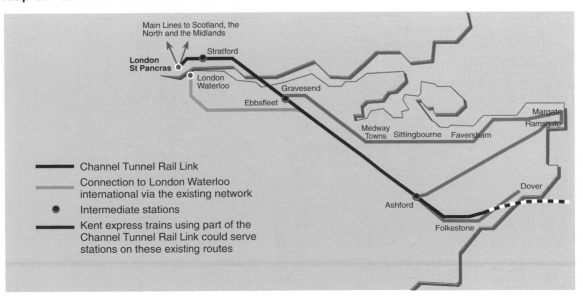

Source: Union Railways

The Stratford station will complement the intermediate station already announced for Ebbsfleet. Whilst Ebbsfleet will be a parkway station with access to the M25 motorway, Stratford is well connected by public transport and a focus for the western part of the Thames Gateway area. Between them the stations will stimulate regeneration across east London and north Kent, bringing the prospect of large benefits for the local economies of these areas. This clearly demonstrates an integrated approach to transport and development.

8.39 Freight trains will be able to utilise extra capacity on the existing network released by the opening of the rail link. They will also be able to use the rail link itself. The rail link will be built to a large European loading gauge, UIC 'C', so that standard European intermodal vehicles will be able to use it if infrastructure is made available to carry it through to terminals in the regions. The rail link thus keeps the options open for the development of international freight services.

8.40 The Hybrid Bill to authorise the project has completed its Standing Committee stage in the Commons and was passed to the House of Lords just after Easter. The Bill has already been significantly amended to reflect a number of route changes required by the Select Committee in the House of Commons.

8.41 The extra rail capacity between London and Europe is an essential need, because without it the growth of both international and domestic services in south-eastern England would be constrained. One consequence of this would be increased pressure for additional airport capacity in the London area, which would be environmentally more damaging. The rail option already offers competitive journey times to Paris and Brussels, especially from city centre to city centre, and the rail link will reduce these by a further half hour.

Road and Rail Access

8.42 As well as the opportunities offered by the opening of the Channel Tunnel and the associated investment in the rail network mentioned above, London also has natural advantages in terms of ease of access to the major south and east coast ports. The national road and rail networks largely radiate from London and offer connections in all directions. The roads programme has provided for considerable improvements to the network linking London and the M25 to Southampton (M3 completed), to Portsmouth (A3 being upgraded), to the Kent Ports and Channel

Tunnel (M20/A20 completed), and to the east coast ports (A12/A14 upgrading). These improvements also contribute to the Trans-European Road Network (TERN). Map 8E shows the roads from London to the South East ports.

8.43 The aim in London is now to ensure that businesses located there can gain easy access onto the national road network, in particular the M25, and travel free from congestion to the ports. The M25 widening programme covered elsewhere in this document will play a major part in this, as will the upgrading of the North Circular road, the A40 in West London and the A13 in East London. These improvements will enable existing businesses in areas such as Park Royal and the Thames Gateway to move goods more easily and should help London to attract new investment in manufacturing.

8.44 In addition, central and local government will need to consider some areas where difficult access onto the M25 and beyond may be having a detrimental effect on regeneration prospects. Areas where this might need to be considered include the Wandle and Lea Valleys.

8.45 Improvements to the road network in London will benefit the tourist industry, much of which makes use of coaches. London Transport, the proprietor of Victoria Coach Station, has invested in improvements to facilities. These have benefitted many travellers on the numerous scheduled services to Europe via the Channel ports. A further review of coach terminal strategy will take place once the effects of rail privatisation on the coach market have been considered.

The Port of London

8.46 The Port of London comprises a series of privately owned wharves, jetties and terminals along the 95 miles of tidal Thames, together with the Port of Tilbury which was privatised in 1992 and recently acquired by Forth Ports plc. The Port of London Authority retains responsibility for conservancy, navigational safety and pilotage on the Thames.

- London handled 51.8 million tonnes of freight in 1994, including 25 million tonnes of bulk fuel. This is the largest operation in the country.

- Tilbury, a Freeport, one of only a handful in the country, attracted £93m of cargo in 1994 and is being expanded.

- All of London's cruise ship operations come under the umbrella of Tilbury, who now operate the prestigious moorings at Tower Bridge and Greenwich.

- Following privatisation in 1992, Tilbury has recorded increasing profits, culminating in 1994 when it recorded a figure of nearly £9m, over twice the 1993 recorded figure.

8.47 The Government's policies for UK commercial ports over the past 15 years have reflected its broad policies on the encouragement of choice and competition, to allow transport to operate as far as possible in an unrestricted market, with intervention limited to areas such as safety and environmental issues. Its objectives therefore have been increasingly to expose the ports industry as a whole to the market place, and to enable ports to compete more fully on an equal footing. By privatisation and deregulation it has largely achieved this, releasing competitive forces which had been dormant for years, and leading to great improvements in productivity.

8.48 One strand of the Government's strategy for the ports industry was the 1991 legislation enabling those ports which had been set up as trust ports to privatise themselves and so have access to normal private sector methods of funding and the discipline of private sector accountability. The Port of London Authority used this legislation to privatise its commercial

Map 8E: Roads from London to South East ports

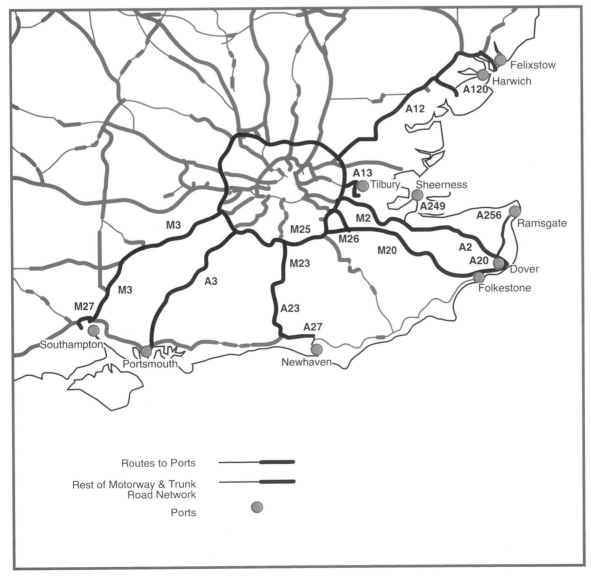

Source: Highways Agency

operations at Tilbury. Tilbury has since seen significant increases in traffic handled and profitability.

Conclusions

8.49 International connections are clearly one of London's great strengths. Our priority is to maintain and enhance them, not to put them at risk.

8.50 Competition for preeminence in aviation is very tough. Many European airports have expansion plans while London's two largest airports Gatwick and Heathrow face environmental constraints on their expansion. Runway capacity, terminal capacity and surface access to both these airports are all pressurised at certain times of the day. The private sector has proved itself very efficient at extracting the maximum from existing facilities, but some major developments may be considered to meet projected demands into the next century. BAA's proposed Terminal 5 at Heathrow mentioned above is the largest single development proposed.

8.51 Regardless of the outcome of the public inquiry on that matter, the Government believes that it must work with the airport operators, local authorities, transport operators and London business to ensure good transport access to the airports. This is a key factor in securing their long term contribution to London's economy.

8.52 The completion of the Channel Tunnel is a major boost to London's surface connections with the rest of Europe. Having provided considerable investment to upgrade existing lines, the Government is committed to enabling the private sector construction of a new high speed rail line between the Tunnel and London in order to take full advantage of the Tunnel's potential for passenger and freight transport. London, and via London the rest of the UK, will be fully connected to the trans-European high speed rail network through this link.

8.53 The Port of London will continue to be a major artery for London's, and indeed the country's trade, with considerable expansion predicted over the next 25 years.

8.54 The links between London and the major ports should not be undervalued. Through an ongoing process of upgrading major routes between London and the ports, through the widening of the M25, and through road improvements within London, the Capital's major industrial areas and boroughs in most need of regeneration will enjoy rapidly improving access.

Chapter 9: Enhancing Services by Rail and Underground

Introduction

9.1 The quality of rail and Underground services has improved significantly in recent years. This is reflected in objective measures of reliability and punctuality and in users' assessments of the cleanliness of trains, helpfulness of staff and quality of passenger information. It is partly attributable to major programmes of investment and to better management, but also to the downturn in London's economy which means that services are less congested today than they were in the late 1980s. As London's economy recovers, demand for transport will increase. This will put both networks under greater pressure.

9.2 Our analysis in Chapter 2 of the underlying trends in London's economy and population does not suggest a resumption of the very rapid increase in demand for public transport which London experienced during the latter half of the 1980s and which produced acute overcrowding and congestion, particularly at the London termini and on the central sector of the London Underground network. Nevertheless, passenger numbers on London Underground have increased steadily in recent years and are now back close to the peak level of 1989.

9.3 Like the business community, we view the enhancement of commuter services to and from the central business districts as a high priority, linked to our objective of promoting the competitiveness of London as a World City.

Rail Services

The Past Performance

9.4 The railway network is very much a national-level transport system, and it is not meaningful to identify separately investment in railways in London. For example, an improvement to a main line will benefit both local and long-distance passengers, as well as facilitating freight movements. Again, London's economy benefits from an improvement to a commuter service, but so do the economies of the towns from which people commute in.

9.5 Although we cannot set a value on the railway investment which benefits London, it is clear that national-level investment has been running at an historically high level - about £1 billion a year at today's prices - over most of the last decade and that London has been one of the principal beneficiaries of this. The

railways are, for example, fully up-to-date in terms of their rolling-stock replacement programme, with no trains being operated beyond their anticipated operational life. The congestion problems of the latter 1980s resulted in a major programme of investment to increase the capacity of commuter services, by buying new trains, by lengthening station platforms and by opening the new cross-London Thameslink service. This last development has cut journey times significantly for those commuting into London from areas which were formerly served only by the Bedford-St Pancras line. Other recent investments which have particularly benefitted commuter services into London include the following:

- On the Chiltern line, major investment in signalling and stations, and in new rolling stock, was completed in 1992. This investment, together with changes to the May 1995 timetable, has resulted in an increase in the number of services to and from London Marylebone.

- SouthEastern, which operates rail services in South East London, Kent and parts of Sussex has recently completed the replacement of all old trains on the inner-suburban service with new Networker trains. This has improved punctuality and reduced cancellations, and it will allow SouthEastern to provide more frequent services in the off-peak period for this part of its operations.

- Thames Trains carried out a programme of total route modernisation which was completed in 1992 and also invested in new rolling stock, including 91 new Networker trains.

The Future

9.6 The Government has embarked upon a policy of rail privatisation, under which the responsibility for maintaining and enhancing services is now passing to the private sector. The privatisation of the railways involves the following allocation of responsibilities:

- The Franchising Director specifies the passenger services which he requires to be operated, including services to, from and within London - the Passenger Service Requirement (PSRs). The PSRs take the BR timetable as a starting point and specify the minimum level of service which is to be provided on each part of the rail network. Operators will run commercial services in addition to the PSR. Overall levels of service will be broadly at those existing previously. The Franchising Director lets a franchise, by competitive tender, which includes the PSR and also puts other contractual obligations on the franchisee, such as compliance with fares regulation, provision of through ticketing, compliance with station standards and co-operation with other operators on timetable planning. The Train Operating Company (TOC) is responsible for operating the service and managing stations as a wholly owned subsidiary of the franchisee.

- The TOC is responsible for the provision of services on a day-to-day basis. The franchise is awarded on the basis of a fixed level of service and other contractual obligations, as well as any service enhancements and investment that the franchisee has committed to as part of the franchise negotiation process. The operator has the commercial incentive to win additional business onto the line by providing a better service to users. In terms of levels of service, it is required to operate at least the PSR set by the Franchising Director, which may not be changed without the Franchising Director's consent. TOCs lease their trains from one of the three rolling-stock leasing companies and pay Railtrack an access charge for the use of the right to run trains along the Railtrack network.

- Railtrack, which is to be privatised shortly, owns the physical infrastructure, including - the stations leased to TOCs, the track and the signalling systems. It is also responsible for maintaining and operating the infrastructure safely. Its track access charges are set at a level sufficient to cover these costs and to provide for a commercial rate of return.

- The Rail Regulator has a role similar to that of other regulators of privatised utilities. In particular, he has to approve the charges which Railtrack makes to train operating companies.

- The Government expects the private sector to play an increasingly important part in investment in the railway. Following the flotation of Railtrack and the franchising of the TOCs, investment should be determined as far as possible by the private sector responding to passengers' requirements.

The Government's role is to channel financial support through the Franchising Director towards the provision of passenger services and to set the framework of objectives for the Franchising Director within which he specifies the minimum service standards to be provided by franchisees. In addition, where the Franchising Director identifies a case for an enhanced service, he can enter into agreements with TOCs and other parties so as to secure new services which are socially and economically efficient and which would not otherwise be provided. We believe that privatisation will greatly increase the incentives to operate passenger services which respond better to users' demands. The operators' fare revenue depends upon their satisfying their customers. Although the Franchising Director has set a minimum service level for all passenger franchises, the true pressures for improvement will be the commercial ones.

9.7 We have already seen examples of this incentive at work in the cases of the first two franchises let:

- The South West Trains franchise, which covers most services into Waterloo, has been let to Stagecoach Holdings plc for a term of seven years. It is maintaining the pre-privatisation level of service, over and above the PSR. Among Stagecoach's financial commitments are £3 million investment in stations in addition to the £2.6 million annual budgeted maintenance and a number of dedicated bus links to South West Trains stations. It will consider the possibility of through ticketing arrangements between the bus link services and train destinations. It also intends to provide rail information at its bus offices in the South West Trains area.

- The Great Western franchise, covering certain services into Paddington, has been awarded to Great Western Holdings Ltd, the management and employee buy-out team with backing from others including the west country based bus operator FirstBus. Great Western Holdings plans to run services over and above the PSR and at least the pre-privatisation number of trains. Its franchise commitments include refurbished rolling stock and co-ordinated bus links with local operators. It will also seek to reduce journey times. The franchise will run for ten years subject to agreement of an investment plan with the Franchising Director within the first two years. The ten year franchise would offer increased service frequencies and further investment in rolling stock and infrastructure improvements.

A further three franchises have now been awarded, opening the way for private sector operation of services to commence during the first half of 1996. These are the Gatwick Express franchise, awarded to the National Express Group plc, the InterCity East Coast franchise, awarded to GNR, a subsidiary of Sea Containers Ltd, and the Network SouthCentral franchise, awarded to London & South Coast Ltd, a subsidiary of the French Compagnie Générale d'Entreprises Automobiles Group.

9.8 Although there is much that individual train operators can do to improve services in their own areas, the investment in the physical infrastructure of the railway remains of crucial importance. Under the new regime, Railtrack has agreements with train operators that require it to deliver a certain level of quality of services. It will have to invest in maintaining the existing physical infrastructure in order to meet its obligations under these agreements. The Rail Regulator's judgement when he fixed track access charges in January 1995 was that Railtrack would have to spend £3 1/2 billion over six years in the renewal of the network to maintain its existing capacity and that this needed to be reflected in the level of access charges. Railtrack will also undertake enhancements in addition to this, such as Thameslink 2000, where it considers that there is a commercial case for doing so. If necessary the commercial justification may include appropriate assurances about future usage and levels of access charges. The Regulator has also provided guidance on how charges can be varied to remunerate investments which enhance services. The pattern of investment will be set out in Railtrack's annual Network Management Statement, the first of which was published in December 1995. The responsibility for rolling stock investment will rest primarily with the three leasing companies, and the terms of the passenger franchises ensure that both they and the train operating companies have incentives not to let rolling stock standards decline. The operator of the Great Western franchise, for example, has plans to negotiate improvements to existing rolling stock or the provision of new trains.

9.9 The existence of the Franchising Director's contractual commitments to support passenger services over the lifetime of each franchise permits the industry to plan ahead with confidence. Franchises are usually for seven years, but with longer terms where operators commit to significant new investment, for example in rolling stock.

Underground Services

9.10 We believe that the priority for London Underground is to concentrate on the completion of the Jubilee Line extension, to tackle the asset health concerns to provide an even better service to users and to further improve the business's financial performance. Although we would not rule out privatisation as a longer-term option, we believe that it would, at present, tend to divert management attention from these more pressing objectives. We have therefore encouraged London Underground to pursue approaches which secure the benefits of greater private sector involvement by harnessing private finance and by contracting out an increasing proportion of the activities involved in the day-to-day operation of the railway.

The Past Performance

9.11 London Underground accounts for the largest share of investment in transport in London. Chart 9A shows the level of investment in the existing network (ie excluding funding for the construction of new lines) since 1960. The increase in investment since the mid-1980s is very obvious. So, too, are the investment trough in 1991/92 and the subsequent hump in 1992/93. Such troughs and humps are inherently undesirable, because they result in a stop-go approach, which is inefficient in both operational and financial terms. Over the last three years, investment in the existing network has been held at a more stable level of a little over £500 million a year. This is more than double the level of annual investment during the period from 1960 to the mid-1980s.

9.12 London Underground has estimated that, as a broad long term average, it would need to invest something of the order of £350 million a year in renewal and repair of the current network to keep it in a stable condition. As the chart shows, investment fell well below this broad level up until the mid-late 1980s, by when a substantial backlog of investment had built up. The much higher investment levels of the last 7 years or so have enabled London Underground to make substantial progress in tackling this.

9.13 The sort of investment which is needed to eliminate the backlog tends to be in parts of the system which users do not see. However, it is of crucial importance in terms of improving the speed, reliability and quality of commuter journeys. For example, if the condition of the track and the permanent way on which it runs is allowed to deteriorate, users will notice a deterioration in the quality of service, because the ride will become uneven. They will also notice a deterioration in reliability, because a poorly maintained track can damage rolling stock, and require it to be withdrawn from service. It may also impact on journey time, because London Underground is already obliged to introduce speed restrictions in the interests of passenger safety.

9.14 Other investments undertaken to improve the quality of assets which had been neglected in the past may be more obvious to users, but may not be entirely welcome. For example, the renewal of escalators has been a high priority in recent years. The short-term effect of this is that the escalators in question have to be withdrawn from service completely, adding to the inconvenience which passengers experience.

9.15 The following major programmes illustrate the types of investment which London Underground has been undertaking and how they benefit users:

- The £800 million modernisation of the Central Line has involved laying new track and replacing outworn signalling and electrical systems, as well as the more visible investment in new rolling stock. The programme has increased the capacity of the Central Line by 16%, making for a less crowded service on what has always been one of the most heavily used lines on the Underground network. It has cut journey times by 12% and will greatly improve the reliability of services.

- All Bakerloo, Circle, Hammersmith & City and Victoria Line trains have been refurbished, and work is under way on refurbishment of the

Metropolitan and Piccadilly Line rolling stock. Refurbishment is a cost-effective way of making trains safer, more comfortable and easier to keep clean.

- The ongoing programme of station refurbishment has a similar mix of benefits. It also provides an opportunity to enhance security, by installing video cameras and help-points, and (which is just as important) to make stations feel safer. As noted in Chapter 6, the perception of public transport as unsafe is not borne out by the statistics, but represents a formidable obstacle to efforts to make more use of public transport and less use of travel by car.

- The £300 million escalator replacement programme has made escalators more reliable, as well as safer. This, in turn, has a significant impact on the speed and reliability of journeys to or from stations where escalator closures used to be a major source of delay.

9.16 Over the last five years, the combination of an ambitious investment programme and management action to improve the efficiency of the operation and the responsiveness of staff to customer needs has secured a significant improvement in the level and standard of service which London Underground provides to users:

- Customer satisfaction with the quality of London Underground services has increased substantially. In 1990/91, only 63% of users were satisfied with the service. By 1995/96, the proportion had increased to 74%. But for the effects of industrial action, the proportion would undoubtedly have

Chart 9A: Underground Core Investment

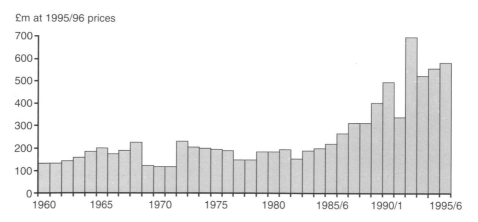

£m at 1995/96 prices

Source: London Transport

been higher. Although a 74% customer satisfaction rating cannot be viewed with complacency by either the Government or London Underground management, it represents a very substantial step in the right direction, and it compares favourably with users' opinions of many other public services.

• The reliability of lifts and escalators has improved. The percentage of escalators in service at any one time has increased from 85% to 93% and the percentage of lifts in operation from 86% to 96%.

• Train services have also become more reliable. In 1990/91, London Underground failed to run 5.3% of scheduled train services. By 1995/96, this proportion was down to 3.7%.

• This improvement in the reliability of train services has taken place against the backdrop of a significant increase in train services run. This rose by about 10%, from 32.8 million train miles in 1990/91 to 35.9 million in 1995/96.

• London Underground has made a significant contribution to the drive to reduce crime on public transport. Crime levels on the Underground in 1994 were some 20% below the 1987 high - see chart 9B. Recorded crime on the network fell consistently for six years until last year, helping make the Underground one of the safest modes of travel in London. Last year's small increase was largely due to a rise in the number of pick-pocketing offences; however the incidence of violent crimes and assaults fell by over 20% last year. London Underground and the British Transport Police are currently undertaking a number of initiatives (such

as Operation Big Dipper, launched in July 1995) to reduce particularly the incidence of pick-pocketing and indecent assaults on the system.

9.17 Over the same period, the financial performance of the business has also improved significantly:

• The business has moved closer to profitability. In 1990/91, revenue was just sufficient to cover operating costs. For 1995/96, London Underground is forecasting a surplus of just under £200 million, which represents the business's contribution to the funding of its capital investment programme.

• In part, this improvement is attributable to growth in revenue, but it also reflects a determined drive to cut costs. In 1990/91, unit costs stood at £12.48 per train kilometre (at 1995/96 prices). In 1995/96, this had reduced by 13$\frac{1}{2}$% to £10.69.

• Staff numbers have been reduced by 6000, ie 27%. This is attributable to an improvement in the efficiency of the business and also to contracting out an increasing proportion of the non-core activities of the railway.

9.18 The combination of improvements in the quality of service and in financial performance is an essential one. The immediate concern of users is, naturally enough, more with the former than with the latter. However, both the Government and London Underground remain convinced that the interests of London at large are best served not only by focusing on quality of service, but also by increasing the financial self-sufficiency of the network and reducing its dependence on financial support from the taxpayer.

Chart 9B: Crime on London Underground

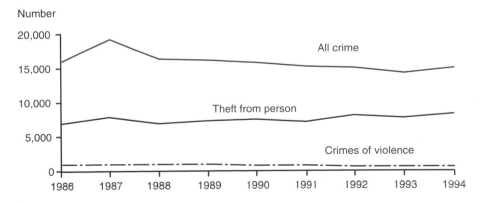

Source: British Transport Police

The Future

9.19 London Underground's forward programme of investment and management initiatives focuses on restoring asset health and improving those aspects of the service which customers value most highly and which contribute most directly to the broader objectives set out in this strategy. London Underground has identified five areas where it needs to concentrate on improving its performance.

9.20 The first area is **journey time**. The aim here is both to reduce the average time which it takes to make an Underground journey and also to make the service reliable, so that users can predict their journey times with greater confidence. As noted in paragraph 3.17, an improvement in reliability can be just as important to commuters and their employers as an improvement in speed. A variety of actions and investments contribute to the achievement of this goal, because there are many points in a Tube journey at which a failure in one part of the system can add delay - an inability to enter a station because it has had to be closed temporarily as a result of overcrowding, ticket machines that are out of order, malfunctioning ticket barriers or an escalator which is out of service. So, an improvement in speed and reliability requires an advance across a broad front. However, the single most important element will be to improve train journey times.

- The major upgrading programmes probably generate the most obvious improvement in this area. The modernisation of the Central Line is close to completion. It was always London Underground's intention that the modernisation of the Northern Line should follow close behind, and work on this programme has now started. The Victoria Line will be next in the queue behind the Northern Line.

- The completion of the Jubilee Line extension is also important, because it takes pressure off existing Underground lines.

- New trains will be brought into operation on the Jubilee Line (covering both the extension and the existing line) and the Northern Line. This will increase the capacity of these lines, as well as making services more reliable.

- Reliability of train services will be improved in the short term by enhancing the signalling systems on the District and Piccadilly Lines, and in the longer term by installing new train control systems on the District and Piccadilly lines and by providing additional reversing facilities at the eastern end of the Piccadilly Line.

9.21 The second area is **safety.** The safety of customers and staff is of paramount importance to London Underground, which has developed a comprehensive approach to safety management, aimed to minimise as far as practicable their exposure to risks. In the wake of the Kings Cross fire, London Underground has applied sophisticated quantified risk assessment techniques to all aspects of its operation, in order to identify the various areas where a combination of system failures could precipitate an incident. Combined with a detailed assessment of the condition of the assets, this permits London Underground to target its safety initiatives and investment effectively.

9.22 Safety and asset health issues tend to be inextricably linked and in turn may have an effect on service quality. London Underground's forward investment programme takes a balanced approach, which aims to continue the process of modernising the Underground network, improving both the safety and the quality of services, while taking account of the need to catch up on the remaining backlog of under investment. Projects with a strong asset health flavour planned in the coming years include:

- Essential tunnel and bridge strengthening works across the network;

- Replacement of the remaining wooden components in escalators;

- Remedial work on embankments.

9.23 Passenger security is an important aspect of safety, particularly for women. As noted above London Underground and the British Transport Police (BTP) have made great progress in reducing crime over the past 10 years and making the Underground one of the safest modes of transport in London. As well as the initiatives planned to reduce crime levels this year particularly in the areas of pick-pocketing and indecent assaults, passenger security will be improved by the relocation of police accommodation at Temple, for the West End and City area stations, and at West Ham for the eastern areas of the Underground. Group Station Control Rooms are proposed for a number of stations, together with help points and improved radio and telephone facilities.

9.24 The third area is the **ambience** of the Underground network. The aim here is to make travel by Tube a more comfortable and pleasant experience. The focus is on the quality of the train and station environments and on ensuring that staff are more sensitively attuned to customer requirements. Key developments in this area include:

- The new train fleets for the Jubilee and Northern Lines, following on from the new train fleet for the Central Line.

- The continuation of the train refurbishment programme for the Piccadilly, District and Metropolitan Lines. At an average cost of £1 million per train, this represents a cost-effective way of improving customers' perception of the service.

- There will be a major programme of refurbishment covering stations such as Elephant & Castle, Oxford Circus, Earls Court and Kennington.

- There will be a programme of congestion relief measures at stations such as Wembley Park, Finsbury Park and Victoria. Such measures greatly enhance the comfort and safety of these stations. The measures also eliminate the need to close stations when they become overcrowded, which presently make journey times on some routes significantly longer and less predictable than they need be.

- There will be improvements to customer information and signing, particularly as part of the Jubilee and Northern Line projects. Further improvements may be achieved if London Underground's proposals for a communications private finance project are successful.

- An improved range of ticket-types, based upon the LT Prestige project, will be introduced, including stored value cards which can be debited automatically as they are used. Prestige will also reduce fraud losses for both Underground and buses.

- Initiatives to encourage interchange between the Underground and other transport modes, in particular at the new Jubilee Line stations at Canada Water and North Greenwich.

9.25 The fourth area is action to contribute to an improvement in the **environment** of the Capital. The most important contribution which London

Underground can make here is through encouraging people to travel by Tube rather than car. However, it can also minimise the environmental impact of London Underground's own activities.

- New trains use systems which are 30% more energy efficient than traditional trains. In addition these trains will be lighter with more efficient motors and better controls. With the introduction of new Central, Northern and Jubilee Line trains almost 50% of the fleet will benefit from these features.

- In future, all normal operational power supplies will be provided by the Regional Electricity Companies via the National Grid. As a result of this, global emissions are reduced, because the more efficient National Grid is used. There is also a particular benefit to London from the reduction of emissions within the Capital from London Underground's dedicated power stations.

- The Metropolitan Line has pioneered the introduction within London Underground of the British Standards Institute environmental standards BS7750. The Line is seeking formal accreditation prior to extension of the standard across the rest of the Underground.

9.26 The last area targeted in the plan is the **financial performance** of the business. The Government has set London Underground demanding financial objectives for the coming three year period. These are intended to continue the progress in improving operating efficiency and reducing costs which have been achieved over recent years, for instance through London Underground's Company Plan initiative. Looking further ahead, London Underground aims to reach the point where the normal investment needs of the existing network can be met without recourse to Government grant. The achievement of this depends on improving revenue through enhanced service levels and service quality, and on reducing costs.

9.27 The overall effect of these programmes is not just to produce a better service for users, but also to enhance service levels. London Underground's current plans include:

- A substantial increase in train miles operated, between now and 2001. By increasing the frequency of the services during the peak period, they reduce average journey times and overcrowding on trains and put themselves in a better position to deal with an upturn in demand. By operating extra services in the evenings and at the weekends, they can encourage people to make journeys by Tube which are currently undertaken mainly by car. This furthers the Government's objective of securing a transfer to a more environmentally friendly mode of transport and improves London Underground's revenue position.

- Reductions both in average waiting times and in average journey times. These improvements in speed and reliability impact directly upon the Government's objective of promoting the competitiveness of London as a World City.

- Significant improvements in the levels of customer satisfaction with the quality of train and station services, and with related issues such as information, cleanliness and personal security. The improvement in the users' perception of the quality of Underground services also furthers our competitiveness objective for the reasons set out in Chapter 3.

9.28 The rate at which the programmes are implemented and the benefits are secured depends, in part, upon the amount of investment undertaken, which is a product of the funding available for investment and London Underground's success in securing value for money on its capital expenditure. There are three principal sources from which funds for investment can be secured: the business's own operating surplus, Government grant funded by the taxpayer and private finance.

9.29 We deal with the prospects for Government funding in Chapter 14 below. However, in order to set that issue in its proper context, it is important to be clear on the prospects for the other two sources of funding.

9.30 We noted at paragraph 9.17 the significant improvement in London Underground's operating surplus over the last five years. This reflects the increase in use of the system, partly as a result of the economic upturn and partly as a result of London Underground's success in making the service more attractive. It also reflects progress in tackling the problem of fares evasion, and reducing costs. However, it also reflects the fact that fares have risen broadly in line with earnings. As noted in the following Chapter, the effect of the Regulator's decision to cap rail fares imposes a constraint on the extent to which

other public transport fares in London can rise. In future, they are likely to rise more in line with inflation than with earnings, implying fares increases lower than in recent years. That development will be welcome to passengers. The Government, too, believes that the combination of steeper increases in the cost of motoring and less steep increases in the cost of public transport send more appropriate price signals to Londoners about the environmental friendliness of the two modes and will help reduce the level of car use and increase the level of public transport use. Nevertheless, smaller fare increases will also have some effect on London Underground's ability to increase its operating surplus.

9.31 Just as internal resources have an impact on investment, so does investment have an impact on internal resources. The investment needed to enhance the safety of the system and to eliminate the backlog of investment in basic assets will be protected even if total investment is cut and could not easily be accelerated even if total investment rose. Hence, the impact of an increase or decrease in investment is felt primarily on programmes which are more obvious to users and more likely to result in short-term increases or decreases in patronage.

9.32 The scope for harnessing private finance has been significantly enhanced by the Government's move from a rule-governed to a deal-driven approach to private finance proposals. Our focus is now on the extent to which a specific proposal represents value-for-money, secures substantial transfer of risk to the private sector and harnesses private sector management skills. The new approach makes it possible to attract private sector money, even where the industry in question remains in the public sector.

9.33 London Underground has been in the forefront of developing private finance, notably through their deal for the provision of over a hundred new trains for the Northern Line. The key features of this deal are that the private sector suppliers bear the upfront capital cost of building the rolling-stock and take responsibility for its maintenance. They will be remunerated on the basis of a payment for having the specified number of trains available, in good order, throughout each working day. There are a number of reasons for regarding this as a particularly attractive deal for all parties:

- Passengers benefit, because the deal permits this £400m investment project to proceed several years earlier than would otherwise have been possible. They also benefit because the terms of the contract mean that the suppliers have a significant financial incentive to maintain trains to a high quality and to maximise their reliability.

- The taxpayer benefits because the private sector bears the risk of cost overruns.

- London Underground benefits because the new trains will complement the other major improvements to the Northern Line described above.

- The suppliers benefit from an order which London Underground would not otherwise have been able to place.

9.34 Maximising the sensible use of private finance is an important goal for the Government and London Underground alike. There are various major projects which appear to have strong private finance potential. These include the power distribution and the LT Prestige ticketing projects identified above. Further private finance opportunities being developed by London Underground relate to communications and Northern Line modernisation works. However, neither the Government nor London Underground is prepared to sign up to deferred payment deals regardless of their longer-term financial implications or without satisfying ourselves that they secure a genuine and worthwhile transfer of risk to the private sector. Doing good private finance deals is not quick or easy. In some areas - such as the use of design, build, finance and operate contracts to fund the construction of trunk roads - it is possible to devise a generic approach to harnessing private finance. The detail of individual contracts will vary, but the broad framework is now well established. As will be obvious from the examples cited above, the London Underground investment programme is much more diverse than this, and each new private finance deal has, in effect, to be brokered from scratch.

9.35 The Government is clear that private finance will be increasingly important to London Underground and that there is considerable potential to exploit it in many areas of the investment programme, but we are clear that it is not a universal panacea. London Underground's investment programme will continue to require some Government funding.

The Government's Role

9.36 The shape of the London Underground investment programme is determined by London Underground management, not by Government. Our role is:

- To monitor London Underground's safety performance and, through HSE and HM Railway Inspectorate, to ensure that statutory safety requirements are met.

- To determine the overall level of financial support for the system. Improvements to the Underground system are extremely expensive - the cost of refurbishing a single Underground station can be as much as £50 million. Although we have demonstrated the high priority we attach to improving the Underground system, on both competitiveness and environmental grounds, this has to be considered against the many other calls on the public purse and the need to restrain public expenditure as a whole.

- To set the investment appraisal criteria. These ensure that investments represent value for money and that it is delivering competitiveness benefit. As noted in Chapter 3, the cost:benefit analysis is a reasonable proxy measure of the net impact of investment on competitiveness.

- To set financial objectives. These are intended to ensure that London Underground has explicit incentives to reduce costs and improve operating efficiency.

- To set quality of service objectives. These ensure that the improvements are being delivered in practice in the areas that matter most to the users of the system.

- To work with London Underground to identify opportunities for exploiting private finance.

Summary

9.37 In recent years there have been significant advances in the quality of services provided by London's surface rail and Underground networks. We have achieved these, together with the industry, through a programme of high investment in capital infrastructure, a rigorous approach to the efficiency of operations, and encouraging London Underground and rail operators to focus on the needs of their passengers. We will build on these improvements, through the privatisation of the suburban rail network, supported by public subsidy, and further capital support to the Underground, supplemented by private finance. Taken as a whole these actions will further our overall objectives of promoting modal shift away from the private car and supporting the competitiveness of London's economy.

Chapter 10: Promoting greater use of less polluting modes of transport

Introduction

10.1 The third of our objectives for transport in London is to promote a modal shift from the more polluting to the less polluting modes of transport. This is an important objective for many reasons; it furthers the objectives of the government's sustainable development and air quality strategies, helping reduce carbon dioxide emissions, and promoting London as a more attractive place both to live and work. This chapter sets out our thinking on which are the more and the less polluting modes; takes a view on the likely future trends in demand for each mode; assesses the effectiveness of the different mechanisms for inducing modal shift; and considers each mode's strengths and weaknesses.

The Hierarchy of Environmental Friendliness

10.2 In terms of the amount of pollution generated per passenger mile delivered, the different modes can be ranked in the following order, taking account of load-factors achieved in recent years in London:

- walking and cycling,
- rail,
- Underground,
- bus,
- motorcycle,
- car,
- taxi.

10.3 Using this hierarchy to try to direct change is not as simple as it looks. The comparative 'friendliness' of modes depends partly on levels of use (a high occupancy car is more environmentally friendly than an empty bus); and partly on the role they play (eg. the Underground's network density makes it more polluting than rail, but it meets demands which rail cannot accommodate). Taxis can be helpful in providing a convenient interchange between modes, and being able to rely on them may convince people to switch to public transport for a greater part of their journey. Moreover, we must be realistic about how far one mode can substitute for another - the car will generally remain the choice for longer journeys not catered for by public transport; and to try to build a public transport network which could cater for all journey permutations would be impractical. More generally, air pollution is not the only measure of environmental

friendliness. Other forms of pollution (such as noise or land take) need to be considered, together with the point of incidence of the environmental damage.

10.4 Against this background, our approach to modal-shift in London is as follows:

- The substitution of a journey on foot or by bicycle for a journey by car or other private transport constitutes an unambiguous environmental gain.

- The substitution of a journey by another mode for a journey by car will generally represent an environmental gain.

- Where car trips are feeders to public transport as a main mode the environmental gain is greater to the extent that the length of the car feeder trip is minimised.

- Other modal-shift effects are treated as neutral in environmental terms.

Future Trends in Demand

Trends in Travel by Car

10.5 The traditional argument is that car ownership rises as economies grow and personal disposable income increases; and that increased car ownership translates into increased car use, partly because the car is more convenient than any other mode and partly because the marginal cost of car travel is low and the perceived marginal cost is lower still. There are reasons for thinking this argument applies less to London than to the country as a whole. In particular London has long had higher average incomes than the rest of the UK, combined with lower levels of car ownership and car use. And, within London, car ownership and use is lowest in the central area where incomes are highest.

10.6 The number of cars available to London residents has been increasing throughout the post-War period. Table 10A shows the number of cars available in different areas of London in 1971, 1981 and 1991, taken from the London-wide transport surveys carried out in those years.

10.7 From comparisons with the 1981 Census of Population, it is believed that the 1981 transport survey was somewhat biased towards car-owning households. There was also under-enumeration (particularly in inner London) in the 1991 Census used to gross-up the 1991 transport survey results. This means that precise estimates of changes in car availability must be treated with caution, although the indications they give of the changes over the 20 year period are nevertheless valid. Growth in household car availability has been higher in outer than inner London, and slightly lower in the 1980s than the 1970s.

10.8 The number of cars per household in London has also been increasing although at a lower rate than the total stock of cars. This is because the number of households has also increased. The best estimates from the surveys suggest that cars per household increased between 1981 and 1991 by 6% in inner London and 9% in outer London.

10.9 Different assumptions on the growth in the number of cars available to London households were used in the two LTS scenarios described in Chapter 2. Growth in the base case scenario was assumed to be 32% between 1991 and 2011, the average of low and high forecasts for London consistent with the Department of Transport's national car ownership forecasts. For the low demand scenario, the low forecast mentioned above was used, which puts

growth in the number of cars available to London households over the period at 22%.

10.10 As can be seen, the increase in household car availability forecast between 1991 and 2011 is less than the actual increase over the preceding 20 years. Most of the forecast extra vehicles will be in outer London, rather than central or inner London, following the pattern of the 1971 to 1991 period.

10.11 Chart 10B shows how the percentage of households in different car availability bands has changed since 1971 and is forecast to do so under the two LTS scenarios in 2011. While the percentage of households with one car available has changed comparatively little over time, much of the growth in car ownership, particularly in outer London, has been the result of many households acquiring a second or third car. In 1971 around 8% of London households had two or more cars available for use. This had risen to 20% by 1991 and is tentatively forecast to be 28% or 31% in 2011.

10.12 These forecasts assume that relationships which had an influence on car ownership levels in the past continue to hold into the future. This is a necessary

Table 10A: Cars available ('000s) to households in London

Area	1971	1981	1991	% change 1971-91
Central	29	29	32	11
Inner	472	502	580	23
Outer	1392	1682	1969	41
All London	1893	2213	2581	36

Chart 10B: London household car ownership

Percentage of households

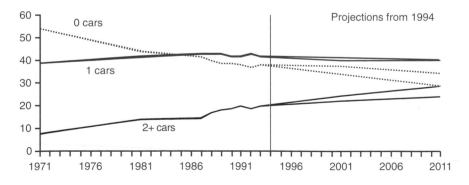

Source: Department of Transport

assumption but a highly suspect one. But changing public attitudes and Government policy towards private motoring in urban areas may alter car ownership aspirations and serve to reduce the growth in the number of cars in London to below even the low demand assumptions. London's congestion problems are a deterrent to car use and possibly also to car ownership. The availability of parking spaces is a major constraint on car ownership growth in central London and, increasingly, in inner London too.

10.13 However, car ownership forecasts are less relevant to the transport strategy than one may imagine. What matters is in car use, rather than car ownership. The correlation between the two is not straightforward as demand for car use in London is conditioned by the high levels of congestion often experienced, low average speeds and the extensive public transport network which provides a good substitute for many journeys by car. For example, the percentage increase in traffic flows on London's major roads between 1984 and 1994 was between one third and two thirds below that experienced in all other English metropolitan areas over the same period.

10.14 The best estimates for future trends in the volume of traffic in London are from the LTS model, as set out in Chapter 2. Within the overall increases in traffic volume reported in Chapter 2, there are wide variations at Borough level. In the base case scenario, the increase between 1991 and 2011 is forecast to be over 50% in Tower Hamlets and Newham, for example, where a combination of regeneration and new infrastructure bring with them a substantial rise in traffic volumes. Other Boroughs seeing large increases in traffic under the base case are in east and north east London where major new highway schemes are assumed to be operational in 2011, including new river crossings. Growth remains well above average in Tower Hamlets in the low demand scenario, as jobs are attracted there from elsewhere in London stimulating transport demand, whereas in other Boroughs demand is much lower due to the exclusion of highway schemes not committed in 1995.

Trends in Travel by Public Transport

10.15 Under the base case scenario described in Chapter 2, the LTS model forecasts that the total number of public transport trips in the three hour morning peak period could rise by 10% between 1991 and 2011. Recent experience suggests growth may also be as strong, if not stronger in the inter-peak period.

10.16 Within this overall growth in public transport trips, there are considerable variations between what is predicted to happen to rail, Underground and bus patronage. In the morning peak, passenger miles by rail are forecast to increase substantially, by 35% between 1991 and 2011. This is due to a combination of new rail infrastructure schemes assumed to be operating by 2011 (Thameslink 2000 and CTRL for example), and continued growth of employment in central London, a major market for rail travel. Passenger miles by Underground are forecast to increase by less, at under 10% while bus passenger miles fall by 10%. Under the base case, public transport has 39% of all person trips in 2011 in the morning peak period.

10.17 The low demand scenario has a different result. Rail passenger miles increase by a more moderate 28% over the forecast period while Underground patronage increases by just under 20%. The decline in bus patronage is halted, with bus passenger miles remaining unchanged. The overall effect of all this is that public transport's share of total trips in the morning peak increases by one percentage point to 40%.

10.18 However, there are considerable problems associated with forecasting public transport demand in general and commuter travel in particular. Chart 2K (see Chapter 2) shows changes in the level of public transport usage since 1975. Underground and rail saw substantial increases in demand in the mid and late 1980s which subsequently declined in the early 1990s. In the last two or so years, Underground patronage has risen again, although not to levels seen in 1988 and 1989. The number of journeys travelled by rail has continued to fall. Bus use declined only slightly throughout the 1980s and early 1990s in London, contrasting with the rest of the country, which saw significant falls in patronage.

10.19 There are no fully satisfactory explanations for the large increase in travel by public transport in the 1980s. Although London's economy was performing well in this period, employment remained broadly constant. However journeys into central London during the morning peak by public transport modes increased markedly. Hypotheses to explain this phenomenon include an increase in morning peak trips for non-work purposes (such as tourism), the expansion of jobs in

Docklands and other inner London areas, requiring a journey into central London in the morning peak but followed immediately by one out again, and labour market effects such as changes in the number of part time employees and contracting out of office services. The introduction of Travelcards may also have been influential. To date it has not proved possible to quantify accurately the contribution of each of these factors, illustrating the difficulties of forecasting public transport demand.

Trends in Walking and Cycling

10.20 Londoners make over 4 million trips on foot each day and a further 4.3 million to or from other forms of transport. Over the period 1985/86 - 1992/94 the average number of walk journeys per person per year fell by about 3%. The most marked decline (50%) was in commuting trips. There were also falls in trips for education and shopping, reflecting the trend for schoolchildren to be driven to school and for shopping to be done by car.

10.21 Each weekday, 140,000 Londoners make around 330,000 bicycle trips, about 1.6% of all trips and about 2% of all 'non-walk' trips. However, there are about 1.2 million bicycles available to London residents, which implies that only about one in ten is used on any given weekday. There is a marked difference in bicycle use across London, with South-West Londoners making three times as many trips as most of the rest of Londoners. Although cycle traffic has declined since the early 1980s there are signs that the decline is slowing or levelling out. Forecasts of trips by foot or on bicycle are not available from LTS, which, at present, only forecasts travel by mechanised modes.

Total Demand Trends

10.22 Under the base case scenario assumptions about the economy, population, relative costs of transport and developments to the highway and public transport networks, the LTS model predicts that total demand for mechanised transport in London, in the form of person trips, increases by 14% between 1991 and 2011 to over 4 million trips in the morning peak period.

10.23 The picture under the low demand scenario is not markedly different despite the significant changes in assumptions about employment and the costs of

motoring and public transport. Total person trips in the morning peak are forecast to increase by 10%, reaching 3.9 million in 2011.

Effectiveness of the Available Measures

10.24 To achieve our objective of promoting a modal shift from the more polluting to the less polluting modes of transport, we need to consider what measures are available and how effective each might be in influencing the trends outlined above.

Cost of travel

10.25 With the sort of price elasticities that we believe to characterise travel behaviour in urban areas, costs of car travel would have to rise considerably relative to public transport costs, for example through a very sharp increase in fuel duty or a big reduction in fares, to make rapid progress in persuading people to leave their cars at home and use public transport instead. It would not be practicable to levy a higher rate of duty on fuel in London than elsewhere in the UK, since it would encourage road users to purchase fuel outside London. The scope for raising fuel duty in London therefore is limited. Nor is direct charging for the use of the road system through some form of congestion charging mechanism likely to be feasible for at least five years. Methods of managing road access, including congestion charging and other means, are considered in Chapter 11.

New Infrastructure

10.26 It is often argued that the provision of new public transport infrastructure is the key to encouraging a shift away from car use to greater use of public transport. However, the evidence from transport models suggests that this is not generally the case. Some recent analysis using the London And South East Region Model (LASER) can be used to illustrate the point.

10.27 LASER is being developed to investigate the interrelation between transport and land-use in London and the South East. Although it covers a far wider area, almost the whole of South East England, and in less spatial detail, it is otherwise very similar to LTS (see Chapter 2) in its representation of transport behaviour. However, it differs in that it seeks simultaneously to explain the impact which changes in transport services and prices will have in the longer term on business and residential location patterns. Because of this 'second-round' modelling of relocation effects, it implies rather higher transport elasticities than LTS. It should be noted that the LASER model is comparatively new, and the long-run elasticity values it implies are not as well-substantiated as the more familiar short- to medium-term ones used in LTS. However, it provides the best available indication of what the full long-term response to changes in transport opportunities will be.

10.28 A LASER scenario test was carried out to examine the combined impact of all the major proposed additions to the rail network post-1996 (except the Jubilee Line Extension and Heathrow Express, both of which are currently under construction). It suggested that with the DLR extension to Lewisham, Croydon Tramlink, CTRL domestic services and Crossrail, the rail mode share of all mechanised am peak trips in 2011 would be less than a half of one percentage point higher than it would be without them (a 5.2% share instead of 4.8%). Although each of these schemes would have a more significant effect in the specific corridor which it serves, the overall combined impact of these schemes on mode share across London and the South East would be quite small.

Speed/reliability

10.29 Work done in the congestion charging research programme suggests that reliability is a significant factor in modal choice. Factors such as overcrowding on public transport are already taken into account by the LTS model when it assigns modal share to particular trips. Further work is being carried out into the value travellers attach to reliability and quality of service. On the evidence currently available, however, it appears that journey time remains the dominant factor in modal choice.

10.30 This is why car travel is so attractive: the door-to-door journey time for most trips is shortest by car, even allowing time for parking at the journey destination. Chart 10C shows the results of a journey time survey. Unfortunately, the scope for changing the relative journey times of the various modes is fairly limited. The one possible exception is buses, where priority measures can help. But, because of the stop/start nature of bus operations, car travel is likely to remain quicker door-to-door. Measures to slow up car movement could be counter-productive since, even with substantial investment in bus priority measures, the nature of London's relatively narrow road system means that buses are frequently caught up with general traffic flow. However, conspicuous self enforcing bus priority measures such as bus gates and priority at traffic signals, together with more effective enforcement of bus lanes, could be expected to have some beneficial impact on patronage by improving the image of the bus. Even then, we have to recognise that increased patronage could be derived from rail and Underground travellers, pedal cyclists or pedestrians as well as from car drivers and car passengers.

10.31 In assessing the scope for modal choice, we must bear in mind the differences between central, inner and outer London journeys. In central London,

Chart 10C: Door-to-door journey times in London 1993-95

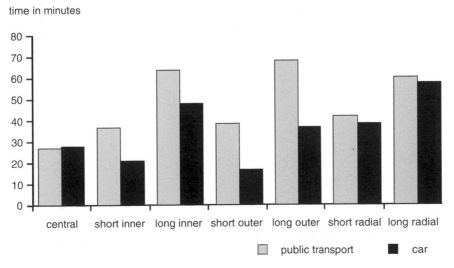

time in minutes

Source: Department of Transport

the coverage and frequency of public transport services means that public transport is a reasonably convenient alternative to the car for very many journeys. But public transport's share of the central London travel market is already dominant, with little scope for bringing about significant further shifts away from car use. In outer London, on the other hand, there is plenty of scope for modal shift, but the odds are stacked heavily in favour of car travel because of the dispersal of development which is difficult to serve by public transport. Inner London may offer most scope for encouraging drivers out of their cars, as car ownership and traffic growth have been more constrained, and there is scope for bus priority and some of the other measures mentioned above.

Modal Strengths and Weaknesses

10.32 Set out below are the estimated average costs for travelling one mile by the main modes of transport in London. Of course, the modes serve different markets; rail is often used for longer distance, radial commuting trips, while many bus journeys are local and quite short. These factors no doubt explain part of the differences in average costs. It must also be remembered that travellers usually focus on the marginal cost of a journey rather than average cost, and so disregard fixed costs such as those associated with owning a vehicle for example. For trips by car in particular, this is likely to mean marginal costs are substantially less than the average cost per mile given here. Marginal costs per mile will also be lower than average costs for users of public transport with Travelcard and similar tickets.

10.33 **Travel by car.** The average cost of running a medium sized car (including depreciation) is estimated by the AA to be 35 pence per mile. The car is generally the quickest form of transport from door to door, with the exception of short journeys in central and inner London, where travelling by motorcycle or bicycle is quicker for most trips. The car is certainly the most comfortable mode. Car journeys can be unreliable because of road congestion, although the relatively fast journey times door to door makes it the most convenient form of travel provided parking is available at the destination at reasonable cost.

10.34 **Travel by bus.** The average cost to the bus passenger is 20 pence per mile. Buses are generally slower and more unreliable than other forms of transport. However they are generally more convenient

than other public transport modes for most journeys in terms of the distance to travel from the bus stops at either end of the journey, and it is a very safe form of transport. Many buses are not particularly comfortable although the new generation of vehicles is a considerable improvement.

10.35 **Travel by rail.** For travel by rail the average cost to the passenger is 13 pence per mile. Rail usually offers the quickest journey times for the routes it serves, particularly over longer distances. Despite a poor public image it is generally reliable. The main inconvenience is the need to get to and from the stations at either end of the journey. It offers a very safe and relatively comfortable journey.

10.36 **Travel by Underground.** The average cost to the passenger for travel on the Underground is 19 pence per mile. Travel by Underground has similar characteristics to travel by rail in terms of speed and reliability, but its stations are often more conveniently located for the start and finish of many journeys. It is a safe form of transport although not always very comfortable.

10.37 **Travel by taxi.** Costs for travel by taxi can vary quite widely, but are around 65 pence per mile for the average journey by licensed cab, reducing substantially if there are two or more passengers sharing. Taxis offer all the advantages of car travel, with the possible exception of comfort, and there are no parking problems at the end of the journey.

10.38 **Travel by bicycle.** Bicycles can be purchased relatively cheaply and the running costs are negligible. This is one of the quickest forms of transport for many trips. And it is exceptionally convenient and generally reliable. It is, however, often uncomfortable in poor weather and not very safe. Most people are unlikely to contemplate cycling other than for short trips.

10.39 **Walking.** This is the ultimate in 'environmentally friendly' travel. It costs virtually nothing, is generally safe and takes you from door to door. However, apart from short trips, or trips for recreation, the time factor makes walking impractical. It can be unpleasant if walking near heavy traffic, on poor footways, or in bad weather.

The Modal Shift Strategy

10.40 From the above analysis, it can be seen that there is no single policy lever which can reverse the underlying trend towards the more polluting modes of transport. Inevitably, therefore, the strategy has to encompass a number of complementary strands. The main ones are as follows.

- Improving the reliability and quality of rail and Underground services and extending the networks.

- Increasing the real cost of motoring relative to the real cost of public transport.

- Adopting traffic management strategies which take more rigorous action to ease congestion caused by general traffic, whilst freeing road space for other users, particularly buses.

- Improving the quality and reliability of bus travel and promoting its use as an alternative mode.

- Promoting walking, cycling and river travel to serve the markets in which they can compete effectively with the car, whilst being realistic about what they can deliver.

- Using the planning system to reduce the overall need to travel and reduce the dependency on the car to make particular journeys.

- Seeking, through education and promotion, to influence travel decisions in favour of the less polluting modes of travel.

10.41 The rail and Underground network is discussed in Chapters 11 and 12. The rest of this Chapter explains in more detail what is being done for the other ones.

The Comparative Cost Lever

10.42 As paragraph 5.24 above explains, the Government is committed to raising fuel duty by 5% per annum in real terms to promote the reduction in CO_2 emissions required to meet the objectives set at the Rio summit. On the basis of the current duty content of the pump price of a litre of petrol, it is estimated that this will increase the perceived cost to the motorist per mile travelled in 1991 prices from just under 8 pence in 1991 to 10 pence in 2001 - an increase of 30% compared to just 15% without the annual fuel duty increase. If the policy continues to 2011, the perceived cost per mile will rise to between 12 and 13 pence. According to LASER, we would expect this measure on its own to reduce the number of car trips which would have taken place in London and the South East in the am peak in 2011 by 2% and car miles by around 10%. Public transport trips and revenues could each be about 4% higher than they would be without the increase in fuel duty.

10.43 There is an important and difficult balance to be struck in determining the level of public transport fares in London. On the one hand, high public transport fares reduce the operators' dependence on the public purse, generate funds to support vital transport investment and enhance the ability to attract private finance. On the other hand, high fare levels add to the cost of doing business in London and discourage the use of public transport at the margins. In Chapter 13, we look further at the important contribution which fares revenue makes to funding of public transport, both existing and new.

10.44 Chart 10D shows the trend in public transport fares over recent decades. There have been periods when fare increases have risen significantly more or less steeply, notably as a result of the GLC's

Chart 10D: Index of London fares and earnings

Real prices index (1971=100)

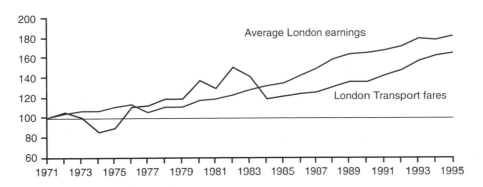

Sources: Office for National Statistics, London Transport

implementation of its Fares Fair policy and the subsequent overturning of that policy by the Courts. However, the clear long-term trend has been for fares to rise broadly in line with earnings. This is understandable: such increases generate the maximum increase in revenue to the operators, in a price-inelastic market, without making public transport less affordable to its customers.

10.45 The Government believes that the policy has resulted in a funding position which is to the advantage of all parties. In particular, whilst accepting the validity of the argument that high public transport fares have an adverse impact on public transport demand, the Government notes that over the short- to medium-term the price elasticity of demand for public transport is modest at about -0.3, while the cross-elasticities between car and public transport are even lower at about 0.1. What this means is that cutting fares by 10% would yield a 3% increase in public transport use, with the majority of this additional demand representing new trips and trips previously completed on foot or by cycle, rather than substituting for car trips. The LASER model suggests that the full effect over the long-term allowing for land-use changes may eventually be bigger than this, but it will take place over a long period of time. The Government's conclusion therefore is that a policy of fares restraint is unlikely on its own to be an effective means of discouraging car use and encouraging the use of public transport.

10.46 The Government announced last year its national-level policy on passenger rail fares. The Government was aware that commuter journeys to and from London would be a major component within the package of regulated fares, and that any decision on rail fares in London would inevitably have a significant impact on other public transport fares. This is partly because rail, Underground, light rail and bus services are all covered by the Travelcard. The Government recognises the high value which Londoners set upon the availability of the genuinely multi-modal ticket and has repeatedly reaffirmed its commitment to preserving Travelcard. Since period Travelcards for the outer zones must fall within the ambit of a policy on passenger rail fares, the Government recognised that the decision to cap rail fare increases at RPI +0% for three years from 1 January 1996 and at RPI -1% for each of the next four years, would inevitably tend to constrain the scope for fare increases for other forms of public transport.

10.47 The LT fares increases for 1996 were announced in October 1995. Across the board, the average increase in LT fares was 4½%, about 1% higher than the rail fares increase. Whilst London Transport will continue to consider on their merits the arguments for fares increases for different types of service and the case for introducing new ticket types, the likely trend will be for rail fares and other public transport fares to increase at a rate closer to RPI than earnings. The LASER model suggests that, taken on its own, the fares restraint policy would slow but not halt the downward trend in public transport's mode share. If without the fare restraint policy fares rose broadly in line with economic growth, by about 60%, the indications are that public transport's mode share of mechanised trips in the am peak would further decline from an estimated 22% in 1996 to under 18% in 2011. But with public transport fares fixed in real terms at 1996 levels, the fall is only to 21%. Likewise, car's share rises from 78% to 79% instead of 82%.

10.48 The model suggests that the combined effect of the fares restraint policy and an annual 5% real increase in fuel duty could be enough to arrest the modal shift towards car. We might expect the public transport share of mechanised trips in the am peak to be the same in 2011 as in 1996 at 22%. Total car miles could be about one eighth lower in 2011 than if previous trends in fares and motoring costs had continued and public transport passenger-miles more than 40% higher. As a result, public transport trips in the am peak would increase by almost 10% between 1996 and 2011, the biggest gainers being bus (13%) and rail (7%). It is important to note however that a very large change in relative travel costs is required to bring this about. The restraint policy implies fares in 2011 about 30% lower in real terms than if the previous relationship of fares with earnings had continued and the annual 5% real increase implies that the pump price of fuel would be about 50% higher. Other things being equal, this should substantially redress the trend over the past ten years, in which public transport fares have risen substantially while motoring costs have barely changed in real terms. Separate motoring figures for London are not currently available, but the comparision of expenditure on travel shown in Chart 10E indicates the divergence. Because of the wider coverage of the LASER model and other factors referred to in paragraph 10.27, these results are not comparable with those given for the two LTS scenarios discussed earlier in this Chapter and in Chapter 2.

The Traffic Management Review

10.49 As will be explained in Chapter 11, The Government Office for London, the Boroughs and operators are working together on a review of the traffic management guidance for London.

10.50 A number of traffic management options are available which might achieve reductions in the impact of the car on road congestion and free road space for other users particularly for bus travel. Traffic management techniques have previously been employed successfully in London and have been shown to moderate congestion and the adverse effects of traffic. Options could be developed to build on the successes achieved by existing policies. A series of modelling tests are being conducted under the auspices of the Traffic Management and Signalling Strategy Group (TRMS) to examine the following:

- area-wide bus priorities and the allocation of road space to buses;

- adjusting traffic signals to inhibit commuting, favour buses, and reduce emissions;

- area-wide traffic calming and the consequences for main road traffic;

- the traffic flow consequences of parking or other car travel restraint measures.

10.51 The tests will involve the use of London-wide and local traffic models. An assessment will be made of the following key parameters:

- network performance and congestion;

- impacts on London's economy;

- vehicle emissions;

- accidents;

- accessibility and choice.

10.52 The initial tests so far suggest that the adoption of individual initiatives alone is likely to be counterproductive. However, a judicious combination of several could help to achieve some of the key aims of smoothing traffic flows, improving the reliability of journeys by bus and easing accessibility for commercial vehicles.

10.53 A considerable amount of work has still to be undertaken to refine further the understanding of what can be achieved with modest traffic management solutions encompassing the sort of combination of initiatives described above. Consideration will have to be given to what would happen at a local level and also whether different approaches should be adopted inter-peak. The TRMS Group will be asked to consider the various alternatives that emerge from this exercise and what the best approach would be for traffic management in London.

Promoting Walking, Cycling, the River and Buses

Promoting Walking

10.54 Walking is one of the most frequently used means of getting about the Capital, particularly in central London and other town centres. Londoners make 4 million trips a day wholly on foot and a further 4 million journeys by other modes begin or end with a

Chart 10E: Family expenditure[1] on travel by London residents

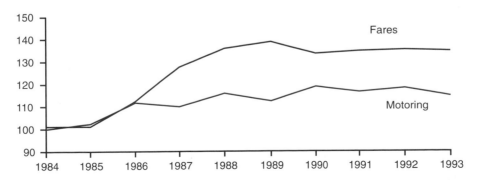

Real prices index (1983=100)

[1] Data are three year moving averages

Source: Family Expenditure Survey (Office for National Statistics)

walk. There are many initiatives in hand to promote walking, such as the City Walks initiative, the provision of a Riverside Walkway along the Thames and proposals for the partial pedestrianisation of Parliament Square and Trafalgar Square. However, their emphasis is very much on promoting walking as a recreational and tourist activity, rather than as a means of getting about London as an alternative to the car. The latter goal is a more important, but more difficult goal to achieve. It means having regard to the detailed layout of roads, pavements and crossings, as has been done by the Traffic Director on the Red Route network. For example, the physical segregation of pedestrians from traffic has obvious safety benefits, even though it can make it more difficult to get around the city on foot, but it sometimes requires pedestrians to make circuitous detours to get from one side of the road to another. Issues such as this will be addressed in the new traffic management and parking guidance on which GOL are currently working. *Strategic Guidance for London Planning Authorities* highlights the importance of Borough action to promote walking, through the planning process. We will also look to the results of LPAC's study into a pedestrian strategy for London, to help us understand better how to promote walking.

Promoting Cycling

10.55 Cycling has significant transport potential. The 1994 journey time surveys show that it is the quickest way of getting round inner London; and it is environmentally friendly. Its main disadvantages are that it is not a particularly comfortable mode, particularly in poor weather, and that cyclists are a highly vulnerable group of road users. The London local authorities are developing the London cycle network which aims to make travel by bike much easier and safer. It will incorporate a safe, convenient and conspicuous network of routes that link local centres and provide for longer distance journeys across the whole of London. The network should provide, in particular, for travel to school and the short commuting trip, where there is the greatest potential for modal shift. The Government will continue to fund the London cycle network, giving this a high priority within the local transport budget for London. Boroughs should develop their own local level schemes to complement the London wide network. They should also promote cycling to school, where they are satisfied that this can be done without compromising children's safety.

10.56 The Government is backing four local authority backed cycle schemes through the London Cycling Initiative. These are:

- The **Friary Lane Cycle Route**, an 8 mile route between Woodside Park and Arnos Grove Tube stations promoted by **LB Barnet**

- The provision of cycling parking facilities, including **350 lockers and 150 stands** in the **RB Kensington and Chelsea**

- The provision of **cycle parking** facilities, at various locations in 11 boroughs, led by **LB Southwark, on behalf of the Central London Partnership**;

- The **Wandle Cycle Route**, a cycle route passing through the boroughs of Sutton, Merton and Wandsworth promoted by **LB Wandsworth**

10.57 *Strategic Guidance for London Planning Authorities* also calls for Boroughs to adopt a radically new approach to transport and development planning in their UDPs to promote cycling, which incorporates the London cycle network.

Promoting River Transport

10.58 Repeated attempts have been made to operate commuter services by river. None has succeeded to date. The main problem is that travel by river is slow, compared with all other commuter modes. This makes it unsuitable for commuter trips, where there is a high premium on rapid journey times, other than for those who both live and work close to the River. The Thames' potential is more for freight and leisure traffic and for shorter distance travel within the central area, although the capacity for increased traffic on the river is limited. It is for business to decide how freight is moved, but Government can do two things to promote use of the River. One is to provide grant for those who want to transfer freight from road to water. The other is to safeguard key berthages via the *Strategic Planning Guidance for the Thames*, on which we shall be consulting shortly. This Guidance, together with *Strategic Guidance for London Planning Authorities*, provide the framework for the local authorities to develop their policies aimed at making the best use of the River.

10.59 The Millennium Exhibition at Greenwich will require good access by river from central London. It should also stimulate riverside development and interest in the River as a tourist destination in its own right. This should accelerate the improvement in the quality of excursions on the Thames which we have begun to see in recent years. A study undertaken by London First on behalf of GOL identified scope for a hopper service, aimed at residents and visitors alike, between the key riverside attractions in Central London. The Cross-River Partnership is working up proposals for the provision of the new piers which these services would require. The Single Regeneration Budget and Capital Challenge may be appropriate sources of funding, if a robust investment case can be produced. The scope for harnessing private finance should not be ignored.

10.60 The Port of London Authority has estimated that the potential exists for freight traffic handled in the Port of London to rise from the 1990s levels of around 50 million tonnes to around 80 million tonnes by the year 2020. Much of this traffic is suitable for transhipment from sea-going vessels to river craft, provided that facilities are available upstream to handle the cargo and that adequate road or rail systems exist on the land side. Local authorities can assist the use of the Thames for freight by protecting existing freight facilities, including those with waterfront access, where these have potential to retain or encourage river-borne freight transport.

Promoting use of Buses

10.61 London's buses carry over 3.5 million people every working day and thus play a crucial role in the life of the capital. The bus accounts for around as many trips in London as the Underground and suburban rail networks put together. Because of the relatively low cost of improvements to the bus network compared to improvements to the rail networks, and because of its flexibility to meet a wide range of different travel markets, the bus stands as a key part of our strategy to encourage modal shift away from the private car. Much has already been achieved to improve the quality and efficiency of bus services, through measures such as the privatisation of London Transport's bus operations, opening up the provision of bus services to competitive tender and the introduction of the London Bus Passenger's Charter.

10.62 The main weaknesses of the bus are its relative unreliability, largely due to traffic congestion, and the time journeys take for all but very short trips. In addition there is often uncertainty about when the next bus will arrive and bus stops frequently offer little protection from the elements. These weaknesses are such that even incentives such as lower fares are unlikely to have anything other than a marginal effect on the number of passengers. In any case many people use a Travelcard to pay for their journeys and some benefit from free bus travel, which limits the scope for opening up a cost-differential between bus and rail/Underground fares. So the main incentives to encourage more people to use buses will be cutting journey times, improving reliability and making sure the buses serve routes on which people want them. Achieving these objectives falls to the Traffic Director for London, in implementing the Red Route network, London Boroughs, who are the highway authorities for most of the routes on which buses operate in London, and to London Transport Buses, a subsidiary of London Transport.

Buses and Red Routes

10.63 As explained in Chapter 11, traffic management measures should help to improve the relative performance of buses. The Red Route network covers the main roads in inner and outer London. The Traffic Director does of course need to have regard to all road users, but bus passengers feature highly in his priorities. Certainly the benefits of rationalising road space through clearer and better enforced parking restrictions, resulting in more smoothly flowing traffic, will impact on buses as much as other road vehicles. In addition the Red Route programme also provides for more effective use of existing bus priority lanes. Thus the pilot red route has demonstrated that bus passengers will be among the prime beneficiaries of this initiative, as explained at paragraph 11.35. The benefits already experienced on the pilot will spread across the whole of London as the network, which covers the main roads in inner and outer London, is implemented.

Buses and the Boroughs

10.64 The Red Route network does not cover all roads used by buses, nor does it extend into central London. The Boroughs are therefore working on a London-wide bus priority network on secondary roads, involving both the introduction of bus lanes and measures to give buses priority at junctions. This network is intended, in conjunction with the Red Route network, to provide an integrated network for buses across the whole of

London. Boroughs have conducted an extensive review of traffic management measures on 500 miles of major bus routes. The network provides for priority for buses through the use of bus lanes and the use of signalling, to allow buses to beat queues. Boroughs are also looking at how to improve conditions for bus passengers at stops and interchanges along major bus routes, and reviewing how waiting and loading restrictions on the network affect bus performance. This programme is supported from within the local transport budget, and is accorded high priority by both Government and Boroughs. Further measures could include improved siting of bus stops, minor traffic management and junction improvements, the provision of advisory bus stop markings on the carriageway, the designation of 'bus stop clearways' and the effective enforcement of yellow line waiting restrictions on bus routes. Using their new powers under the 1991 Road Traffic Act the local authorities intend to concentrate their parking enforcement efforts on the bus network.

10.65 Such bus priority measures are designed to minimise the impact on the flow of traffic generally. The main purpose of a bus lane, for instance, is to get the bus to the front of the queue at junctions, not to reduce the capacity of the junction for other traffic. Although it could be argued that the psychological impact of delaying cars, as well as freeing up bus movement, would double the impact of the measures in terms of attracting people to switch from cars to buses, it would almost certainly increase congestion and pollution as well. And it is debatable whether buses would gain overall since it is difficult in practice to insulate them from the effects of general traffic congestion.

London Transport Buses (LTB)

10.66 Action by Boroughs and the Traffic Director to maximise the ability of roads for which they are responsible to meet the needs of buses is complemented by that of London Transport Buses (LTB). Its key roles are:

- to determine the routes which make up the bus network, service frequencies and fares;

- to manage contracts for over 700 bus services;

- to manage bus related infrastructure (stations, bus stops and shelters); and

- to promote and advertise services.

LTB is implementing a wide range of measures designed to further its key objectives of providing a high quality and comprehensive bus network to meet London's bus travel needs, and maximising passenger benefits and usage. Among these are initiatives to address the image problem of buses. They may be a 'friendly' mode, but they don't always look that way - they tend to be judged by those at the kerb side and motorists by the black and smelly fumes that a small minority of buses emit. LTB is addressing this problem and considering how best to reduce bus emissions through the tender process. It is currently reviewing existing emission standards and plans progressively to increase the percentage of vehicles with Euro 1 and 2 certified engines. LTB plans to complete its preliminary evaluation during this year. A number of recent contracts have been awarded to companies offering vehicles equipped with engines to Euro 2 specification. In addition routine smoke checks are now being carried out by all operators. In the longer term, LTB is planning trials involving low sulphur fuels and oxidising catalysts on a number of vehicles operating in central London.

10.67 The design and condition of the vehicle fleet is crucial to promoting a positive image of bus travel as well as being critical to the provision of reliable and safe services. As service contracts are renewed, roughly half are expected to involve the provision of new buses. This will result in an increasing proportion of London's buses featuring attractive modern designs outside and in and greater comfort and accessibility for bus users.

10.68 Another way of increasing bus patronage will be to improve the level of information available about services. London Transport's Travel Enquiry Service operates Travel Information Centres at major locations, including Heathrow and interchanges such as mainline stations. It also offers a comprehensive 24 hour telephone travel enquiry service and distributes area bus guides, containing maps and route service frequencies. An innovative development is the Countdown system which provides passengers waiting at bus stops with real-time information about when the next bus will arrive, similar to dot-matrix displays at London Underground stations. In 1995 LTB launched a network trial on 30 bus routes centred on the Nag's Head junction on Holloway Road in North London. LTB will monitor its effect on bus use. If successful, LTB intends to approach the Department with proposals to extend the system across London. In addition to the Countdown trial, LTB has a programme to improve the presentation of timetable information at bus stops and also to provide clearer, easier to use bus maps at bus shelters and stations. It also has an ongoing programme of bus stop improvement work.

10.69 The environment where customers wait is an important part of their journey. LTB is responsible for some 17,000 bus stops, 9,000 shelters, 100 off-highway stands and 36 bus stations. A major improvement programme, the London Initiative, is under way. The package includes improved shelters, involving the replacement of existing ones and where practical the provision of new ones where they do not exist, throughout London. Investment in the shelter development programme will continue at a rate of up to 1,200 shelters per year. The initiative aims to replace all existing shelters by 2000/01. Modern advertising shelters are being provided in partnership with More O'Ferrall Adshel. Non-advertising shelters will be enhanced to a similar standard, generally to include seating and lighting. At many shelters the programme also provides improved weather protection, seating and enhanced information provision. All new shelters will be fully compatible with the Countdown system. In addition, in some areas of London the provision of shelters does not rest with LTB, but with the Boroughs, who have agreements with J C Decaux.

10.70 Most existing bus stations have had partial or full refurbishment, for example West Croydon and Harrow. Elsewhere completely new facilities have been provided, as at Hammersmith and Stratford. Major new bus stations will be constructed in connection with the Jubilee Line Extension at Canada Water, North Greenwich and Canning Town. In addition a new bus link is planned at Canada Water together with replacement bus facilities at Tenison Way, Waterloo. LTB's plans also feature the redesign and refurbishment of Turnpike Lane and Morden bus stations, and improved or enlarged facilities at Crossharbour and Walthamstow Central bus stations. Furthermore, LTB is seeking to secure the provision of major new bus stations at Victoria, Brent Cross and White City in connection with commercial developments, at no cost to LT.

The Planning System

10.71 A progressive tightening up of parking standards for new developments, in circumstances where alternative options of travel are available, will also be helpful in promoting greater use of less polluting modes. Through its *Strategic Guidance for London Planning Authorities*, the Government is encouraging local authorities to develop a coherent approach to all forms of parking within their areas and, in particular, to minimise the amount of traffic generated by new developments by placing maximum limits on the level of off-street car parking spaces permitted. This approach is also espoused in *PPG13 A Guide to Better Practice* published in October 1995, which, in turn, reflects the Government's *Sustainable Development Strategy*, originally published in 1994 and updated in March 1995.

10.72 However, the main contribution that the planning system has to make is in reducing the overall need to travel and the dependency on the car to make particular journeys. PPG13 sets out the national framework for the development of transport and land use policy by local authorities. In line with this framework, the Government has recently issued strategic planning guidance which is encouraging the London local authorities to prepare urban development plans which seek to accommodate economic activity and new development at locations which are accessible by public transport and, where possible, are near to locations where people live and can therefore walk or cycle to work. The Authorities are also being asked to consider the use of appropriate conditions and to negotiate planning obligations to ensure that public transport facilities and improved traffic management arrangements are associated with new development.

10.73 Over time, the implementation of the guidance should lead to a better match between development and the public transport systems which serve them, and this in turn will enable London to become less reliant on private road transport. This will be particularly relevant to problems in outer London where, at present, developments tend to be inaccessible by public transport and in many cases people have no alternative but to use the car to reach them.

10.74 However, better integration of land use and transport will not guarantee a gain in modal split. Even if developments are located more conveniently for public transport, people may still choose to make the journey by car. If they do switch to public transport, there is a risk that others will simply fill the road capacity which has been released to make car journeys which would otherwise have been suppressed. There is therefore a need for complementary action, such as parking restraint, to ensure that the benefits of modal shift are sustained.

Education and Promotion

10.75 If modal shift is to be achieved, attitudes about travel will need to change. Education and promotion has proved successful in influencing purchasing decisions towards more environmentally friendly choices in other markets, and in encouraging activities such as recycling paper, glass and other materials. Thus far there is little evidence that most people are willing voluntarily to modify their own travel habits in the interests of the wider environmental good - though the environmentally damaging impact of car travel is now widely recognised, and there is a general desire to see lower traffic levels. The Government believes that public opinion would be receptive to an educational and promotional campaign, perhaps focusing first on short trips which can be made conveniently on foot or by bicycle, where there are also potential health benefits. This is an area where we believe local authorities together with operators are best placed to take action. There may, however, be a case for some form of co-ordination between their activities across London. GOL will initiate discussions with the ALG, Boroughs, and LT on the scope for action in this area.

Chapter 11: Managing Road Access

Objectives

11.1 Busy streets are a sign of economic vitality and prosperity. However, roads in many parts of London are excessively congested with the result that travel is slow and frustrating, pollution is exacerbated, journey times are unpredictable, and drivers are inclined to divert to less suitable roads. This Chapter looks at how we achieve objective 4: simultaneously facilitate the access which businesses need to the central business districts and preserve ease of movement within and between those districts. By central business districts we mean not just the City of London and the City of Westminster, but also the locations to the east and west which internationally mobile businesses have occupied in recent years - particularly the Western Corridor and Docklands.

11.2 Successful business centres require reliable access arrangements for employees, suppliers, visitors and service providers. The focus of our initiatives to provide access for employees is enhancing rail and Underground services (see Chapter 9). Bus and cycle can also play a part, albeit a more modest one. Nevertheless access by road is essential for goods and service vehicles.

11.3 On the other hand, as noted in Part One, the main reason why firms locate in major cities, despite the higher cost of doing business there, is to secure the advantage of proximity to a wide range of customers, suppliers and competitors. That advantage depends upon ease of movement within and between central business districts. As one moves towards the centre of London, roads are more congested, traffic speeds are slower and the problems of vehicle emissions increase. Congestion impacts upon competitiveness both by impeding ease of movement and aggravating air quality problems. It also has a particularly damaging effect on the reliability of bus services, which adds to the difficulty of inducing greater use of this more environmentally friendly mode of transport.

11.4 There is, therefore, an inherent tension between facilitating access to central business districts and facilitating ease of movement within and between them. It is aggravated by the fact that business and commercial trips, travel by taxi, commuting by bus, and journeys by local residents all contribute to the congestion problem alongside car commuters. Over the last ten years, there has been a 35% increase in taxi numbers and a 30% increase numbers of vans

entering central London - two types of vehicle which are particularly likely to be making multiple trips within business districts. It is also possible that a growing proportion of cars are being used for commercial purposes and are making the same multiple trips as vans.

11.5 Partially offsetting this, London does start with the important advantage that it is rated highly by international businessmen on ease of movement, ranking ahead of all other major European cities. This is not because they are blind to the congestion problem, but because they are comparing London with other busy cities and are probably focusing particularly on the modes (taxi, Underground and walk) which businessmen are most likely to use for short trips within the central area.

11.6 Pursuing either of the two objectives described in paragraph 11.1 in isolation would be relatively straightforward. Pursuing them in parallel is more difficult. In addition, we must ensure that the solutions which we propose to help areas closer to the centre do not compound either the environmental or the regeneration problems of areas further out. We also have to ensure that we respect freedom of choice and do not compromise safety. The result is a complex access management problem.

The Options

11.7 Against this background there are a number of ways in which we can seek to achieve our objectives:

- promote rail alternatives to road travel into the centre;

- promote bus and coach alternatives to travel by car;

- reduce the overall need to travel through better land use planning;

- seek to facilitate orbital flows, so that road traffic does not need to come further into the centre than its journey requires;

- improve the quality of road access into business centres through selective road junction improvements and/or priority route traffic management measures;

- take traffic management and enforcement measures to ease the flow of traffic within the more central areas;

- ration road access to the more central area by price, ie the congestion charging approach;

- ration access to the more central areas by traffic management measures;

- suppress demand for road travel to the centre by further constraining parking provision, through either constraints on public parking and on private non-residential parking.

The first two options involve the promotion of modal shift to public transport and are explored in Chapters 9, 10 and 12, and are mentioned below only where bus priorities can sensibly be incorporated in the other options. The third option, where local authorities are in the lead, is taken up in *Strategic Guidance for London Planning Authorities*. Changes to land use are necessarily longer term. Consequently the delivery of this objective in a balanced way, at least in the short term, has to rely predominantly on making imaginative and sensible use of the ways in which we can develop and manage the 10,000 miles of the road system of London. It is appropriate, therefore, to consider the regional road system and its functions.

The London Road Hierarchy

11.8 The Government Office for London proposed last year in the consultation draft of *Strategic Guidance for London Planning Authorities* a new functional hierarchy for roads in London. The original proposals found favour and were further developed with support from a working group of officers from boroughs in North West London.

11.9 The strategic roads, Tier 1 - motorways, primary routes and Red Routes - carry about a third of all road traffic in London, half of all commercial vehicle traffic, but amount to only 5% of the road length. Tier 2, London distributor roads - A roads which are not in the top tier - constitute 10% of the network and carry another third of London's traffic including much of London's bus services. The remaining 85% of the network is largely access and residential roads, together with locally important Borough distributor roads.

11.10 The roads in each tier have distinctly different functions. Strategic routes are intended to attract and serve strategic longer distance traffic. They are part of the national motorway and primary route network. Within the M25 an extensive programme of re-signing the primary route network is about to commence.

Distinctive green background directional road signs will all be renewed, following extensive planning and consultation and a pilot scheme on the A4.

11.11 Tier 2 roads provide a district distributor network. They often have significant lengths of frontage development so the balance between catering for movement and access will be not be easy. These roads should attract appropriate traffic from lower tier roads, while not attracting unsuitable traffic from strategic roads.

11.12 The local distributor and access roads in Tier 3 are for local traffic. Speed limits of 30mph or even 20mph will prevail. Calming measures on access roads can reinforce this function by helping to deter unnecessary through traffic. These roads can also serve as pleasant and safe routes for pedestrians and pedal cyclists.

Facilitating orbital movement

11.13 If one could design a strategic road network for London, with carte blanche to build new roads wherever they were needed and to demolish or decommission existing roads where necessary, what would it look like? The question is worth posing in this form, even though its premises are manifestly false, because it helps to cast light upon the role of the strategic road network in London.

11.14 Map 11A illustrates what such a hypothetical strategic road network might look like. It pictures a 'ring-and-spoke' network, in which the width of the route is an indication of the relative attractiveness to drivers, in terms of door-to-door journey times. The two key principles are that attractiveness increases as one moves further out from the centre and that, for a given distance out from the centre, the attractiveness of the orbital route exceeds the attractiveness of the radial route. Such a network could accommodate different types of traffic movement as follows:

- Movement A is a through-movement, beginning and ending outside the region, and diverted round it, rather than across it

- Movement B is a shorter through-movement originating within London. The hypothetical road network will divert such traffic around the centre by offering a better outer network.

- Movement C is an essentially radial movement which exploits an orbital link.

- Movement D is an essentially orbital movement which exploits a radial link. The better the quality of the strategic road network, the less risk there is of movements C or D being made by diverting onto local roads.

- Movements E, F and G are typical local movements, which ideally would not degrade the attractiveness of the strategic road network

11.15 Diagrams along the lines of Map 11A have been drawn before. From the perspective of the goals which we are trying to achieve in this strategy, the environmental and competitiveness gains of an attractive strategic road network are obvious, but it is also worth mentioning the regeneration benefits. As noted in Chapter 1, a good strategic road network can facilitate access to areas with development potential.

11.16 For economic, environmental and historical reasons, a road network like the model at Map 11A has long since ceased to be possible. However, in framing a road strategy for London and in looking at individual schemes, it is worthwhile to consider whether the strategy or scheme results in the network becoming more like the model. At the strategic level, this leads us to three tests, which we have applied alongside the economic cost:benefit analysis and consideration of regeneration effects in reviewing the London component of the national roads programme and in dealing with proposals from Boroughs for other strategic road improvements. The tests are:

- we should endeavour to increase the capacity of orbital routes in outer London;

- on the outer parts of the radial routes we should endeavour to increase the capacity of congested sections;

- on the radial and orbital routes within inner London and where substantial local traffic is unavoidable we should endeavour to make movement more efficient, but should not increase the capacity of the route other than at key junctions;

Map 11A: A hypothetical strategic road network for London

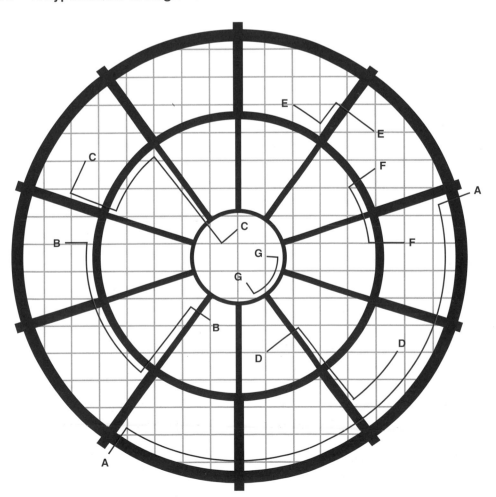

Let us look at how the application of these tests works in practice.

11.17 The M25 is London's outer 'ring road' and remains extremely effective in keeping lorries and other long-distance traffic out of London. However, key sections are often heavily congested, which could tempt through-traffic to cut across the Capital. A comprehensive and long-term widening programme is therefore under way. At the next level in, the North Circular meets London's orbital needs reasonably well and there are plans for plugging the few remaining gaps in it, ie the junctions which still constitute bottlenecks. However, the South Circular runs too close to the centre, varies enormously in terms of quality and capacity and could not easily be upgraded. Nor is there any scope for widening the inner ring road. Turning from the orbital rings to the radial spokes, the summary position is:

• The **eastern quadrant** is the main target for enhancement of the trunk road network. A comprehensive improvement programme is being implemented along the A13 and the new A12 link, with the aim of facilitating traffic flows to (but not beyond) the intersection with the A102 and Blackwall crossings. No further improvements are needed to the A12 and A127 or, south of the River, to the A20 or A2. The widening of the Thamesmead Spine Road as far as the M25 will make that area much more readily accessible. The addition of these schemes will give the eastern quadrant a network of radial routes which corresponds reasonably well with the model at Map 11A, but their ability to foster orbital flows of traffic will be hampered by the dearth of river crossings.

Map 11B: The strategic road network: existing motorways and primary routes

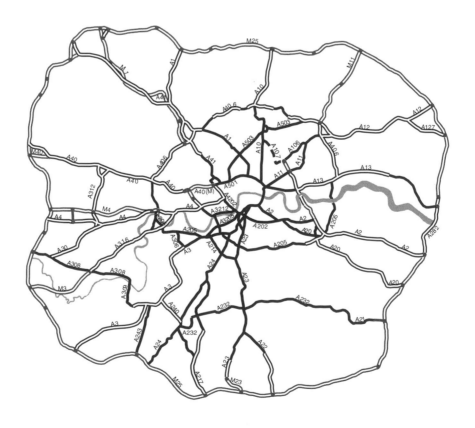

| Motorways & junctions | ====●==== | Primary route dual carriageway | ======== | Primary route | ▬▬▬ | River Thames | ∿ |

- The **southern quadrant** poses particular problems. The A23, which is of indifferent standard, is currently the only trunk road between the A3 and A20. It runs through heavily built-up areas of London and the economic and environmental cost of upgrading it would be prohibitive. The only scope for improvement is the elimination of some of the worst pinch-points and, in the longer term, the Coulsdon inner relief road. The A21 is a possible candidate for primary route status but this and other strategic roads provide for only limited access from the south.

- The **western quadrant** is much better served and its radial routes generally comply with the principle that relative attractiveness should reduce on the inner stretches. The top priority in this quadrant is to maintain existing capacity, particularly by tackling the problems with the elevated section of the M4. The only schemes planned to increase capacity are the widening of the M4 between Junctions 3 and 4B (which would be required if Heathrow's Terminal 5 is built) and the elimination of the remaining bottlenecks on the A40.

- The picture in the **northern quadrant** is reasonably good. The M1, A1 and A41 provide reasonable access to the North and Midlands and the M11 provides good access to East Anglia. The A10 performs a more limited strategic role.

A more detailed discussion of London's strategic road network is given in Chapter 12.

Map 11C: The strategic road network: improvements planned or under construction
(excluding longer term Schemes)

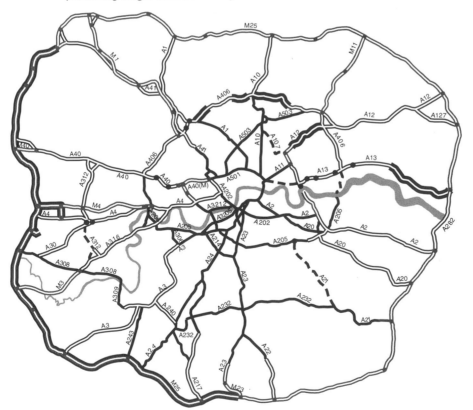

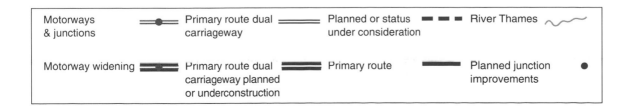

Motorways & junctions	●━━	Primary route dual carriageway	━━━━	Planned or status under consideration	■ ■ ■	River Thames
Motorway widening	▤▤▤	Primary route dual carriageway planned or underconstruction	▬▬▬	Primary route	▬▬▬	Planned junction improvements ●

Summary of strategic road provision

11.18 Maps 11B and 11C show the strategic road network in terms of the provision of attractive high quality, mostly dual-carriageway roads and the extent to which this network will be improved once the schemes in the current national and local roads programmes have been completed. Map 11D shows further roads that could be improved in the longer term if finance were readily available and where improvements are likely to prove acceptable to those that live locally. The maps indicate that the existing network and planned improvements should form a reasonable network of orbital and radial roads in north, west and east London. But they also highlight the inadequacies of the River Thames crossings and the problems of strategic road access to centres in south London and parts of north London. Crossings of the

Thames are discussed in Chapter 12.

11.19 In terms of objective 4 the improved strategic road network will help to facilitate orbital traffic flows in many sectors of London. This will improve road access to established and developing business centres in outer London and assist efforts to ameliorate the penetration of traffic into inner and central London. But only a proportion of the new capacity discussed here could be in place within the ten year horizon of this transport strategy. The reduced pace of investment in road improvements will mean that road traffic conditions in inner London could get worse before they get better. This adds to the priority we must give to bolstering the performance of the strategic road network and the effectiveness of the second tier network through traffic management and other measures.

Map 11D: The strategic road network: longer term schemes
(excluding east London river crossings)

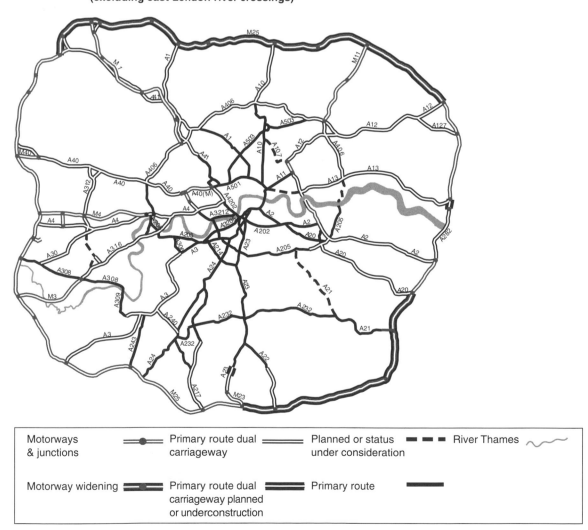

Motorways & junctions	Primary route dual carriageway	Planned or status under consideration	River Thames
Motorway widening	Primary route dual carriageway planned or underconstruction	Primary route	

Traffic management: getting into and around central business districts

11.20 There are a number of traffic management measures that can be taken to improve the quality of road access to business and retail centres, or to ease conditions within congested areas. We focus here on:

- Road user information

- Urban traffic control

- Selective network enhancements

- Better enforcement of on-street parking controls

- Automatic detection of potential traffic offences

- Utilities' street works

- Red Routes

Road user information

11.21 We know from market research that drivers rate highly the provision of better direction signing, better street naming and better information about parking and loading facilities. The primary route re-signing programme is expected to be complete within the next four years. It is probably the largest single urban direction signing programme ever undertaken. The investment by the Highways Agency will amount to £20m covering both trunk and borough roads. Better directional information will reduce lost travel, improve the use of the strategic road network and reduce driver stress. The Government Office for London will be discussing with the Agency and the Boroughs how to ensure that the quality and continuity of the new signs is maintained. GOL is also keen to encourage complementary *London Local Signing Strategies* from individual or groups of Boroughs and is leading the development of guidance on tourism signing within the M25. The local signing strategies would cover directional, information, tourism and regulatory signing and street naming.

11.22 New technology has opened up the possibilities for electronic information systems which could provide drivers, road network managers and operators of vehicle fleets with a wider range of information, including potentially up to the minute reports or even forecasts of conditions across the road network. There will doubtless be opportunities for a range of information providers in a region as large as that within the M25/A282, but the contribution of new systems to general traffic management has still to be established.

There is more to understand about the supply and management of traffic information, driver reactions to advice or warnings and the scope for sensible diversion routes within inner London and the possibilities for providing such information as part of a wider service for travel on all modes of transport. In the medium term it would appear that the priority for central and local government is to ensure that conventional signing systems on strategic and district distributor roads are brought up to date and properly maintained.

Urban traffic control

11.23 This is the name given to the systems of central control of traffic lights. About half of all traffic signals within Greater London, including those at pedestrian crossings, are connected to a central control. Half of these are under 'SCOOT' control, a highly advanced system which automatically copes with changes in traffic conditions. Recent developments of SCOOT have added new facilities, including a bus priority capability, systems which allow the location of queues to be managed and features which can detect the presence of probable incidents. The Police continue to have an important role in the operation of the control systems.

11.24 The Department of Transport's research programme is seeking to stimulate the development of a new generation of urban traffic management systems. In time these could enable traffic authorities to adopt more sophisticated traffic management strategies, such as giving comprehensive priority to public transport, improving the safety and convenience of pedestrians and cyclists, restraining traffic in sensitive areas, giving priority to traffic on defined routes, and reducing the impact of traffic on air quality.

11.25 Urban traffic control has a vital role in securing the most efficient performance of the road network within congested areas but its strategic contribution may be rather specialised. Nevertheless, along with electronic road user information systems, it must continue to be considered as a potential longer term component of a more comprehensive set of traffic management and control arrangements for improving access into or conditions within central business districts.

Selective network enhancements

11.26 Urban traffic control relies for its success on the fact that it is the junctions and other comparable features which effectively control the performance of urban road networks. Selective more significant enhancements of the performance of key intersections or pinch points can have a pronounced impact on improving the access to central business districts, opening up bypass routes, or allowing other measures to be introduced which get to the heart of the problems within a congested area. Examples are the introduction of additional lanes at a narrow bridge, extra capacity at a key junction or a flyover at an important roundabout. The Highways Agency's programme of Network Enhancement Projects on motorways and trunk roads will have a crucial role in this respect. Moreover, it will be addressing accident blackspots and other locations where safety can be improved and through its recently announced landscape strategy for London's trunk roads helping to improve the visual amenity of strategic routes.

11.27 Alongside other traffic management programmes selective enhancement projects at the right locations on Tier 1 and Tier 2 roads within London will be one of the most effective ways of securing easier access to business and other centres for lorries and other vehicles being used for commercial purposes and for supporting local objectives to manage conditions within centres.

Better enforcement of on-street parking controls

11.28 Illegal and inconsiderate parking is one of the main causes of congestion in London and the Government's aim has been to provide more effective and efficient enforcement. The Road Traffic Act 1991 provided for a new system of decriminalised parking enforcement in London. All London local authorities are now responsible for the enforcement of 'permitted parking' at meters, residents' bays and so on and for most of the enforcement of waiting and loading restrictions denoted by yellow lines. The local authorities retain the income from parking penalties to pay for their enforcement activities. The Police and their traffic warden force now concentrate on the enforcement of the restrictions on London's Red Route network.

11.29 The London local authorities have established a joint committee (the Parking Committee for London) to help co-ordinate their new parking enforcement responsibilities under the Act. The Committee runs the parking adjudication system where a driver can contest the issue of a parking ticket. It has produced a Code of Practice on Parking Enforcement which offers practical help to the local authorities in providing a responsible and consistent approach to parking enforcement. Public acceptance of the new system depends on it being seen to be fair and impartial.

11.30 The new system has been in operation on most roads in London since July 1994 and has substantially increased the level of resources for parking enforcement in London. Compliance with existing controls has improved and there is less meter feeding, parking on yellow lines and illegal occupancy of residents' bays. Better parking enforcement is contributing to smoother traffic flows and better journey times. The new system has allowed London local authorities to tailor parking enforcement more closely to local needs. Many yellow lines and other restrictions no longer have much relevance. Where they are not needed we encourage local authorities to remove them, but where they are needed (whether for safety reasons or to facilitate traffic flow) they should be properly enforced.

Automatic detection of potential traffic offences

11.31 The Government is also looking at ways in which new technology can contribute to road safety and easing congestion. Red light and speed cameras are already producing substantial reductions in accidents. The Traffic Director for London has started a project to investigate the scope for using camera technology to improve enforcement of bus lanes. The scope for using cameras to enforce yellow box markings and other traffic management measures is also being pursued. The use of cameras is signed, to increase their deterrent effect. The intention is not to catch drivers out but to improve compliance with traffic restrictions.

Utilities' street works

11.32 A common cause of traffic congestion on strategic, secondary and local roads is street works associated with the utility companies. The Highways Authorities and Utilities Committee (HAUC) meet to discuss co-ordinating streetworks activities at a strategic level. Co-ordination is important, but it needs to be backed by decisive action. Boroughs as street authorities have powers under the New Roads and Street Works Act. They must be prepared to use them to restrict further street works for a one year period after substantial works have taken place.

Red Routes

11.33 The development of the Red Route strategic traffic management initiative goes back to 1989 when Ministers ruled out any substantial programme of new road construction in London as a way of solving the problem of congestion. The emphasis switched to making the best use of the existing network of main roads. The Government announced its intention to establish the Red Route network once the necessary legislation was in place. The network would aim to improve the movement of traffic on the main roads in London so that people could make longer distance journeys more easily, reliably and safely. A pilot scheme was created to work out the practical details of the project, such as how to cater for the needs of local residents and traders and how the benefits could be used to help buses.

11.34 The 7.8 mile pilot red route commenced in January 1991. The route selected was the A1 trunk road from the north end of Archway Road in Haringey to the Angel, Islington and then on local roads round the Inner Ring Road (City Road - Old Street) and on to A13 Commercial Road in Tower Hamlets as far as its junction with Butcher Row. The pilot scheme involved reviewing all existing traffic management measures, such as pedestrian crossings, traffic signal phasings, waiting and loading restrictions. The locations where kerbside parking and loading could be located without disrupting the flow of traffic were thoroughly reviewed. Several road safety schemes were implemented. Most critically, the new restrictions were strictly enforced by a substantially increased police and traffic warden effort.

11.35 The results from the pilot were very encouraging. A notorious congestion blackspot at Muswell Hill was removed. Surveys showed improvements in general traffic and bus journey times and reliability, and a reduction in accidents. The number of passengers using the 43 bus route and the X43 (introduced in 1992) increased by about 11,000 a week, an increase of some 10% compared with a small overall decline in bus patronage in London over the same period. Eleven new or improved crossing places were installed for pedestrians and three for cyclists; 107 side road

entries were made safer; traffic calming measures were installed in the surrounding area to deter rat-running traffic; and 620 new free short-term parking spaces were provided throughout the pilot scheme where only a few meters existed before.

11.36 The Road Traffic Act 1991 provided the legal framework for the Red Route project. The Secretary of State designated the 315 mile Priority (Red) Route Network in June 1992. The network was based on a review of the Primary Route Network - the Tier 1 roads in the new London road hierarchy - characterised by green background directional signs. It includes all 220 miles of trunk road within Greater London and 95 miles of borough roads. The Traffic Director for London was appointed to design, implement, maintain and monitor traffic management measures on these routes. His approval is required before a highway authority can implement any measure which might affect the traffic flow on a red route. He has produced a *Network Plan* which sets out his aims for the network and provides the framework for the local plans which determine red route controls along particular stretches of routes.

11.37 One of the Traffic Director's objectives is to achieve, as far as is practicable on the priority route network, results comparable to those on the pilot route, where similar characteristics apply - perhaps 125 to 150 miles. This would mean a 17% reduction in accidents; a 10% reduction in general traffic travel times with a 40% improvement in the reliability of journey times; and a 10% reduction in bus journey times with a 33% improvement in the reliability of bus journey times; together with improved facilities for cyclists and pedestrians and disabled road users. Compliance with the regulations should make deliveries and servicing more reliable, but businesses may need to change their schedules to fit with the operational conditions applying in the vicinity of their premises. Side roads will frequently receive treatment to demonstrate that they lead to residential areas, unsuitable for strategic traffic.

11.38 In preparing his plans, all existing waiting and loading restrictions have been reviewed by the Traffic Director. Locations are identified for loading, unloading and parking where the flow of traffic permits. Extensive bus priority measures will be introduced. The aim is to strike a balance between the needs of local residents and businesses and traffic on the strategic road network. Extensive consultation on local plans has provided ample opportunity for local residents and residents' associations, businesses and amenity groups to put forward views. Implementation will include amenity measures such as tree planting.

11.39 On the Red Route network the measures should bring substantial benefits to buses, pedestrians, cyclists, residents, shoppers and local businesses. Proper enforcement is a key to the success of the Red Route initiative and the Metropolitan Police Service, who play an essential part in keeping traffic moving in the Capital, are taking a joint approach with the Traffic Director to ensure that there will be sufficient police and warden effort devoted to securing proper enforcement of the new arrangements. Several sections of the Red Route network are now fully operational; the full network should be substantially operational by 2000.

Congestion Charging

11.40 It has long been suggested that traffic levels should be managed by charging road users for moving within congested urban roads. Proponents argue that charging would make for quicker and more reliable journeys, and ensure that the limited road space available is put to its most efficient use. In November 1991, the Government commissioned a comprehensive study into both the theoretical effectiveness and the practical feasibility of implementing congestion charging in London. A full report on more than three years' research by leading experts was published by the Government Office for London in 1995.

11.41 The study developed and used state-of-the-art transport modelling techniques, and confirmed that charging road users would indeed reduce congestion significantly. It estimated, for example, that a £4 charge to enter the central area would reduce traffic there by 15%, average journey times by 20% and emissions of carbon monoxide within central London by 35%. Charging would also yield high financial and economic surpluses. At 1991 prices the £4 charge would raise net annual revenues of £270 million for the charge operator and recoup the initial capital investment in road-side and in-vehicle equipment within two years. For the community as a whole total economic benefits would exceed total resource costs by some £70 million a year. There would be substantial benefits to existing bus travellers through quicker and more reliable journeys.

11.42 However, most drivers would not gain sufficiently to offset their charge payments and those living near a charge boundary would be particularly hard hit. Some rail and bus travellers would experience increased overcrowding. Such losses could be mitigated by a combination of charge privileges (exemptions, free credits or 'caps') and redistribution of the charge operator's surplus, but any worthwhile scheme which reduced congestion for the majority of travellers would be likely to leave a significant number of individuals worse off than they were before charging.

11.43 On the practical side the study investigated the technology and the administrative systems which would be required. It found that while electronic technologies are already available which have many of the necessary features, no complete system has yet been proven which would be suitable for application in London. A key problem is ensuring that the enforcement arrangements are adequately rigorous and fair for the system to command public respect. Further development is needed to ensure that charging could be effectively enforced in London's very demanding traffic conditions and to make the roadside equipment acceptably unobtrusive. It also found that complex procedures would be needed to distribute in-vehicle units and to administer charge exemptions and privileges.

11.44 One further important conclusion was that for charging to work effectively it would be important to achieve from the outset a high degree of consensus that it represented both a necessary and a reasonable transport policy for London. The very high level of compliance required could depend on it. But as many surveys have shown, congestion charging is not one which currently holds much appeal for Londoners.

11.45 The Government believes that the price signal is the most efficient method of influencing transport demand in the desired direction, preserving freedom of choice to the maximum extent and ensuring that road space is used by those who set the highest value upon it. However, the study made it clear that congestion charging is not a viable option now. The Government's assessment is that suitable technology of the necessary accuracy and reliability to handle the huge volume of transactions that would be generated by a charging scheme, even just for central London, is unlikely to be available for a minimum of five years and possibly longer. Accordingly, a congestion charging system for London could not be operational much before the end of the period covered by this strategy. It would, therefore, be unrealistic to assume in this ten-year transport strategy that congestion charging will resolve London's problems. It will not.

Rationing access by traffic management measures

11.46 The Road Traffic Regulation Act 1984 gives local authorities extensive powers to make Traffic Regulation Orders (TROs) prohibiting, restricting or regulating vehicular traffic or particular types of vehicular traffic. The Environment Act 1995 extended the purposes for which TROs can be made to cover explicitly pursuit of air quality objectives. In London the unco-ordinated exercise of these powers would be damaging in economic terms and potentially counter-productive in environmental terms. This issue needs to be addressed at the strategic, London-wide level. (See Chapter 15).

Managing demand by constraining parking provision

11.47 In the absence of congestion charging, controls on the availability and price of parking remain the principal means that the demand for travel by car can be restrained or managed without creating additional congestion and pollution. This is because parking controls can fundamentally affect the choice of destination or mode of travel. There is nothing novel about their use with this end in mind. For example, the Corporation of London and the City of Westminster have for a long time limited the amount of on-street parking available, and maintained fairly tight controls on the levels of parking provision at new office developments. With the spread of the use of wheel clamping during the early and mid 1980s there was a substantial improvement in compliance with on-street controls in central London. These policies have resulted in less congestion than otherwise would have occurred, because there is more effective use of road space and some limitation of the number of terminating car driver trips. In central London the effect of reducing parking availability to commuters is generally to encourage travel by public transport rather than to suppress economic activity.

11.48 In any review of parking controls it is important to consider the various types of parking which constitute locations to 'store' a vehicle. These are

- on-street parking: which can be divided by time or user controls and where convenience remains an important factor; loading and unloading facilities for frontage premises is another consideration.

- off-street public parking: which can be publicly or commercially provided and operated with a variety of regimes from contracts to pay and display and controlled by time limit, user type or even day of the week.

- off-street private parking: this is generally provided for the users or occupants of specific premises or dwellings, but again a variety of management regimes can apply; there is also scope to use the resource for informal 'public' parking; some space is generally reserved for loading or servicing activities.

- other spaces: everybody knows of land used to 'store' vehicles which does not fit into any of the above categories; roadways within hospitals or universities; Horseguards Parade in central London; 'service areas' behind shops; open spaces in housing estates; and so on.

A study commissioned in 1988 into parking availability and demand indicated that demand for parking exceeded supply. We believe that there are still shortcomings in our knowledge about the overall availability of parking spaces. This is a serious gap in our knowledge, and the Government will therefore commission a study to remedy it. We wish to progress this work in tandem with LPAC's revised supplementary advice on parking, which we expect to receive this Summer.

On-street parking

11.49 Existing traffic management and parking guidance sets an overall framework for local authority policies, but exercises a light touch on the question of the extent to which they should use on-street parking to restrain traffic. This is appropriate because Boroughs are best placed to make trade-offs between restraining car demand and ensure parking is provided to meet a minimum of the economic needs of an area. However in general terms we also think it is right to introduce a general presumption against increases in on-street parking in inner London, to further the environmental objectives we have set out above.

11.50 Increased levels of enforcement are giving local authorities much greater power over the effectiveness of parking controls. The new powers to manage on-street parking available to London local authorities have radically altered the scope for making use of more conventional techniques to limit the amount of commuter parking in business centres. They now have the ability to stop all-day parking on-street. This means that fringe areas can be controlled - inhibiting park and walk while protecting space for residents, loading and short term parking. In considering the balance on parking provision, the importance of providing suitable access for deliveries to commercial premises should be given due weight. Selective parking controls could be introduced where necessary to ensure deliveries can be made at certain times of the day.

11.51 One critical difficulty is the spread of double and even triple on-street parking. Anecdotal evidence suggests that this is occurring particularly in inner London, but to a lesser extent both in the central area, where car ownership is lower, and in outer London where there is generally more space for parked cars. Enforcement effort needs to target this problem as a priority, in view of the potentially serious difficulties for the emergency services. We will ask the Parking Committee for London, in conjunction with the Traffic Director, to monitor this problem, the need for local authority and police action to remedy it, and report on this in the proposed *Annual Report* on the Transport Strategy.

11.52 A second area where Borough action will be critical in bringing improvements is the congestion caused by commuters parking on-street around rail stations. Research carried out by TRL in 1993 showed that 'informal park and ride', where commuters leave their vehicles parked on-street near at rail stations all day, undertaking the rest of their journey by rail, contributed to the problem of congestion in certain areas, along with overspill residential parking and parking by local workers. Co-ordinated action by Boroughs to give priority to local parking needs around rail stations may help to encourage longer distance commuters to undertake the whole of or a greater proportion of their work journey by public transport.

Off-street parking

11.53 In 1985 it was estimated that nearly 50% of off-street **public** parking in inner London was under local authority control. The general presumption against an increase in the amount of on-street parking in inner London we propose above would therefore seem to be appropriate to apply also to this category. In some areas there will be strong arguments for transferring sites to non-parking uses. The emphasis in *Strategic Guidance for London Planning Authorities*, on not increasing travel by car, will also mean that new proposals for commercially provided parking will be unlikely to be acceptable either.

11.54 New guideline limits for **private** non-residential parking at new developments are set out in *Strategic Guidance for London Planning Authorities*. The restraint of new parking provisions through the development control process in accordance with planning guidance is important throughout London. It should help to reduce the number of car trips, as new offices with few parking places replace older buildings having generous parking provision. The planning mechanism may be an effective means of controlling the provision of private parking but it is not quick.

11.55 Largely because of the time taken for the planning system to deliver a reduction in private non-residential parking, there have been calls for action to be taken to reduce the amount of existing private parking provision. This might be done by requiring spaces to be relinquished, or by taxing them. The Government does not currently propose to do this. It is possible that a relatively high levy per space would be needed to generate modal shift away from private car usage for commuting. That would impose substantial costs on businesses, and weaken London's competitiveness. We have however undertaken to research the subject further, and to discuss it with the local authority associations.

Selecting and blending options: towards a traffic management and parking control strategy for London

11.56 The role for strategic traffic management within Greater London is being examined by the Traffic Management and Signalling Strategy Group (TRMS) - which was set up by the Government Office for London in Spring 1995. It comprises all the organisations involved with traffic and public parking management within London. Its work, already mentioned in Chapter 10, addresses the scope for securing reductions in congestion and pollution, and freeing up road space for buses and other users.

11.57 The TRMS group will be reporting to Ministers at the end of the year. Their work will bridge strategic and local considerations and matters such as the intensity with which particular objectives can sensibly be applied.

Summary

11.58 In pursuing proposals to reduce the penetration of road traffic into central business areas there are risks that the centres could become less accessible, leading to an erosion of their competitive position. It may be the case that for small areas, road access could be denied to all vehicles other than those servicing the area - but this is only likely to be tenable where there is comprehensive public transport access or where the area is small enough to be accessed on foot, and where there are suitable diversion routes for through traffic. In most of the London business centres there will be a need to strive to balance the two strands of objective 4 by attempting to reduce the volume of traffic that does not strictly need to be in the areas concerned while at the same time easing the flow of the remaining essential traffic.

11.59 To facilitate access by road to the central business districts and ease of movement within them will require a judicious combination of improvement to the strategic road network, to ease orbital movements with a balanced approach for radial routes and dealing with bottlenecks as summarised in this Chapter with more detail in Chapter 12; and traffic management measures, of which there are a host of possible alternatives to deploy as described above, requiring careful consideration by the TRMS Group. Ensuring that the Red Route network is substantially operational by 2000 remains a key target and focus of traffic management activity on the strategic upper tier of London roads hierarchy. The adequacy of on-street parking enforcement and measures incorporated into the London bus priority network will be critical for the functioning of the middle tier of the hierarchy.

11.60 Managing demand by constraining parking will require careful consideration of the extent by which it is justified to reduce parking for commuters in business districts but taking full account of the need not to suppress economic activity. Employing more severe traffic management proposals will need to be approached with caution to avoid causing severe economic and environmental disbenefits that may result if traffic is made to queue.

Chapter 12: Plugging Gaps in the Network

Introduction

12.1 The base case scenario at the end of Chapter 2 envisages modest growth in employment and little, if any, growth in population, with greater downside risk than upside risk in both areas. On that basis, we have set ourselves the objective of promoting the competitiveness of London as a World City, to which the main contributions from transport will be via maintaining the quality of the international links, reducing air pollution and improving the quality of commuter travel to the central business districts. The last of these objectives is a particularly costly one, and leaves little headroom for investment in new infrastructure. Nor, on the basis of the base case scenario, is new infrastructure urgently needed in order to deliver additional transport capacity. The concerns that underlay the Central London Rail Study do not apply today, and the concerns that underlay the London Assessment Studies apply with diminished force.

12.2 However, we have also stressed, as London Pride did, that we are 'planning for success'. We assume that the measures we are taking to promote London's competitiveness and foster regeneration will succeed and that the result might be further strong growth in transport demand. We likewise assume that our measures to promote modal shift will succeed and that an increasing proportion of the total demand for transport in London will be in the form of demand for public transport. Having embarked upon such policies, the Government would be foolish not to have plans ready to deal with their success. Additionally, as we stressed in Chapter 2, the economy of London - and the transport market, in particular - has surprised forecasters in the past and is perfectly capable of doing so again. This, too, points to the need to be ready to shift the emphasis of the transport strategy as rapidly as possible from the promotion of economic growth to the accommodation of transport growth. Since the lead-times of major new projects are long, a switch of emphasis is not easy. The least we can do, however, is to plan well ahead and to ensure that worthwhile schemes are ready to take forward.

12.3 Additionally, the case for building new infrastructure does not turn exclusively on the need to accommodate future demand growth. In Chapter 4, we looked at the regeneration needs of London and concluded that a good network of strategic routes was an essential precondition for local-level regeneration initiatives. There are some conspicuous gaps in the London road network, particularly in the Thames Gateway area. There are also areas of London, some of them in urgent need of regeneration, which are not well served by the existing rail or Underground networks.

12.4 Last but not least, there are major rail schemes which could make a material contribution to the competitiveness of London by cutting commuter times and facilitating airport access.

12.5 Accordingly, whilst plugging gaps in the existing transport network cannot be our top priority, it is a priority, and we would expect to be able to make some progress on it over the ten years covered by this strategy.

Background

12.6 London is often thought of as a collection of villages, and the main requirement of the transport system for many of its inhabitants is simply a means of moving around safely and easily within their local areas. But the majority of Londoners also want to travel regularly beyond the boundaries of the locality where they to live, whether to go to work or to pursue their leisure activities. And as a Capital city and a major focus of employment and business activity, many people need to travel into London from outside, either on a daily basis from the south east region or from further afield. Over and above this, London is a major tourist destination and a World City which large numbers of people need to reach from all parts of the globe. Last but not least, goods and services have to be delivered efficiently to shops and other businesses which together generate more economic activity than many small countries.

12.7 London's transport system therefore has to serve a whole spectrum of needs from villages to the international community. This is a very tall order since it means that the transport network has to cater for everything from walking to air transport. And it has to do it in a way which allows London to continue to be a pleasant place in which to live and work.

12.8 The result is a very complex system involving many different modes of travel and inter-connecting networks and there are considerable constraints over how the system can be modified and expanded. Nevertheless significant development of the networks has been achieved over the last 10 years.

12.9 Major rail developments include the opening of the Thameslink cross-London line (1988), the construction of the new rail link at Stansted Airport to connect Liverpool Street (1991), the opening of modernised stations at Liverpool Street and Angel (1992), the completion of the new international station for the Channel Tunnel services at Waterloo (1993), the opening of the Docklands Light Railway (1987) and the extensions to Bank in 1991 and to Beckton in 1994. Major road improvements include the completion of the M25, the Docklands road network including the Limehouse Link, and the upgrading of parts of the A40 and the A406.

Looking Ahead

12.10 For the future, upgrading the existing transport infrastructure - such as the resignalling of the Northern Line - will make an important contribution to responding to future patterns of demand. It makes sense economically and environmentally to make the best use of the existing transport infrastructure before embarking on the disruption and cost of creating wholly new links. But undoubtedly additions to the existing road and rail networks will be needed to serve new markets, and to ensure that there is sufficient capacity to provide acceptable travelling conditions, not only in response to demand as it is today, but in response to demand as is expected to be in the years ahead as the London economy returns to the prosperity enjoyed in the late 1980s.

12.11 A substantial programme of investment in new infrastructure will be necessary in the years to come. In carrying this forward, many practical constraints have to be taken into account. These include the financial and economic costs of particular transport schemes, and the social and environmental impact which they will have on the Capital city. It is clear, for instance, that Londoners would find a Los Angeles style transport system wholly unattractive, even assuming it could be afforded.

12.12 The development of London's transport networks must be a realistic balance between, on the one hand, satisfying the growing demand for travel and, on the other, pursuing a programme which is sustainable both economically and environmentally. The different modes all have their part to play. Rail travel is best suited to carrying large numbers of passengers, longer distances between areas of concentrated activity. Cars, on the other hand, carry people to their destinations without interchange. They are best suited to travel patterns where there is a low density of development and diffuse patterns of trips.

12.13 It would be completely impracticable, for instance, to try and impose a public transport solution for the myriad of inter-suburban trips which have developed since the advent of the motorcar. Equally it would be as wasteful to try to provide enough road capacity to enable the majority of central London workers to get to and from work by car.

Gaps in the Rail Network

12.14 In general, London is already well provided with railways - certainly compared to most other major cities in Europe. Its external rail connections are particularly good. Eurostar services began in 1994 from Waterloo International Station providing regular direct rail services to Paris and Brussels. These will be further upgraded with the completion of the Channel Tunnel Rail Link early next century, when travel times from central London will be cut further - see Chapter 8.

12.15 London is at the hub of Britain's inter-city rail network. Regular high speed train services operate direct to London from the north along the East Coast Main Line and West Coast Main Line and from the west along the Great Western Line. And high speed domestic services to the south east will start once domestic rail services begin to operate along the Channel Tunnel Rail Link to St Pancras.

12.16 Within London itself, the Underground and surface rail networks provide extensive coverage throughout most parts of London. But there are a number of significant deficiencies.

12.17 The first is that the surface railway system terminates at the edges of the central area, and the Underground system has extensive suburban coverage without matching capacity in the central area. As a result, passengers suffer the inconvenience of having to change from one transport mode to another at the mainline termini. This was one of the concerns addressed in the Central London Rail Study and it remains a valid one. Additionally, the already busy central sections of the Underground system remain at serious risk of acute overcrowding if the demand for transport turns up again.

12.18 Three projects - Crossrail, Thameslink 2000 and the Chelsea-Hackney Line - are designed to overcome this problem. This new generation of lines across the City and West End, mainly in new tunnels, would connect most of the mainline rail termini and would be built to allow through running of trains onto Railtrack's network. As well as relieving congestion on the existing system in central London, they would allow fast new services from outside London to deliver passengers direct to the central area. They would also enhance the quality of London's international links by providing excellent direct rail connections between the centre of London and the three main airports for business travellers and tourists.

12.19 These new lines might also help to counteract the tendency for development and employment to disperse to outer London and the rest of the south east, since they would improve the accessibility of central area. And there will be some direct regeneration benefits in inner London and on the fringes of the central area. The Chelsea-Hackney Line would bring new areas into the Tube network, opening up new development opportunities for Hackney (the remaining inner London Borough not presently served by the Underground system) with its acute problems of deprivation, and - depending on the final route chosen for the line - to the riverside area to the south west of the central area. Similarly Thameslink 2000 - in conjunction with Crossrail and the Channel Tunnel Rail Link - will enhance the accessibility and therefore attractiveness of the northern fringes of the City and the King's Cross area. The timescale for taking forward these major projects is discussed in Chapter 14.

12.20 The series of studies undertaken in the late eighties into improving London's rail network also identified an ambitious range of other rail improvements, which, if added to the projects contained in this strategy, clearly could not all be afforded in their totality. The schemes in this document represent both what LT, who are responsible for planning the Underground network, believe is the right strategy, and what Government believes could offer good value for money and be afforded. It follows that large schemes which are not included here are not being promoted, since they are either not affordable or they do not represent good value for money.

12.21 The list of schemes at Chapter 14 does not claim to cover the whole of LT's future investment programme. It is concerned with those schemes which continue to be promoted and which have such a significant impact on public expenditure that the Government retains an interest in them. LT, as the promoter of Underground schemes, is able to come forward with additional schemes, which the Government would need to consider both in terms of their value for money and affordability.

12.22 The second deficiency concerns the need to integrate the new business area in Docklands into the rail and Underground networks. The completion of the Docklands Light Railway (DLR) and the Jubilee Line Extension (JLE) will largely put this right:

• The DLR now links the City of London with the Isle of Dogs, Stratford and Beckton. New signalling technology has been introduced together with a through service from Beckton to Bank, and last year full evening and weekend services were resumed. The DLR's connection with Bank Station provides access to the four Underground lines serving the City. There are also connections to mainline rail services at Stratford and Limehouse, and to the East London Underground line at Shadwell station. A further extension to the DLR is planned between the Isle of Dogs, Greenwich and Lewisham. The concession to design, build and maintain the extension is expected to be let towards the end of the year with the aim of completing construction by 1999.

• The JLE, which is due to open in 1998, will establish important new transport links between Docklands and the East and West Ends, linking into mainline rail services at Waterloo, London Bridge, and Stratford. The scheme involves 10 miles of new Underground line and 12 stations. Four of these stations (Southwark, Bermondsey, Canada Water and North Greenwich) are completely new. There will be interchanges with the DLR at Canary Wharf and Canning Town.

12.23 The third major deficiency is the lack of orbital rail connections in inner suburban areas, in contrast to the predominantly radial connections currently provided by the rail system. Schemes such as the East London Line Extension, the Croydon Tramlink and improvements to the West London Line are examples of how it is possible to provide a rail alternative on heavily used orbital corridors, especially where existing rail infrastructure exists which can be developed or turned to good effect. Croydon Tramlink will be a $17\frac{1}{2}$

mile light rail system linking Croydon with Wimbledon to the west, Woodside and Beckenham to the east and New Addington to the south. For much of its length it will use disused railway lines or replace existing heavy rail services. Within central Croydon it will run on-street following a one-way circulation of the town centre. In total thirty-six tram stops are proposed. The private sector will build and operate Tramlink, but the system will be integrated with the rail, Underground and bus networks and offer joint ticketing arrangements.

Gaps in the Road Network

12.24 Chapter 11 described a hypothetical road system for London, and put forward a series of tests derived from that to assess the current state of the road network in London. The next paragraphs go through the orbital and radial routes in London and see how far they match the test requirements, and thus how far they meet the needs of London.

Orbital Roads

12.25 First, the tests suggest we need to provide for orbital movements around outer London. The M25 is London's 'ring road'. It keeps longer distance through traffic, particularly lorries, out of London. The statistics show a marked drop in lorry traffic in London when the M25 was built, and volumes have not returned subsequently to pre-M25 levels.

12.26 However, significant stretches of it sometimes suffer from serious congestion problems. If the position is allowed to deteriorate, through traffic will be increasingly tempted to cut across outer London or to divert onto inappropriate local roads beyond the M25. A comprehensive widening programme is planned to try to prevent this. The sections most requiring widening were in the western and south western sectors and at the Dartford Tunnel. Substantial investment has taken place, including the successful private sector arrangements for the Queen Elizabeth II Bridge at Dartford. Work is currently in hand which will provide a dual four lane motorway from Junction 7 to Junction 16. This policy originally led to proposals for parallel link roads alongside certain sections of the orbital motorway. However, after balancing the environmental disbenefits against economic considerations, the Government has decided not to proceed with these further plans. The result is that most of the M25 will become a dual four lane

motorway with sections of dual five lane and dual six lane motorway only in the western sector.

12.27 The construction of Heathrow Express and the study of surface access improvements at Heathrow (see Chapter 8) show the Government's commitment to promoting a balanced environmentally sustainable transport solution. This is particularly important for a location such as Heathrow Airport, which is the biggest single traffic generator in Europe.

12.28 The model system and the resulting strategic level tests suggest that the outer orbital should be complemented by at least one intermediate orbital route to serve outer London and attract longer distance movements out of inner London. Both orbitals should be connected by good quality radial routes. The improvements to the A406 North Circular Road, the A312 Hayes Bypass and the A102 route can be seen to relate to this model. When the improvements to the North Circular Road are completed, orbital movements within much of north London will be relatively well catered for. The A205 South Circular Road, however, is far from the hypothetical network, being located much closer to the centre and with a wide variation in its attractiveness along much of its length. As with the A232, the other south London orbital route, many sections cannot readily be differentiated from the rest of London's local road network. Other than perhaps improvements at the most congested junctions, there is little likelihood that the fundamental attractiveness of these roads can be enhanced in the foreseeable future.

12.29 The hypothetical model would also point towards the establishment of a lower capacity inner ring road skirting central London. The actual Inner Ring Road is largely within central London and consists of an assortment of roads connected by some of the most highly stressed junctions in London. Comprehensive improvements in the heart of London are out of the question and there are long term concerns about the ability of Tower Bridge to continue to provide a link of the ring road. The best that is likely to be achieved is adequate signing and better traffic management which will help ensure that the ring road operates to the maximum practicable efficiency. But unless a comprehensive traffic management strategy is adopted that reduces the volume of traffic entering the ring road at the most congested junctions, there is little likelihood of the Inner Ring Road performing as an attractive alternative for through traffic.

12.30 The River Thames in east London constitutes an obstacle to orbital road movement. It is discussed later in this Chapter.

Radial Roads

12.31 Turning from the 'ring' to the 'spokes', the outer radial routes in the southern quadrant pose a particular problem. Between the A3 and A20 there are few good quality strategic radial roads, with just one trunk road, the A23, which is of indifferent standard. A bypass of Bromley centre on the A21 has been constructed and on the A23 a bypass to Coulsdon centre is currently included in the national road programme, but as a longer term category scheme. There is no prospect of a comprehensive up-grading of the strategic radial routes in the southern quadrant and the best outcome that can be expected is some minor improvements to pinch points.

12.32 The west London strategic radial routes - the A40, M4/A4, A30/A4 and M3/A316 - provide reasonably attractive movement through outer London and generally follow the notion of capacity constraint within inner London. The final junction improvement schemes proposed for the A40 will provide a high quality route into the Park Royal and White City regeneration areas, a better connection to the cental London business districts, remove two of the more notorious congestion and accident blackspots within London and remove strategic traffic from local roads.

12.33 The capacity of the M4/A4 corridor in London has already been comprehensively expanded. The only further improvement planned is the Junction 3 - Junction 4B widening which would provide for access to Terminal 5 at Heathrow if this development were to proceed. Like the adjacent M25, the M4/A4 road capacity is stretched by the volume of Heathrow traffic. Traffic management measures providing greater operational flexibility between the M4 and A4 may offer some relief in the future. But the commitment to provide for improved public transport access to Heathrow and seek further modal shift through LASAS must mark the way forward. To ameliorate the impact of the volume of traffic using this corridor, environmental improvements are planned, including a comprehensive tree planting programme.

12.34 The strategic radial routes in north London present a mixed picture. The A1/M1/A41 corridor provides high capacity for northbound movements

which is heavily used. The A10 performs a limited strategic role and does not provide an adequate means of access to the Lea Valley development areas. The M11 corridor provides good access to the M25 and areas to the north east of London and beyond to Cambridge and East Anglia. Inside London the new A12 link between the A11 in Hackney and the M11 will improve access to east London including the development areas in the Lea Valley and Docklands. Further improvements on the outer London stretches of these roads are unlikely to be made in the foreseeable future.

12.35 In East London the strategic radial routes comprise the A12/A127, A13, A2 and A20. The A12 and A127 have been improved in the past; and no further up-grading of these routes in outer London is planned. A comprehensive improvement programme is being implemented on the outer reaches of the A13 which accords with the general test mentioned earlier and is of great importance in facilitating access to the Thames Gateway area. Within the North Circular Road the A13 improvements are focused on the key junctions and facilitate access to the newly constructed Docklands Highways.

12.36 On the south side of the Thames in east London, the investment in the A2 and A20 trunk roads and the comprehensive improvements being made to the Thamesmead Spine Road as far as the M25 will mean that access to the area is relatively well served. The main problems remain at the point where these radial routes link to the approaches to the Blackwall crossing. Relieving these stress points is contingent on sorting out the way ahead for the river crossings.

Summary of strategic road provision

12.37 The maps in Chapter 11 indicate that the existing network and planned improvements should form a reasonable strategic road network in most of London, but they also highlight the inadequacies of the River Thames crossings and the problems of strategic road access to centres in south London and parts of north London. Crossings of the Thames are discussed separately below.

12.38 Regarding strategic road access in south London, in the absence of large scale improvements to the network, we need to ensure that the key orbital routes, the A205 and A232, function as effectively as possible. Careful thought needs to be given to what priority should be given to these roads at junctions with radial routes. Small scale improvements to the A23 are likely to be needed to provide a better radial link between the A232 and the M25 and facilitate the southerly access to Croydon and the Wandle Valley.

12.39 In sum, improvements already made or planned within the timescale of this document should provide a reasonable network of strategic roads and level of service, consistent with the overall national policy of making adequate provision for the use of strategic traffic while taking account of the likely availability of public and private finance for major road improvements within the region. Additional investment in south London radial and orbital routes would be particularly helpful to securing a more effective strategic network and a way forward must be found for better crossings of the River Thames in east London. In the much longer term, it has been suggested underground roads might provide an opportunity to remove through traffic from areas of London and still meet many of the key objectives. However, financing such an undertaking and the technical difficulties would present formidable challenges.

The Thames Gateway Area

12.40 The *Thames Gateway Planning Framework* (RPG9a), published in 1995, articulates clearly the Government's view that new and improved cross-river links in East London are *"essential if the area is to function more effectively and fulfil its development potential"*. New crossings would bring with them improved levels of accessibility in the eastern Thames Gateway that would help to attract residents and employers to the area and retain those that are already there. However, there are also sound transport reasons that support the case for the provision of additional crossing capacity. These include concerns about the future lifespan of ageing crossings in West Docklands, the absence of orbital public transport links encouraging modal shift and the transport benefits to be derived from the relief of congestion associated with the existing crossings at Blackwall, Rotherhithe and the Woolwich Ferry, which is among the worst in London.

12.41 A number of new public transport projects are already in the pipeline:

- The Jubilee Line Extension (JLE), which alone will provide three new crossings of the Thames, is under construction and due to open in 1998;

- tenders have been received for the DLR/Lewisham Extension;

- a promoter has been appointed for the Channel Tunnel Rail link; and

- the Government has announced its support for Thameslink 2000, which brings with it the prospect of some improvement to cross-river rail services in East London.

12.42 The case for bringing forward other cross-river schemes, such as extensions to the East London Line are also being explored. LUL have applied for powers for a northern extension to Dalston and are considering a southern extension; but whether and when either project can proceed will depend on the availability of sufficient private finance.

12.43 It is recognised, however, that these crossings will not meet all of East London's needs. They do not, for example, provide improved crossing facilities for commercial vehicles. There are height restrictions northbound through the Blackwall Tunnel and capacity problems at the Woolwich Ferry. The East London River Crossing (ELRC) and the high-level bridge option proposed at Blackwall were two schemes which would have improved access for this type of heavy commercial traffic and addressed already significant congestion problems at Blackwall and elsewhere, but they have not been progressed due to their environmental impact (particularly in the case of ELRC) and the absence of any substantive public support for them.

12.44 In September 1994 it was announced that alternative options for crossings at Blackwall and Gallions Reach would be considered afresh in the context of an overall strategy for river crossings in East London. With this in mind, the consultation document *River Crossings East of Tower Bridge* was published in June 1995 with the aim of seeking views on the options available and initiating a process of consultation from which a measure of consensus about the siting and form of all types of new crossings might be derived.

'River Crossings East of Tower Bridge': Consultation Response

12.45 As the first step in this process, the consultation produced an encouraging response. The consultation revealed strong support for the idea of preparing a coherent River Crossings Strategy to provide a framework against which to assess individual crossing schemes and package proposals. It also confirmed the Government's view that it would be desirable to match and prioritise the provision of new crossing capacity, as far as possible, to Thames Gateway planning and environmental objectives. This should help to ensure that the resultant development benefits are maximised without adverse impact on the environment.

12.46 The objective framework for new river crossings set out at Annex 3 of the consultation document was also well received, as were some of the 'sustainable' transport concepts it put forward. The use of the river as a highway for the movement of people as well as goods, as advocated in the draft *Thames Strategy*, mixed mode links and the adoption of a balanced approach towards transport provision are among the cases in point. Despite their potential to promote modal shift, Park and Sail/Ride were greeted more cautiously, principally because of their potential for drawing commuter traffic further into London.

12.47 New ideas suggested by consultees which merit further consideration include the use of traffic management information systems (eg remote traffic monitoring and variable message signing) to manage traffic distribution between alternative crossings, and the development of interchanges to link principal and intermediate public transport modes and offer radial and orbital services via new crossings. There were also a number of interesting proposals for new crossings or alternatives to existing proposals which were considered when preparing the Crossings Strategy.

12.48 In addition to support for new crossings, the consultation exercise also highlighted plenty of concerns, amongst which were:

• deteriorating air quality, increased noise and visual intrusion arising from higher traffic levels on the approaches to a new crossing. These are particularly important issues in the context of new crossings at Blackwall, Gallions Reach or in West Docklands, where they provide additional capacity;

• land-take, blight, road safety and the prospect of attracting additional long distance commuting traffic.

12.49 The Government has had to balance these concerns against the area's transport and regeneration needs. For example, a number of consultees argued

for a strategy that would support new public transport crossings and prioritise existing road crossing capacity in favour of buses, with the aim of suppressing the use of the private car for both radial and orbital journeys in London and encouraging modal shift.

12.50 While, in line with its broader sustainability objectives, the Government wishes to see as much use as reasonably possible to be made of public transport, it is not always possible to meet even a substantial proportion of travel demand by public transport, particularly in the outer parts of Greater London. In certain locations, if regeneration and economic development are to be facilitated, there may be a need to improve accessibility and therefore add to the capacity of the surrounding road network. East London is one area where there would appear to be a *prima facie* case for additional road capacity to accommodate local cross-river movements.

12.51 The Government also has to think about the consequences of not providing additional crossing capacity. These include continued or worsening congestion at existing crossings and their approaches, poor accessibility for local residents and businesses and the reduced competitiveness, longer journey times and higher transport costs this imposes. These aspects are indirectly also likely to cause adverse impacts on inward investment, local jobs and the local environment. For example, if no new crossing were built at Blackwall increased queuing times at the existing tunnels would only add to the diversionary pressures contributing to the congestion, noise and poor air quality in Greenwich town centre. These adverse consequences can be regarded as running counter to the objectives of sustainable development.

12.52 Last but not least, the Government has to bear in mind its broader objective of discouraging the inward penetration of through traffic, towards the central parts of the Capital. For example, height restrictions at the Blackwall Tunnels means that overheight HGV's with destinations north of the river either have to use the Woolwich Ferry and accept the delays that often entails, or use other upstream crossings, irrespective of whether they are heading to central London or not. Additional orbital capacity at Blackwall should reduce the need for these large vehicles to have to manoeuvre their way through the middle of London.

12.53 Some of the crossing options highlighted by the consultation document were received more enthusiastically than others. The JLE, East London

Line Extension and DLR/Lewisham schemes have few detractors, save for those impatient to see them completed. The Woolwich Rail Tunnel proposal was also enthusiastically acclaimed by many consultees. The prospect of a local multi-modal crossing at Gallions Reach attracted a mixed reaction. A third crossing at Blackwall was the least popular of the three options, although it had supporters who recognised its economic importance to the Gateway.

The River Crossings Strategy

12.54 There is a problem upstream of the Greenwich Peninsula. The JLE and the new rail crossings in the pipeline should help to reduce short distance car-based commuting between the areas they serve, but they do little for business access; both Tower Bridge and the Rotherhithe Tunnel have limited capacity. Moreover, if they continue to operate at current capacity their projected lifespan, recently estimated to be 20 and 50 years respectively, will be greatly reduced. Since Blackwall seems incapable of providing a viable alternative for much of the traffic currently using Tower Bridge and Rotherhithe, as structural and maintenance problems make it increasingly necessary to restrict the type and volume of traffic they can handle, it seems likely that there will ultimately need to be at least a partial replacement of existing crossing capacity in West Docklands.

12.55 The position between Erith and Dartford is the converse of that in West Docklands, since it is the absence of any significant demand rather than the desire to restrain it, which provide the case against a new crossing. Potential demand is limited by the paucity of high density development along the river corridor and in areas immediately adjacent to it. This, combined with the cost of spanning the substantial reach presented by the Thames in this location, make the prospect of any new fixed crossing between Gallions Reach and Dartford extremely remote. Potential promoters of other crossings will also welcome this reassurance.

12.56 The concept of providing a tunnelled rail connection linking the LT&S and North Kent Lines between Rainham and Erith was put forward by a number of consultees. Since this proposal is no more than an idea at this stage, with no feasibility study of economic or financial case to support it, and since the Woolwich Rail Tunnel would be capable of fulfilling a similar function at a significantly lower cost, it is not a proposal that can be supported in this strategy.

12.57 The target zone for new crossings, therefore, lies between Greenwich and Erith. Within this area there are a variety of crossing movements which it is either necessary or desirable to accommodate; there are also others which it is not. In the former category are local movements of people for work, shopping and leisure purposes and intermediate or sub-strategic commercial movements encompassing longer distance journeys with origins or destinations in East London. At the other end of the spectrum are the undesirable movements, such as commuting flows from the home counties and long distance traffic such as lorries and holiday makers coming from Scotland, the North and Midlands through to the Channel ports and Tunnel, which would be better routed around Greater London than through it.

12.58 The Government's intention is to encourage commuters from the Home Counties and the outer London suburbs to use public transport, wherever possible. It also regards the natural route for long distance traffic to be the M25 and wishes to see it remain so. To reinforce both objectives it is important that it should not be made cheaper or easier for this traffic to use crossings upstream of Dartford.

12.59 There are substantial brownfield sites suitable for commercial development throughout the Thames Gateway corridor. By restricting the hinterland of these development sites to one side of the river or the other, the absence of adequate crossing capacity reinforces the role of the Thames as a major obstacle to commerce between them. Similarly, for people living in deprived residential areas both north and south of the river, such as Thamesmead, Woolwich, Canning Town or Silvertown, the lack of convenient opportunities to cross the river inhibits access to labour markets outside their immediate area. Additional provision for local movements of goods and service vehicles and better local public transport provision would help enormously. These are journeys which in outer London typically cover 2-5 miles, are relatively easy elsewhere in the Capital, but very difficult in East London especially if they are orbital or involve a cross-river destination.

12.60 Accommodating cross-river sub-strategic movements, many of which are commercial, is vital if the Thames Gateway and Lea Valley are to be opened to inward investment and local businesses are to be allowed to thrive. Currently significant diversions via Dartford and the A13 or Central London are required for northbound traffic. Frequently there is also substantial queuing at Blackwall and the Woolwich Ferry in the morning and evening peaks.

Potential New Crossings

12.61 To meet the demand for this type of movement and facilitate increased numbers of local trips by public transport, or where necessary by car, while discouraging transient long distance journeys, the Government believes the most promising option is a **package** of the following crossings which could include:

- a third road-based crossing at Blackwall;

- a multi-modal local crossing at Gallions Reach; and

- a Rail Tunnel connecting the North London and North Kent Lines at Woolwich.

The role, form and prospects for each of these schemes are considered below.

12.62 In addition to the core schemes, the possibility of establishing a new ferry crossing, primarily targeted at HGV traffic, between Belvedere/Erith and Havering Riverside to service the substantial riverside industrial and warehousing developments proposed for this part of the Thames Gateway, may also merit investigation and further consultation. In this context and given the prospect of new fixed crossings up and downstream of Woolwich, the case for maintaining the existing subsidised Ferry operation also requires careful examination.

12.63 If, as seems likely, the capacity of the existing West Docklands crossings need to be constrained, the need for partial replacement of lost capacity may also merit re-evaluation against the background of a third crossing at Blackwall. The logistics of providing a new crossing in this area are extremely difficult, however. Most of the better crossing points have been lost to development, and the impact of significant changes in the distribution of traffic on local roads could have significant adverse implications on areas linked by a new crossing.

12.64 Partly for this reason and partly because there is no immediate need for replacement capacity to be provided, the Government would not support proposals for additional road crossing capacity between Tower Bridge and Blackwall in the short or medium term. To do so might encourage additional traffic to travel further into the centre of London than

would be desirable. The position will need to be periodically reviewed, however, with an eye to the longer term. In the interim, there may be as yet unidentified opportunities to improve cross-river pedestrian and cycle connections. These would certainly merit further consideration if they could be financed without relying on a Government contribution.

Blackwall III

12.65 At Blackwall, there are three principal transport objectives:

- to provide more capacity for local movement;

- to reduce congestion and thereby secure quicker and more reliable journeys for sub-strategic commercial traffic travelling to and from the area; and

- to improve cross-river public transport connections.

Realisation of the latter objective could involve introducing bus priority measures on the approaches to both existing and new crossings, for example.

12.66 Following the decision to consider alternatives to the May 1993 high-level bridge scheme, the Government is not wedded to a particular engineering solution to deliver a new crossing at Blackwall, but any schemes which come forward will need to address the aforementioned objectives. They will also need to be feasible in engineering, operational and financial terms and provide a solution which is environmentally acceptable.

12.67 Off-line alignments, tunnelled and bridge-crossings, uni-directional and tidal flow operation, could all form part of a wide range of options which may merit further investigation. It is important to recognise, however, that a low-level lifting or swing bridge across the Thames could provide a significant impediment to both river and road-based traffic if not very carefully designed and located. Tunnels are typically (though not always) more expensive than fixed high-level bridges such as that previously proposed for Blackwall, but they potentially offer advantages in terms of environmental impact which a fixed bridge cannot match. It would be inappropriate, therefore, to rule out any of these options at this stage, although further work is being undertaken by GOL to identify which corridors and engineering solutions appear to be the most promising alternatives to the 1993 proposals.

Gallions Reach

12.68 Gallions Reach is envisaged as a multi-modal crossing providing a dual two-lane road connection alongside dedicated public transport provision (eg a DLR spur, light rapid transit link or guided busway) and possibly pedestrian and cycling facilities as well. LDDC and Thamesmead Town are leading a team examining the case for the public transport component of the scheme and what its optimum form might be. A new crossing in this location would offer the kind of improved accessibility that is badly needed in this part of the Thames Gateway. Its strategic location, multi-modal format and the scope it offers for linking public transport networks either side of the Thames mean that it should have the potential to contribute significantly to local regeneration.

12.69 In all likelihood, the crossing would need to utilise the published East London River Crossing (ELRC) alignment across the river between Beckton and Thamesmead, which is regarded as optimal in this location. However, it would terminate on the south side of the river at the A2016 Thamesmead Spine Road, because its aim is to cater for local and sub-strategic journeys, rather than long distance through traffic. As such it will provide the kind of improved specification for a crossing in this location, that the Government has been seeking to replace its ELRC proposals.

12.70 With this in mind the Secretary of State proposes to revoke as soon as possible the Line Orders relating to the ELRC scheme. The intention is to replace the revoked orders with proposals for the multi-modal Gallions Reach crossing on the same alignments as the ELRC scheme.

Woolwich Rail Tunnel

12.71 The Woolwich Rail Tunnel as currently envisaged would run between Silvertown and Woolwich linking the North Kent Line and North London Line on the Railtrack network. It could potentially serve several functions:

- improving accessibility by rail between the station catchment areas along the North Kent Line, North London Line and Lea Valley Line corridors, within the Royal Docks and around Stratford;

- facilitating otherwise difficult orbital movements by public transport in east and south east London;

- enhancing access to those parts of central London more easily accessed from the key radial routes which interchange with the North London Line at Canning Town, West Ham and Stratford; and related to this;

- helping to secure better employment prospects for residents within the hinterland of connecting stations.

There could also be scope for linking the scheme to London City Airport.

12.72 Initial assessments point to an Abbey Wood to Stratford shuttle as the best option for a core service utilising the new rail crossing. However, there might be scope for subsequent development of additional capacity on the North Kent Line, to permit services to be extended beyond Abbey Wood to Dartford and ultimately Ebbsfleet, thereby creating a secondary rail spine linking the two main growth poles of the Thames Gateway, Ebbsfleet and Stratford/Royal Docks.

12.73 The scheme is currently being examined by a joint team consisting of Railtrack, London Transport, British Rail and London Docklands Development Corporation. This group is looking at engineering feasibility, possible train service patterns, overall issues of costs and benefits and the scope for private finance. The results of this work are expected later in 1996.

12.74 It seems clear that the scheme would need a significant proportion of public finance to be taken forward, and the Government can make no commitment that public funds will be available. The Franchising Director, too, would need to be satisfied that he should give financial support to train services through the tunnel.

12.75 The scheme would clearly have implications for Railtrack, since it links parts of the Railtrack network. Railtrack has given a clear indication that in the future, as a private company, it will be ready to consider enhancements to its network where such projects are economically viable from Railtrack's perspective. But at this stage neither Railtrack, nor any other private sector investor, is committed to participation in the Woolwich Rail Tunnel project.

The Package Approach

12.76 Whilst each of the above schemes has its own attractions, no one of them would be sufficient on its own to achieve the level of improved accessibility required to meet the transport and regeneration needs of East London and the rest of the Thames Gateway.

Nor, individually, would they produce the kind of balanced transport strategy which the Government is seeking to promote in London. It is equally unrealistic to assume, even if the Woolwich Rail Tunnel and the East London Line Extension were taken forward in conjunction with JLE and the DLR Lewisham Extension, they could provide an acceptable substitute for Blackwall III or vice versa.

12.77 Blackwall III does little to help the travel to work needs of areas of high unemployment such as Thamesmead, Woolwich and Silvertown; nor does it encourage modal shift or improved orbital movements by public transport. Equally, the Woolwich Rail Tunnel would do little to entice business into the Lea Valley and Thames Gateway, reduce delays on the approaches to the existing Blackwall tunnels (frequently the single worst congestion point in London), or alleviate the current restrictions on cross-river HGV movements west of Dartford. Moreover, neither Blackwall nor Woolwich will do much to help secure early development in the eastern end of the Royals, Beckton, Thamesmead and Barking Reach. A multi-modal crossing at Gallions Reach would address these objectives, but could not by itself provide an adequate substitute for either of the other two proposed crossings.

12.78 The Government therefore considers each of the three schemes has the potential to contribute something to a package of new crossings for East London, provided that detailed evaluation confirms a sound economic and financial case can be made for it. The package should also include traffic management measures designed to accompany the new crossings, prevent diversion and facilitate access to Park & Ride sites associated with the public transport components if suitable sites that do not encourage additional commuting can be identified. The concept of a package was well received during the River Crossings consultation and would therefore seem to provide the way forward.

12.79 One option for delivering a package would be for its component schemes to be procured through one contract, although new construction might need to be phased. Alternatively they could be promoted separately, but co-ordinated so as to meet the broader package objectives advocated in this strategy. Whichever approach is adopted, an economic and financial case will have to be made for each scheme,

both individually and in terms of its contribution to the package as a whole. Railtrack, the Frachising Director and any private sector partners would also need to be willing to participate in respect of the Woolwich Rail Tunnel.

12.80 The prospect of a package of crossings, raises question marks over the need to maintain a ferry crossing at Woolwich. The Government is clear, however, that until such time as Gallions Reach or a full height northbound crossing is in place at Blackwall, a subsidised ferry crossing must continue to be provided. Once a viable alternative is available to HGVs, then it would be prudent to re-evaluate the continuing need for a service that would no longer be essential and the public subsidy it requires. That review might also consider whether the boats and equipment at Woolwich might not more profitably be used elsewhere - for example between Havering Riverside and Belvedere/Erith.

Funding Arrangements and Tolling

12.81 With many competing priorities, finance for publicly funded transport projects is likely to remain hard to come by. First indications are, however, that at least some of the proposals for new crossings present opportunities for investment by means of private finance. Other major crossings, including Dartford, have been funded by private investment recouped by means of tolls levied on users of the facility.

12.82 Further careful work is required to investigate these possibilities in the context of East Thames river crossings and to consider the potential of the various options for private finance arrangements. This work is under way and will include assessments of the traffic effects of tolling some or all of the proposed road crossings. The effects of differential tolls relating to time of use and local exemptions will also be examined.

River Crossings: The Way Forward

12.83 Subject to appropriate public and private sector finance being available, the construction of new crossings and the tolling of new, and possibly existing crossings, would require statutory powers to be secured. Although these could be sought separately for each element of a package using existing legislation (eg the Transport and Works Act 1992 and the New Roads and Street Works Act 1991), a package might more conveniently be promoted via a single hybrid Bill. The Government will need to reflect further on this.

12.84 Further work is also needed to define and evaluate the three principal new crossing schemes before private sector interest is sought, possibly in the early part of 1997 or more realistically at the start of a new Parliament. The Government and other parties involved in the promotion of particular crossings will be undertaking further work on scheme definition in parallel with the preparation of an Appraisal Framework to assess the economic and financial case for new crossings and their potential traffic, socio-economic and environmental impacts. It will therefore have an important role in facilitating comparative evaluation between the proposals that come forward from the private sector. Consultants are to be appointed shortly to prepare the framework and consult upon it.

12.85 The Government would welcome views on the approach to new river crossings in East London advocated in this strategy. Under the aegis of the Government Office for London, the Government will establish a programme of on-going consultation with local authorities, private sector representatives and other interested parties. The purpose of these meetings will be to discuss the development of the Appraisal Framework, review comments received on the Crossings Strategy and seek feedback on associated option and scheme definition studies.

Millennium Exhibition

12.86 Since the publication of the *Thames Gateway Planning Framework,* the Millennium Commission has announced that Greenwich will host the Millennium Exhibition. Access to the site will be transformed by the Jubilee Line Extension, due to open in 1998, and other projects, such as the DLR Lewisham Extension, will improve the surrounding public transport network. The 'escape ramp' promoted by the Highways Agency which will reduce the amount of time it takes to divert overheight lorries as they approach the Blackwall Tunnel will also improve road conditions in time for the Exhibition. In addition to these planned improvements, the Greenwich Millennium Trust have also worked up a wide range of proposals to enhance access even further. Now that the Greenwich site has been chosen, the Trust and the prospective organisers of the Exhibition can work together in partnership with public transport operators and highway authorities to plan what further improvements are required. One attractive

scheme is the introduction of a river service, linking the exhibition site with other visitor attractions such as the Tate Galleries (see paragraph 10.59). We will work closely with the promoters of the site and partners to assist them in developing an access strategy for the Millennium Exhibition.

Gaps in the Bus Network

12.87 Given the fairly limited road construction programme outlined above, it is clear that public transport services will have to bear a greater burden than they have in the past. As explained above, major additions to the Underground and rail network in central and inner London are in hand or planned, but these are very expensive and building them is a slow process. In outer London coverage of the rail and Tube networks is patchy, particularly for orbital movement. Light rail (see paragraph 12.92) mainly using existing infrastructure can bring extensive benefits but will have limited coverage given the costs. This is why the development of London Transport's network of bus services is a key priority.

12.88 Ten years ago London Transport provided and operated almost all the bus services in London. Progressively services have been competitively tendered and now bus services are provided under contract by private bus operators, with London Transport specifying the routes, frequencies, service quality standards, fares and ticketing arrangements. Bus services have been restructured and developed to meet the needs of passengers and reduce their vulnerability to traffic congestion. The 'big bus' network has been rationalised, and smaller midi-bus services have developed to improve frequencies on lightly used routes. Partly as a result of these improvements, the number of bus miles being run has increased by more than a fifth over the last decade.

12.89 Bus services will continue to develop in the future to serve changing markets and improve frequency, punctuality, speed and convenience. Initiatives include:

- further extension of services using smaller vehicles at more attractive frequencies;

- making the network more coherent and easier for passengers to understand and use;

- 24-hour bus services, a recent initiative which may be extended further if proved successful;

- low-floor accessible buses for all types of mobility impaired people;

- new Smartcard ticketing schemes.

12.90 Central and inner London remain very dependent on buses. London Transport is developing local area network studies to reorganise services in response to the market and changes in travel patterns. Sometimes this means shorter routes, linking to rail and Underground interchanges, and smaller midi-buses running more frequently. Midi-buses can improve the viability of low demand, low frequency services and enable the network of routes to be extended to provide more local services.

12.91 About 9% of Underground journeys in London start with a bus trip. This bus 'feeder' traffic enlarges the catchments of the railway stations and supports some bus services which would otherwise have insufficient demand to be viable. When reviewing routes and services London Transport Buses seeks new opportunities to improve the range and quality of this feeder role. And feeder services are positively planned when new lines are built. Studies are in progress in relation to both the Jubilee Line Extension and Croydon Tramlink projects.

Light Rail and Intermediate Modes

12.92 To bridge the gap between conventional rail and bus services, the development of new intermediate forms of transport is being considered. The wide range of systems available makes it possible to optimise the choice of mode for different levels of passenger demand and local circumstances, ranging from guided bus ways through to fully automatic light rail. As well as improving orbital links in inner and outer London, these new systems could serve the peripheral centres and suburban towns and offer residents new connections and a real choice to using the car. Improving public transport to these areas could further the wider planning objectives in PPG6 and in *Strategic Guidance for London Planning Authorities* of enhancing and revitalising town centres. London Transport is now working with local authorities on twelve preliminary case studies in outer London areas, looking at the likely level of demand for new services and assessing the likely economics.

Park and Ride

12.93 London Underground currently owns 65 commuter car parks, providing approximately 11,400 spaces, mainly located in outer London. Railtrack provide a further 75,000 spaces in the former Network South East area, most of which are outside London. At present 5% of rail passengers start their journeys by car. Of these nearly 60% park and ride. Sufficient parking spaces at the right locations at railway stations and bus termini enable public transport to attract passengers from a wider catchment and reduce daytime on-street parking. However car parks in the wrong locations encourage motorists to drive further into the urban area than is desirable, exacerbating road traffic congestion. Attention to safety of vehicles in car parks, for example by CCTV or supervised controls, could increase confidence and usage, diverting pressure from street parking. London Transport is reviewing the scope for a number of 'gateway' park and ride schemes, most of them associated with property development proposals, and opportunities for bus park and ride facilities in outer town centres are also being investigated, including at Bromley and Kingston.

Conclusions

12.94 Most of the above proposals for improving London's transport infrastructure have a wide measure of support amongst all the key players involved in planning and providing London's transport systems. Few people would argue, for instance, with the policy announced by the Government in the late 1980s that the upgrading of the trunk road network in south London was not a practical option. And despite a high propensity to travel by car, most Londoners would accept that the emphasis should be put on improving the already extensive public transport networks, so that they can provide an attractive alternative to the car for many journeys.

12.95 Criticisms are, however, made about the lack of certainty about the pace at which the various elements in the strategy will be pursued. Whilst there is a considerable degree of certainty about the timing of projects which are under construction such as the Jubilee Line Extension and the Heathrow Express, and a fair degree of certainty about the timescale for projects which are in the final planning stages such as the Channel Tunnel Rail Link and the A13 road improvement schemes, timing on projects such as Crossrail and the river crossings in east London remain less certain.

Chapter 13: Funding Transport in London

Introduction

13.1 In Chapter 1, we stated the underlying goals of our transport policy for London and looked at how they related to one another and to the specific circumstances of London. However, we deliberately set to one side the question of affordability. We must now bring it back into the equation.

13.2 There are three main sources from which London's transport systems are funded:

- the revenue from fares, tolls, penalties and other charges levied on transport users;

- public expenditure, borne by central or local government, for which the bill is ultimately footed by the taxpayer;

- private finance, in the form of either a developer contribution or an up-front capital contribution which is remunerated over time by the users of the system or the taxpayer or a combination of the two.

In addition to these established sources of finance, it has been suggested that funding for transport infrastructure in London might be generated by the establishment of a supplementary levy on businesses. This Chapter looks, in turn, at these four potential sources of funding.

13.3 However, before doing so, it is worth stressing that there is no 'free lunch' concealed within any of these approaches. Ultimately, the cost of funding London's transport system is borne by the user and the taxpayer. Additionally, however the bill is apportioned between user and taxpayer, it represents an addition to the cost of doing business in London.

13.4 This does not mean that the question of how the transport system is funded is a matter of indifference to the Government or to London. By harnessing private sector contributions to the capital cost of new works, for example, we aim to secure the benefits of private sector management of projects and risks. We are particularly keen to involve the private sector during the early stages of project-design, in order to secure a 'whole-life' view of the balance between capital costs, operating costs and revenues. Similarly, when it comes to the recovery of the cost of the transport system, we have a strong preference for mechanisms which send clear cost-signals to those who use it or benefit from it. Since transport imposes significant economic and environmental costs on the community

at large, it is important that it does not come to be perceived as a free good. Our overall goal is to strengthen such price signals, wherever possible. Hence, the attractions of congestion charging, if it can be made to work and to command public support, as a means of controlling access to the more central areas. Hence, also, our acceptance of the principle that the cost of enforcing the controls on on-street parking should be borne by those who use the service and, in particular, by those who abuse it.

Revenue from Charges

13.5 Revenue from fares is an important source of funding for London Transport and for other public transport operators. In 1995-96, it is estimated that London Underground will earn traffic revenue of about £765 million and London Transport Buses will earn traffic revenue of about £245 million, excluding revenue to bus operators on net cost contracts. London Underground will generate an operating surplus approaching £200 million, which will be used towards the operating costs of the business and the maintenance of the system and the funding of the capital investment programme. London Underground could not claim to be profitable, in the conventional sense of that word, because its operating surplus falls far short of what would be needed to cover depreciation and renewals properly, let alone to generate an adequate rate of return on capital employed. Nevertheless, fares revenue is of vital importance, and London is unusual in having a metro system which is capable of fully covering its operating costs in this way. For LT Buses, revenue falls short of operating costs by about £33 million, which means that there is an implicit operating subsidy from the taxpayer equivalent to about 16p per bus mile. However, this average figure conceals wide variations between individual routes. Some of the busiest routes are capable of fully covering their operating costs, while some of the less well-frequented routes require high levels of operating subsidy, which are justified by the vital role which such services play in meeting the Capital's transport needs. The nature of that contribution is explored more fully in Chapter 10 above, and need not be rehearsed here.

13.6 What is said above about the fare revenue of London Transport applies equally to other operators of public transport services, such as the train operating companies who will provide passenger services on behalf of OPRAF. As noted at paragraph 10.46, the likely effect of capping rail fares is that the likely trend for all public transport fares will be to increase broadly in line with RPI and with each other, rather than with earnings. The ability of a public transport system to generate a revenue-stream is of particular importance in attracting private finance for the construction and operation of new railway lines, such as the DLR Lewisham Extension and the Croydon Tramlink.

13.7 The Government believes that the public transport operators will be able, like businesses elsewhere, to secure efficiency gains which are broadly sufficient to offset the effects of inflation. The Government also expects the operators to pursue the scope for attracting additional revenue by the introduction of new services, the introduction of new ticket types, the more effective marketing of existing services and the more effective exploitation of revenue from advertising and related sources.

13.8 On the above basis, it is a prudent assumption that the long-term contribution which revenue from fares makes to the funding of transport in London will increase slowly. There will continue to be upturns and downturns in revenue, reflecting the upturns and downturns in the London economy, which greatly add to the short-term problems inherent in managing the finances of a public transport business, but which cancel one another out in the longer-term.

13.9 A further potential source of revenue is tolls on river crossings. This is considered at paragraph 12.81 above.

13.10 Lastly, it is worth mentioning revenue from parking charges and from penalty charges. At the time of the transfer of responsibility for parking enforcement from the Metropolitan Police to the London Boroughs, the Government agreed that the revenue which the Boroughs generated from these activities should be applied to fund the enforcement costs. Allowing local authorities to retain revenue from charges and penalties is now being considered in the context of local authority enforcement of emissions offences, for which regulations under the Environment Act 1995 are being drawn up.

Public Expenditure

13.11 In paragraphs 13.22-13.28 below, we deal with the significant contribution which private finance has already made to the funding of transport infrastructure in London and reiterate our view that there is considerable private finance potential still to be tapped. However, the Government recognises a continuing need for public expenditure on transport in London.

13.12 Table 13A sets out the Transport Departments' forward expenditure plans for the next three years.

13.13 Much of this expenditure is essentially national in nature and could not sensibly be disaggregated by region. The running costs of the Department of Transport's headquarters and of the DVLA fall within this category, as does the Government's expenditure in relation to international transport by air, rail and sea. The balance of the three Departments' expenditure can, with varying degrees of difficulty, be apportioned on a geographical basis. Thus:

- OPRAF support for train operating companies which provide services within London and for commuter services to and from London, but excluding those which provide long-distance services, is forecast at about £620 million in 1996-97. This is, however, subject to two important caveats. First, the precise expenditure figure will, of course, depend upon the bids actually received from prospective franchisees. Second, the support for commuter services clearly represents a benefit to the communities where the commuters reside as well as to London, but there is no obvious method of apportioning the benefit between the two.

- The Highways Agency typically spends between £225 million and £250 million a year on the construction and maintenance of trunk roads in Greater London and on minor schemes to improve traffic flow and to reduce road casualties. Again, there are two caveats. First, the scale and make up of the programme varies from year to year depending on the timing of the larger improvement schemes and the major road and structure maintenance works. Second, by focusing narrowly on investment which takes place within the Greater London boundary, we are ignoring the significant benefit which London undoubtedly derives from schemes such as the M25 widening programme. Although it lies predominantly beyond the London boundary, the M25 is, as noted elsewhere in this strategy, London's ring road and the Capital benefits greatly from any improvement to it.

- Some £2 billion is planned to be provided over the next three years to fund London Transport's

Table 13A: Transport Departments' Summary[1] Cash Plans 1996-97 to 1998-99

£ million	1996-97	1997-98	1998-99
Across the Modes			
DOT administration and miscellaneous services	98	98	94
Credit approvals for local authority expenditure	500	482	482
Executive Agencies	263	259	247
Other[2]	61	63	63
Total	**921**	**901**	**887**
Roads			
National roads	1,569	1,495	1,488
Local roads[3]	245	236	236
Other	107	112	108
Total[3]	**1,921**	**1,843**	**1,833**
Public Transport			
National Railways[4]	-1,355	-385	-385
Other rail privatisation costs	4	1	1
Other railway related	56	53	53
London Transport's EFR[5]	953	660	441
Other public transport[3]	40	38	38
Total[3]	**-303**	**367**	**148**
Air Transport[3]	**-13**	**-22**	**-22**
Sea Transport[3]	**0**	**-1**	**-1**
TOTAL DEPARTMENT OF TRANSPORT	**2,527**	**3,089**	**2,845**
Office of Passenger Rail Franchising[6]	**1,651**	**1,566**	**1,561**
Office of the Rail Regulator[7]	**8**	**8**	**7**
TOTAL TRANSPORT	**4,185**	**4,663**	**4,413**

[1] Detailed information on the spending plans of the three Transport Departments (DOT, OPRAF and ORR) is contained in the Transport Report 1996, published by HMSO.

[2] Includes research and development; ERDF grants; roads and local transport grants; freight grants; transport security; Government Office programme and administrative expenditure and miscellaneous services.

[3] Excluding credit approvals.

[4] Including the External Financing Requirement of British Rail and Railtrack and privatisation effects.

[5] External Financing Requirement. The amount of finance, whether by central Government grant or borrowing, which the industry may raise during the financial year.

[6] OPRAF became a non-ministerial Government Department on 8 November 1993.

[7] ORR became a non-ministerial Government Department on 1 December 1993.

core business and the construction of the Jubilee Line Extension. Supplemented by the operating surplus which London Transport forecasts, it should be sufficient to fund investment of around £500 million per year in the core Underground business.

- The plans provide for £104 million of support in 1996/97, via Transport Supplementary Grant and Credit Approvals, for local authority transport initiatives within the London area. Included within this is £9 million of support for the London bus priority network and £4 million of support for the London cycle network.

- Some £75 million of funding is planned over the next three years for other London-specific purposes. This includes £17 million for Red Routes in 1996/97, rising to £22 million in each following year, and £4 million a year for the Woolwich Ferry. It also includes modest provision for traffic surveys, modelling work and consultancies.

- provision for the public sector contribution towards Croydon Tramlink, the level of which will be decided in the light of the outcome of the current competition.

13.14 On the basis of the above figures, London's share of the total Transport Departments' budget for the coming three years is between 30 and 40%. Because of the caveats which are entered in relation to OPRAF and Highways Agency expenditure, this range has to be treated with a degree of caution. Nevertheless, it gives a helpful feel for the extent to which London benefits from the Government's transport investment programme. The fact that London appears to do disproportionately well should not come as a surprise to anyone. It reflects the fact that the transport expenditure programme accords priority to expenditure on public transport and the fact that London is more heavily reliant on public transport than the rest of the country.

13.15 The public expenditure plans which the Chancellor unveiled in his Budget last December involved a reduction of 7% compared with the comparable plans which were set out in December 1994. Faced with the need to find significant reductions in the Transport Departments' budgets, it has not been possible to exempt London from the need to find savings. However, the London component of the transport programme is expected to remain steady, and we have protected four key programmes in London: London Transport, Red Routes, the bus priority network and the cycle network.

13.16 For LT, the Government has provided a substantial increase in funding to offset the additional costs on the Jubilee Line Extension project which resulted from the problems which the Heathrow Express project experienced with the New Austrian Tunnelling Method. This led to delay on some of the key Jubilee Line Extension works, where the same tunnelling method was being employed, whilst London Underground and the Railways Inspectorate satisfied themselves that it was safe to proceed. Inevitably, it also led to increased costs, because contractors were unable to complete works to schedule. We concluded that, even in a difficult public expenditure round, we should find additional funds to offset these costs. The costs clearly arose from circumstances which were beyond London Underground's control and it would have been wrong to penalise them or, indirectly, their passengers for a problem which arose on a completely different project. We have stressed to London Underground the importance which we attach to the new line opening, as scheduled, in March 1998. London Underground has, for its part, given assurances that it remains on course to meet this timetable.

13.17 Funding for London Transport as a whole, including the existing bus and Underground networks, has been held at the same level in the 1995 Budget as it was in 1994. We have not felt able to increase funding for these networks. We have, however, taken seriously the message which both LT and London First have stressed about the consistency of funding being as important as the level of funding, if not more so - a point to which we revert below. We have also borne in mind the fact that improving the existing London Underground service contributes most directly to our primary goal of promoting the competitiveness of London as a World City.

13.18 By preserving the level of Government support for LT at a time when other transport programmes have had to take substantial cuts, we believe we have sent a clear signal about our investment priorities in London. However, we cannot completely insulate LT, or any other organisation, from the risks that are inevitably associated with taking forward a major construction project, nor from the pressures on public expenditure in general. This, too, is a point to which we revert in Chapter 14.

13.19 In the 1994 Budget, we set expenditure on the Red Routes programme on a firmly rising trend. Provision was increased from £11 million in 1994/95 to £12 million in 1995/96, £17 million in 1996/97 and £22 million in 1997/98. In the 1995 Budget, we have preserved the Red Routes funding intact. This should permit the programme to be operational in 2000. Funding for the London bus priority network and London cycle network was increased by £1 million. The priority attached to all three programmes reflects the fact that they are, by transport standards, relatively low-cost initiatives, with important contributions to make to freeing traffic flows and securing modal shift.

13.20 However, the protection of these key programmes inevitably increases the pressure on other areas of expenditure.

13.21 We have dealt in previous chapters with the review of the national roads programme and its implications for London. The Government welcomes the more pragmatic approach which Boroughs are adopting towards local transport problems and their efforts to secure local-level ownership of solutions to difficult transport problems. In the event, having funded existing commitments and the increases for the bus and cycle networks, we were unable to support any new major road schemes and were able to support only the following 'package' bids: West London Line stations; Stratford Station Eastern Concourse; SWELTRAC (access in south west London); Park Royal Transport; Cross River Transport; Wood Green Spouter's Corner; Aberfeldy Estate traffic management; and Bexleyheath town centre.

Private Finance

13.22 London has already demonstrated convincingly that investment in transport infrastructure has considerable private finance potential. Private finance also brings with it private sector management skills. There are three main ways in which a project can attract such finance.

13.23 First, there are contributions from developers or other businesses, who stand to gain directly from the provision of a new transport service or the improvement of an existing one. This is the basis on which the promoters of Canary Wharf agreed to contribute £400 million towards the cost of the Jubilee Line Extension and on which BAA plc agreed to join with BR in funding the Heathrow Express. Developer

contributions are also an important source of finance for smaller road and rail schemes, such as road access to new major retail outlets in north west London and the proposed stations on the West London Line. Developer contributions do not fall within the scope of the private finance initiative and there are many transport projects where it will not be possible to secure them, because the benefits of the new investment are highly diffuse. Nevertheless, the Government believes that developer contributions will continue to have an important part to play in the funding of some transport schemes, and will continue to press hard for them. Local authorities' dual responsibilities for land use and transport matters in their local areas make them well placed to negotiate contributions from developers to public transport improvements.

13.24 Second, there are arrangements under which the private sector bears some or all of the capital cost of a project and is then remunerated by its users. This approach is most appropriate for public transport schemes and for tolled estuarial crossings, because such projects are capable of generating the revenue-stream from which the promoters can be remunerated. This is the approach that was adopted to the funding of the Queen Elizabeth II bridge between Dartford and Thurrock, and which might also be applied to the funding of a new road crossing for through-traffic at Blackwall and for the proposed crossing at Gallions Reach which would serve both local road traffic and the Docklands Light Railway. Estuarial crossings are particularly suitable candidates for private finance, because they possess a degree of natural monopoly, which allows the private sector promoter to be reasonably confident that revenue will not be disrupted by changes elsewhere in the transport network. East London is unusual, within the UK, in having a significant need for additional estuarial capacity.

13.25 Third, there are arrangements under which the private sector bears the capital cost of a project and is then remunerated over time by a public sector body. At the national level, one of the most important examples of this type of deal is the Design, Build, Finance and Operate (DBFO) approach to the construction of new roads. Under DBFO schemes a private sector consortium designs and builds roads and is responsible for the financing and operation of that infrastructure together with an associated package of trunk roads over 30 years and is remunerated principally by reference to the volumes of traffic which use those roads. This approach is to be employed for the A13 trunk road and will help deliver the urgently needed improvements along this important strategic route. London also stands to benefit significantly from the Northern Line rolling-stock deal, under which GEC-Alsthom will build and maintain a fleet of trains which will then be provided for London Underground's use under a service agreement. The DBFO and Northern Line rolling stock approaches illustrate ways in which private finance can be harnessed even where there is no revenue-stream or where the link between the new investment and the revenue-stream is indirect. The latter point is a particularly important one for London, given that much of the investment required by London Underground, in particular, is not to provide new services, but to maintain and enhance the quality of existing services.

13.26 The Government does not accept the criticism that investment in transport is a matter of accepting high risks and low returns. We have stressed repeatedly that our approach to the private finance initiative is deal-driven, that we shall strive to secure the best deal we can on behalf of the taxpayers and that we expect the private sector to do likewise on behalf of their shareholders. At the end of the day, the balance of risks transferred and returns earned will have to be mutually advantageous. Such balances should not be difficult to achieve in the transport sector, where major projects are capable of generating significant benefit. The extensions of the Jubilee Line and the Docklands Light Railway illustrate the significant benefits which can be delivered in terms of enhanced land values. Similarly, in relation to revenue-generation, traffic levels on the Dartford-Thurrock bridge have outperformed the forecasts and the project now seems set to recover its cost over 12 years, rather than the 20 years originally envisaged. Publicly funded schemes, such as the M25 and Victoria Line, have also demonstrated that there can be significant upside risks on major transport schemes.

13.27 In some important respects, the Government believes that the private finance initiative has exceeded expectations. We know that more can be done, and therefore welcome the fact that London First, following the first meeting of the Joint London Advisory Panel, has offered to explore actively with the business community in London the scope for further private finance deals on transport projects, and to present them to Ministers. Already it has proved possible to

construct deals, which represent value for money and secure a sensible transfer of risk to the private sector, in areas where the potential for such deals looked questionable. In the light of experience to date, the Government is not prepared to say that there are any types of transport project where it is impossible to conceive of private finance making a contribution. However, some areas are more obvious candidates than others:

- Projects with their own revenue-streams (such as the new Thames Gateway crossings and Croydon Tramlink) are highly attractive candidates. They appear to have significant demand-growth potential. There is, additionally, the prospect (in some cases) of capturing developer gain.

- DBFO road projects which involve genuine and substantial transfer of risk to the private sector, offering value for money for Government and a package of construction and long term operational responsibilities attractive to the private sector have good potential.

- Projects such as London Underground revenue collection and power generation are promising candidates because they are discrete parts of the London Underground operation, even though they are not free-standing projects with their own revenue stream. There will be some difficult issues to resolve along the way, but we have resolved such problems in the context of the Northern Line rolling stock deal and are reasonably confident of being able to do so again.

- Some local authority schemes, other than straightforward joint ventures and financially free-standing projects, may be less suitable for private finance, although we would not want to rule any possibilities out *ab initio*.

13.28 Since private finance is unlikely (in the short term, at least) to help meet some types of investment need, that makes it all the more important that we tap the contribution it can make. Our inherent preference is for the more highly leveraged schemes and for those which do not pre-empt funding in future years.

The Proposal for a Transport Infrastructure Levy

13.29 As noted at paragraph 13.23, developer contributions can be attracted only in cases where the beneficiaries of a new scheme are few in number and readily identifiable. For most transport projects, the benefits are diffuse and the beneficiaries are difficult to identify. Recovery of the capital cost via the farebox is the obvious way of funding such schemes. However, it does not help with the upfront capital cost. If there remains a requirement for public sector funding, after the private finance potential has been explored, the new schemes will have to compete for funds with a number of other calls - some of them very pressing - on the London transport 'budget'.

13.30 This has prompted London First to propose the introduction of a levy on London businesses to assist with the funding of major capital projects such as Crossrail. Such a scheme would have a significant impact on property values and business prospects in the West End and the City. The levy would be payable in the form of a supplement to the unified business rate by all businesses falling within the scope of the scheme. London First has suggested that the scheme would cover only businesses in the central and inner areas and that small businesses would be excluded. The levy would help support named public transport schemes. It would not become payable unless a majority of the businesses who would fall to pay it voted in favour of it. In this way, London First seeks to preserve the principle of voluntariness, whilst dealing with the obvious temptation for businesses to "free-load" on the contributions of others.

13.31 The idea is an interesting one. It sends a clear signal to us about the high importance which the business community attaches to improvements in the public transport system and its willingness to pay for them. It reinforces the message which London First has put to us about the clear linkage between public transport quality and London's competitiveness. Unless it were genuinely voluntary for all those who paid it, the levy proposed would represent a tax and the expenditure which it supported would therefore score as public expenditure. The Government commitment to restrain public expenditure therefore bites, as the City would, in its other manifestation, expect it to bite. Hence, it does not solve the public sector's funding difficulty.

13.32 That is not a reason for rejecting the levy proposal out of hand. We have no wish to discourage London First from working up their ideas further. Since businesses in London are major beneficiaries of transport investment, there may be a case for seeking to recover some of the cost of the programme from London employers, in the same way that public transport in Paris is supported by employers there. However, in working up their proposals, it is important that the London business community does not labour under the misapprehension that the Government will be able to accept a scheme that will raise the level of taxation as such.

Chapter 14: The Investment and Expenditure Timetables

Introduction

14.1 This Chapter looks at the timetable for delivery of further improvements to transport in London. It distinguishes between two main types of initiative:

- making better use of existing transport systems, keeping them in a decent state of repair, improving the service they provide, minimising their impact on the environment and, where appropriate, increasing their capacity;

- providing new infrastructure to plug gaps in the network, to improve international links, to foster regeneration or to accommodate growth in transport demand.

14.2 The Government believes that it will be possible to make good progress on both fronts in the period covered by this strategy. It also notes that there is often a synergy between the two types of initiative - for example one of the main benefits from the construction of new rail and road links in London is the extent to which they take pressure off existing networks.

14.3 Nevertheless, the Government has also consistently stressed that it attaches the higher priority to making better use of existing networks. That assessment of relative priorities was endorsed in the London Pride *Action Programme*. It is also reinforced by the analysis in Chapters 2 and 3 of this strategy, which suggests that the need to promote the competitiveness of London as a World City is likely to be a more urgent priority, in the short to medium term, than the need to accommodate the sort of rapid growth in transport demand which the Capital witnessed in the latter half of the 1980s. Accordingly, whilst the Government is clear that there is a need for investment in new infrastructure, we are equally clear that the public sector contribution to such infrastructure cannot be made at the expense of depriving existing transport networks of the funding which they need.

14.4 The Government treats public expenditure on new infrastructure as separate from expenditure on the existing networks. For example, when authorising the Jubilee Line Extension, the Government was at pains to stress that the funding of the new line would neither displace nor enhance the funding for the existing Underground system. To that end, the Jubilee Line funding was subject to a separate ring-fenced external financing limit. It is not the case that there is a 'baseline' for transport expenditure in London, within which projects such as the Jubilee Line must be accommodated. The concept of a 'baseline' is a valid one for expenditure on existing networks, but not for major new projects. Such projects are considered on their merits. To the extent that they require public funding, they are competing not with the existing transport networks, but with other expenditure priorities nationwide.

Affordability

14.5 In framing their *Action Programme*, London Pride did not have to take into account the question of the affordability of the improvements which they proposed. Over the 14-year period covered by their *Action Programme*, London Pride envisaged investment of £23 billion, requiring public expenditure of £11 billion. Although the total public expenditure requirement of their programme was not significantly out of line with existing expenditure provision, it did require a very substantial increase in the short term - of the order of £800 million over the three years 1996/97 to 1998/99. London Pride envisaged a significant proportion of this increase being devoted to accelerating the investment programme of London Underground, which would bring forward the point at which the business would achieve financial self-sufficiency, thereby freeing-up public funds to support other schemes.

14.6 Although the Government fully recognised the merits of the investment programme, it was obliged to conclude that the increases sought by London Pride were not affordable at the time of the 1995 Budget. We have to take account of our commitment to reduce public expenditure in both absolute terms and as a proportion of GDP and to take account of the relative strength of the competing claims on the expenditure totals. London is already the beneficiary of a very substantial proportion of the total budget for the Transport Departments, including the £950m investment for 1996/97 in London Transport, six of the seven new trunk road schemes given the go-ahead in the revised national road programme, £104m of the Local Transport Capital Settlement, and a substantial proportion of the investment for national railways. In addition to these, the Private Finance Initiative is providing new trains for the Northern Line, will develop the Channel Tunnel Rail Link, and is expected to construct several new trunk road schemes in London.

14.7 The 1995 settlement was a good one for London.

It sends a clear signal about the high priority which the Government attaches to transport in London generally and to public transport in particular. It also reflects the Government's recognition of the importance which those responsible for managing transport programmes attach to stability and certainty about budgets. Key London programmes, such as London Underground investment and the Red Routes network, were protected at a time when the overall transport budget was cut steeply. Total provision for public expenditure on London's existing transport system was set to remain broadly constant over the three year period covered by the settlement.

14.8 We have considered carefully London Pride's concern that uncertainty about future finding levels causes inefficiency in the management of investment programmes and their request that *"the Government should commit itself to a consistent level of investment for the medium term"*. We have concluded that this is possible for some of the smaller programmes and have spelled out our longer term plans for expenditure on the Red Route, bus priority and cycle networks at paragraphs 14.14 to 14.17 below. The Government does not, however, believe that this is a practical approach for the larger programmes. While the value of stability and predictability of funding is fully recognised, we believe that it is important to retain the flexibility provided by the present system to allow funding needs to be reviewed in the light of changes in circumstances over time. For instance, funding decisions may need to be revised to take account of unforseen changes in the level or pattern of demand and revenue, or in the availability of private finance. In addition, given the scale of public expenditure represented by these programmes, there is no escaping the fact that the Government also needs to be able, if necessary, to adjust funding levels - whether up or down - to take account of changes in macroeconomic circumstances and in the priorities which have to be placed on the calls on the public purse.

Improving Existing Transport Systems

14.9 In the earlier chapters of this strategy, we have identified a variety of different measures which need to be pursued in parallel to achieve the objectives which we have set ourselves. For example, the most significant impact on air quality in London is likely to come from the progressive tightening of regulations on the construction and use of vehicles, backed by tougher enforcement of vehicle emissions standards. However, in order to maintain that improvement, it is necessary to take measures which encourage the use of more environmentally friendly modes of transport. The combination of increases in fuel duty and restraint of public transport fares increases ensures that the price signals sent to transport users reflect more accurately the environmental costs of the different transport modes. The Red Route and bus priority networks will improve the speed and reliability of bus services, whilst Countdown will improve the quality of passenger information. At the same time London Transport is progressively improving the standard of bus shelters. And privatisation, combined with the tendering of bus routes and franchising of rail services, will give operators stronger incentives to respond quickly to changes in passenger requirements. The quality of London Underground services will continue to be improved, partly via investment (both publicly and privately financed) and partly via new management initiatives (such as the progressive contracting-out of non-core operations). It is important to stress that the achievement of each of our transport objectives for London depends upon a similar mix of initiatives - some major and some more modest, some with expenditure implications and some without. Although this chapter focuses primarily on investment and expenditure plans in general and on major programmes in particular, many of the initiatives which will benefit London have little if any expenditure implication.

14.10 There are three priority areas of expenditure on the existing transport networks: the funding of London Underground; the completion of the Red Route, bus priority and cycle networks; and the maintenance of roads.

Improving the Existing Underground Network

14.11 Chapter 9 summarised the problems which London Underground confronts as a result of the backlog of under-investment which built up during the period of GLC control. It dealt with the progress which London Underground has already made in remedying these problems and mapped out their forward plans. The rate at which these plans can be implemented depends critically upon the availability of funds. In broad terms, London Underground estimates that, as a long term average, they would need to invest something of the order of £350 million per annum in renewal and repair of the existing network to keep it in a stable condition. To the extent that annual investment exceeds this level, London Underground can make inroads into the backlog of under-investment in basic infrastructure or it can invest in measures which will increase revenue or cut costs in the longer term. The balance is a matter for the management of London Underground. In practice, it will wish to do all three of these things. Whilst eliminating the investment backlog has the highest priority, measures to boost revenue or cut costs will often have a rapid payback period, generating the funds that will allow London Underground to accelerate its investment in basic infrastructure.

14.12 Chart 14A shows the past trend in investment in the existing Underground network (ie excluding the construction of new lines). On the basis of the level of public expenditure provided for in the 1995 Budget and likely future levels of fare revenue, the sums available to support London Underground investment would increase steadily over time to about £670 million by 2000/01. So, if public expenditure were maintained at its present level, the elimination of the investment backlog and expenditure on new assets to bring the existing network up to a very high standard, would be achieved around 2008. Around a year later, LUL would become financially self-sufficient, in that it could generate enough revenue from its own activities to fund the renewal of the network without further Government grant. At that point, any Government grant would be for improvements to the network or extensions to it.

14.13 The above scenario is provided for the purpose of exemplification. Since the London Underground

budget is a major component of total expenditure on transport in London, its future funding is very much subject to what is said at paragraph 14.8 above about the Government's balancing of competing pressures on public expenditure. However, the Government would hope to maintain London Underground investment at broadly the current level until the investment backlog has been eliminated. This goal should be facilitated and the scope for accelerating the investment programme should be increased by the determined efforts which London Underground are making to harness private finance to secure improvements to the existing Underground system. The London Regional Transport Bill now before Parliament will extend London Transport's powers, enabling LT to make full use of private finance.

Making Better Use of the Existing Road Networks

14.14 The importance of making better use of the existing road networks has been stressed at many points in this document. This encompasses a variety of initiatives which are being taken forward by the Boroughs (such as the extension of the SCOOT traffic control system) or the Highways Agency (such as the vitally important programme for re-signing the priority route network in London). In their *Action Programme*, London Pride identified three ongoing programmes - Red Routes, the London bus priority network and the London cycle network - as particular priorities. All three of these programmes are relatively modest compared with the programme of investment in London Underground or the cost of new infrastructure. The benefits are potentially very great. The future work

Chart 14A: Total investment in London Underground existing network 1986/87 to 1995/96

£ millions

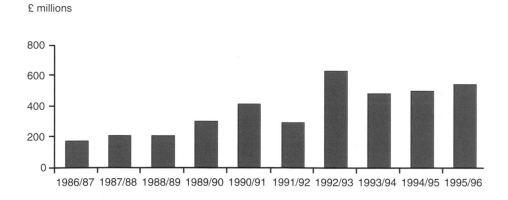

Source: London Transport

programme, particularly for the Red Routes, is very clearly defined. It is therefore possible to make expenditure commitments to these programmes that would not be possible for those which are larger and less well defined.

14.15 The Government remains firmly committed to having the Red Route network substantially operational by 2000. The Government intends to provide the Traffic Director for London with sufficient funding to ensure this timetable is met.

14.16 The Government has considered carefully representations by London Pride and others that the timetable for the completion of the London bus priority network should be accelerated and that responsibility for the funding of the network should be transferred to London Transport. However, our discussions with London partners confirm that this approach does not command widespread support. Nevertheless, the Government recognises that uncertainty about the availability of funds in future years constitutes an obstacle to the implementation of the network and has implications for the Boroughs' ability to secure value for money. We make two proposals for remedying this uncertainty:

- We can confirm that it is our intention to maintain funding sufficient to permit the network to be completed not later than 2003, that we shall use our best endeavours to secure more rapid progress than that, and that we shall look to the Boroughs to do likewise.

- We recognise that in order to manage the implementation of the project efficiently, Boroughs need to be assured that, where consultation on traffic orders is initiated, funding will be available to let the relevant contracts within a reasonable period. To meet this legitimate concern, when we decide on the allocation for any given year, we will undertake to provide 75% of that allocation in the following year, and 50% in the year after that.

14.17 Similar arguments about implementation and commitment also apply to the London cycle network. Subject to the Government being satisfied that the progress on the network remains satisfactory, it is our intention to provide funding sufficient to permit the network to be completed not later than 2005. In addition, we are also undertaking to provide continuity of funding, on the same basis as for the bus network, so that local authorities can manage the implementation of the project efficiently.

Maintenance of the Road Networks

14.18 The maintenance of local roads and the strengthening of bridges were amongst the areas where expenditure in the next year or so has had to be reduced. The Government is, however, fully aware of the need to ensure that, in tackling a backlog on the Underground and other transport needs, adequate funding is provided to local authorities to maintain and safeguard their roads and bridges, provided care is taken to prioritise and manage the available resources.

14.19 The structural maintenance of local authority principal roads is funded through the TPP process. The bids made by local authorities in London have been assessed with a view towards steady and planned maintenance throughout the capital. The historical level of allocation in London (around £19m) for carriageways, has helped ensure that the maintenance activities have kept reasonably in step with the rate of deterioration. However given the higher priority which both the Boroughs and the Government attach to completion of the bus priority and cycle networks, some reduction on road maintenance spend will be required in the short to medium term. Accordingly, this strategy proposes that the least cost maintenance options are pursued up to the middle of the next decade.

14.20 The level of funding will be maintained to ensure that all bridges on London's principal roads are assessed by 1999. The exact position on how many still require strengthening is not known and data about the number of bridges that have been strengthened to date has not been collected centrally. Local authorities are being encouraged to form sectors within which the programme and priorities for strengthening can be fully considered. Such an approach would enable strategies to be developed covering routes and corridors and matters such as resourcing and timescales to be explored. Meanwhile available resources are being targeted on bridges carrying priority/primary roads and other key locations such as Thames crossings.

14.21 For trunk roads and bridges substantial sums have been spent on maintenance in London. The strategic importance of these roads means that, while the levels of expenditure may fluctuate from year to year as a result of budgetary considerations, substantial sums will continue to be spent. For example major maintenance projects such as the refurbishment of the M4 elevated section and Blackwall

Tunnel Southbound, will need to be carried forward by the Highways Agency and will require substantial expenditure over several years.

Other Expenditure on Existing Networks

14.22 Accommodating the three priorities identified at paragraphs 14.11 - 14.21 means that there is unlikely to be funding available within the London component of the local transport settlement for new starts on local roads or public transport projects for some years to come. The funds that can be made available to support package bids are also likely to be severely constrained. In order to avoid nugatory effort on the part of Boroughs, the annual guidance on the preparation of TPP bids will give a clearer steer on the likely availability of funds for new starts. At the same time it may be possible for boroughs to seek funds for transport schemes from the Capital Challenge fund, if we decide to take this initiative forward. This would allow local authorities to make integrated bids across the whole of their capital funding programme, including transport projects.

14.23 On the Motorway and Trunk Road Network the Highways Agency - in addition to its maintenance and major scheme expenditure - has a substantial programme of *Network Enhancement Projects* (NEPs). These are smaller scale projects which will typically focus on an individual junction or section of trunk road. They are generally aimed at an accident or congestion blackspot or at a location where additional traffic management or facilities for pedestrians or pedal cyclists are appropriate. One of the advantages of a NEP is that it can be implemented during maintenance activity, thereby minimising the occupation of the road and subsequent traffic disruption which the work might otherwise have caused.

14.24 NEPs will make an important impact on the Highways Agency contribution towards the Government's target to reduce road accident casualties in London by 2000. The 115 road safety schemes completed on London Motorways and Trunk Roads between 1991 and 1994 have achieved more than a one-third reduction in accidents, valued at nearly £50m.

Provision of New Infrastructure

14.25 We can distinguish between the projects to which the Government has made a formal financial commitment and the rest. We seek to maximise private sector involvement and finance in all of these schemes, where possible.

14.26 The first tranche of schemes to which the Government is committed consists of projects which are already under construction. Their future timetables can be mapped out with a considerable degree of confidence, subject only to the caveat that they do not encounter major technical problems during the remaining stages of the work. The projects are:

- The *Jubilee Line Extension*. Contracts were let in the autumn of 1993, since when much of the civil engineering work has been completed. The next major phase will be installation of the electrical and mechanical equipment. There have been some problems, due partly to precautions connected with the New Austrian Tunnelling Method, but London Underground's target opening date remains March 1998. Developer contributions of £400 million towards the total cost of £2 billion have been secured.

- **Heathrow Express.** This project is a joint venture between BAA and BR. Construction of the project by BAA and Railtrack is now generally well advanced. Services are due to begin in mid-1998.

- **Orbital road schemes**. The schemes already under way to widen the south west sector of the M25 and improve the North Circular, to be completed by the end of 1997.

- Radial road schemes. The Hackney-M11 Link (to be completed by mid-1998) and the A13 Thames Avenue to Wennington improvement scheme (to be completed by mid-1997)

14.27 The second tranche of projects are those which have not yet reached the construction stage, but for which the Government has made a firm financial provision or commitment, and where private finance, as appropriate, is either committed or under discussion. The precise nature of the commitment and status of the project varies. The timetable for these schemes is necessarily slightly more tentative. The projects concerned are:

- **Channel Tunnel Rail Link (CTRL).** The Government announced in February its choice of the private sector consortium to build and operate the new line. The CTRL Bill is expected to secure Royal Assent at the end of 1996 or early 1997. Subject to maintaining satisfactory progress with the Bill, the Government would expect construction of the line to commence in 1998, and the line to be completed by 2003. While the Government will provide financial support with a present value of £1.4 billion, London and Continental Railways will be responsible for the construction and commercial risks of the £3 billion project.

• Thameslink 2000. The Government announced the go-ahead for the Thameslink 2000 project in February 1996. It is Railtrack's intention to submit an application under the Transport and Works Act in early 1997. If the application is successful, Railtrack expect work to commence, at the earliest, in 1998, with Thameslink 2000 operational by summer 2002. However, this timetable is dependent on the timetable for the construction of the low level station at St Pancras as part of the CTRL project. In line with the PFI, this project will be joint-funded, with Railtrack and London and Continental Railways taking the construction risk for the project.

• **Road schemes.** The six new schemes scheduled to start in 1996/97 are the remaining Hackney - M11 Link and outer A13 (Heathway - Mar Dyke) contracts, and the A40 Gypsy Corner and Western Circus improvement schemes.

• **The DLR Lewisham Extension.** The PFI competition to choose a private sector consortium to finance, build and maintain the DLR extension to Lewisham is nearing completion. Construction is expected to start by the end of 1996, and the extension to open in 1999.

• **Croydon Tramlink.** A PFI competition has been held to select a private sector consortium to

finance, build and operate the system and at the time of publication of this strategy bids for grant are being evaluated to see if they offer value for money and are affordable.

14.28 An illustrative timetable for these committed schemes in the first and second tranches is shown in Chart 14B. The timings shown represent the current best view, but for the second tranche in particular they may be reviewed as the schemes progress. They constitute an ambitious programme of investment for London, with an estimated total cost of £7 billion, funded via around £4 billion of public expenditure and around £3 billion of private finance.

14.29 As noted at paragraph 14.8 above, affordability will inevitably have a significant impact on the timing of new infrastructure projects. However, there are other reasons why these schemes would have to be taken forward on a phased basis. Major projects put a degree of strain upon some supplier industries. They make significant demands in terms of project management skills. They are also likely to have, to varying degrees, a disruptive effect upon existing transport services and, thereby, on the economy of the Capital. The Government therefore believes it is likely that, as in the past, new infrastructure projects will tend to be taken forward in tranches, with no more than one large-scale rail project in each tranche. The Government feels that it would be misleading to set out timetables for the start and completion of these projects, but has endeavoured to give a steer on the likely order in which additional schemes might be tackled.

Chart 14B: Indicative timetable for committed transport schemes

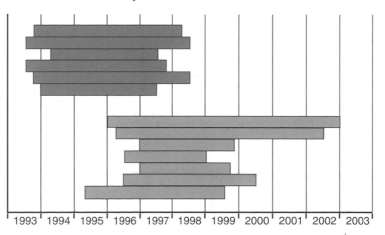

First Tranche	
Jubilee Line Extension	
Heathrow Express	
M25 south-west widening	
A406 North Circular Road improvements	
A12 Hackney-M11 Link contracts 2 and 4	
A13 West of Heathway-Wennington	
Second Tranche	
Channel Tunnel Rail Link	
Thameslink 2000	
A12 Hackney-M11 Link contracts 1 and 3	
A13 Heathway-Mar Dyke	
A40 Improvements	
Croydon Tramlink	
DLR Lewisham Extension	

1993 1994 1995 1996 1997 1998 1999 2000 2001 2002 2003

14.30 In establishing this ordering, we have had particular regard to:

- **The ratio of benefit to cost.** Although it is difficult to make like-for-like comparisons between different types of project, the benefit:cost ratio remains an important measure of the resource costs of a scheme compared with the wider benefits. Other things being equal, there is advantage in tackling first the schemes with the highest benefit:cost ratios.

- **The ability to harness private finance.** Given the constraints on public funding, this is clearly an important consideration. There is a strong case for seeking to tackle first those schemes which are most highly leveraged in terms of their ability to harness private finance, where this provides value for money.

- **Affordability.** Even schemes able to attract a high proportion of private finance may still require a substantial public sector contribution. Going ahead with a single very expensive scheme might mean that several small schemes have to be delayed.

- **The regeneration benefit.** Some schemes, notably the East Thames Crossings and East London Line, are of particular importance to the achievement of the regeneration of the areas of London identified in Chapter 4.

- **The state of preparation.** Some projects are more well-defined than others, are better costed or at a more advanced stage in terms of securing the necessary statutory powers. Again, other things being equal, it would be sensible to tackle these schemes first.

- **Synergy between schemes.** It is often necessary or desirable to tackle one scheme ahead of another or in parallel with it. For example, the timetable for upgrading of the A13 and constructing Thameslink 2000 needs to take account of the timetable for the Channel Tunnel Rail Link.

- **The disruption factor.** Just as there are advantages in tackling some schemes together, there are good reasons for tackling other schemes separately. As noted at paragraph 14.29, major transport construction works can cause serious problems on existing networks. It is sensible not to inflict two such projects on a given area of London at the same time.

14.31 The Government has applied these criteria in reviewing its national road and rail priorities and in framing the plans set out in this strategy. In doing so, it has leant heavily upon the expertise of the Highways Agency and the railway operators, although the final decisions have, necessarily, rested with Ministers. Our conclusion is that there are three further broad tranches of infrastructure project which we would expect to see taken forward within London.

14.32 The third tranche is expected to comprise:

- **The inner A13 road schemes.** These schemes will improve junctions between Ironbridge, Canning Town and Movers Lane, and have been identified as DBFO schemes in the revised national roads programme. We aim to let a contract for this scheme in 1997.

- **A package of three new East Thames Crossings:** The Government believes that there is a case for a tolled, multi-modal crossing at Gallions Reach, a third, tolled road crossing at Blackwall, and the Woolwich Rail Tunnel. All three crossings have PFI potential - Blackwall as a free-standing project, Gallions Reach as a predominantly private sector financed joint venture, and Woolwich Rail Tunnel as a railway project requiring significant public sector support. They also have potential regeneration benefits. Initial indications suggest positive benefit:cost ratios for all three crossings. Their inclusion in this tranche would depend on privately funded options arising from the recent consultation exercise. The timetable for these schemes is difficult to predict, but work on the third Blackwall crossing could not start until after the Millennium Exhibition.

- **The East London Line Extension.** Powers have been sought for a northern extension, from Whitechapel to Dalston Junction, and a southern extension from New Cross Gate is under consideration. There are likely to be regeneration benefits but progress and timing will depend on the availability of private finance.

14.33 The fourth tranche is expected to comprise:

- **Crossrail.** The Secretary of State for Transport has said that he expects Crossrail to come after the Jubilee Line Extension, Thameslink 2000 and the Channel Tunnel Rail Link. He has asked London Transport, Railtrack and British Rail not to proceed for the time being with an application under the Transport and Works Act for powers to build Crossrail. He has also invited Railtrack to consider the project further, once Railtrack is in the private sector, in the light of the Government's continued firm policy that Crossrail should proceed only as a joint venture with a substantial private sector contribution.

- **Orbital roads.** These major improvement schemes would widen the M25 in the western sector, plug the final gaps in the upgrading of the North Circular and relieve Catford Town Centre.

14.34 The fifth tranche is expected to include the **Chelsea-Hackney line** as it is feasible to undertake only one major project at a time. It has long been announced policy that Chelsea-Hackney should follow Crossrail, provided that the project continues to represent a sound investment at the point where a final decision to press forward with it has to be taken. The national road schemes would comprise the remaining widening projects on the **M25** and the other longer term London road schemes in the national programme. As to smaller schemes which might also form part of the fifth tranche, London Transport are currently studying with local authorities and others the feasibility of light rail and other intermediate modes in 12 corridors in outer London. It would be premature to attempt to assess whether any of these would be justifiable or to assess their relative priorities.

14.35 It is not possible to map out a clear timetable for the projects in the last three tranches in the same way that it was possible for those in the first two tranches. However, the ordering of projects within these tranches does give the best steer possible at present on the relative timings of the different projects. Absolute timings of these projects will depend partly upon affordability, but also (and increasingly) on the commercial judgement of the various private sector players, and therefore the Government can give no indication of a conclusive timescale.

Private Sector Investment

14.36 The projects and investment programmes listed above are dependent in whole or in part on public sector finance. But purely private sector funding is becoming increasingly important to London's transport system. BAA alone are planning to invest nearly £5 billion in their airports at Heathrow, Gatwick, and Stansted over the next 10 years. Bus operators in London, who are now all in the private sector, are expected to replace about 50% of their fleet over the next 10 years at a cost of approximately £275 million. And Railtrack has announced a £1 billion a year investment programme to maintain and renew the network over its first 10 years in the private sector. Much of this will be of direct benefit to track, stations, signalling, bridges and other structures in London. The train operating companies will not be required to pay additional charges to fund the work, although they will be able to change the terms of their contracts with Railtrack to finance additional investment to enable them to offer service improvements.

Chapter 15: Who Delivers the Strategy

Introduction

15.1 This Chapter looks at who is going to do what in order to secure delivery of the transport strategy mapped out in this document. In other words, it is about the allocation of responsibility for transport in London. It starts by setting out the Government's reasons for believing that a strategic transport authority for London would be both undesirable in principle and unworkable in practice. It sets out the Government's own proposals for allocating transport responsibilities within the Capital and for ensuring that there is proper co-ordination between them.

The Concept of a Strategic Transport Authority for London

15.2 There is a widespread belief that the co-ordination of transport in London would be facilitated by the creation of a strategic transport authority. Views on the precise nature and role of such a body vary significantly. However, there are three common themes. The first is that the strategic transport authority would be responsible for all aspects of transport in London. The second is that it would hold a transport budget for London and be responsible for its apportionment. The third is that it would secure the co-ordination of transport services.

15.3 We look at these three aspects in turn.

Responsibility for all Aspects of Transport in London

15.4 There are three more or less distinct tiers of transport provision in London.

15.5 At one end of the spectrum, there are the national networks of railway lines, motorways and principal trunk roads, at whose hub London lies. Although they converge on London and have an important part to play in facilitating the movement of goods and people to, from and within the Capital, these networks constitute a national asset, meeting the requirements for inter-regional and international transport movements. Responsibility for these networks must, in the Government's view, rest with national-level bodies. Thus, the responsibility for framing the national roads programme rests with Ministers and the responsibility for implementing it rests with the Highways Agency. Similarly, responsibility for provision of rail infrastructure rests with Railtrack, responsibility for specifying the passenger services with the Franchising Director, and

regulatory responsibility with the Office of the Rail Regulator.

15.6 At the other end of the spectrum, there are the essentially local transport networks, which exist primarily to facilitate movement within a single Borough or between adjacent Boroughs. The vast majority of London's roads fall within this category. So do some public transport networks, such as the proposed Croydon Tramlink or the local bus networks. Much of transport activity in outer London generally fits into this category. Outer London is dealt with in more detail below.

15.7 Between these two extremes, there are London-wide networks. The London Underground system clearly falls within this category. So does much of the bus network. There are also roads which are of more than local importance, even though they could not properly be categorised as forming part of the national road network.

15.8 This intermediate tier is an extremely important one, and much of this strategy is devoted to it. Much of our investment programme is, likewise, devoted to improving the quality of London Underground services and much of our action programme concentrates on facilitating longer distance movement of traffic within London, particularly by bus. Nevertheless, it is not the only tier. A strategic body that concentrated only on these issues would not be taking the overview which proponents claim to require. And its responsibilities would overlap, to a very significant extent, with those of LT.

A Transport Budget for London

15.9 The Government's forward expenditure plans are reviewed annually by a Cabinet Committee, EDX, which is chaired by the Chancellor of the Exchequer. On the basis of advice from EDX, Cabinet collectively determines the apportionment of public expenditure between Government Departments. It is then for the Secretary of State for Transport to determine what provision he makes, within his budget, for London Transport and for other areas of transport expenditure (of which the most substantial are OPRAF, the national roads programme and support for local authority transport schemes). In the case of London Transport, the Secretary of State sets four separate budgets. Three of them cover specific projects or responsibilities the construction of the Jubilee Line Extension, the preparation of the Crossrail scheme and the operation of the Dial-a-Ride service. The fourth covers the operations of the existing bus and Underground networks. It is up to London Transport to determine how they apply this fourth budget plus the revenues earned from fares and other sources. In doing so, they must have regard to the financial, safety and quality of service objectives which they have been set and the investment appraisal criteria which Government has laid down. However, decisions on how their budget is to be spent and on what the priorities are rests firmly with the Board of LT and its subsidiaries. Over the past three years LT has invested over £500 million each year in the existing network.

15.10 On the basis of this explanation of the existing funding regime for LT (which has similarities to the regimes for OPRAF, the Highways Agency and the local authorities, although there are also some important differences), what would the role of the new strategic authority be? Would it take decisions which currently rest with Ministers? If so, that would be unacceptable to Government. Or would it take decisions which currently rest with LT? If so, that represents an unacceptable encroachment into their day-to-day management responsibility.

15.11 It is sometimes suggested that the route out of this *impasse* is to create a separate transport budget for London. The suggestion is that Ministers would decide what level of funding to allocate **to** this budget and the strategic authority **within** it. However, as noted in paragraph 13.13, there are many areas where the attribution of transport expenditure between London and the rest of the country is difficult. Since their principal purposes is to link communities up, transport infrastructure and services cannot be expected to respect arbitrary geographical boundaries. The rail and road networks straddle the Greater London boundary and so do the public transport services which use them. Although we believe it is sensible to take stock periodically of the level of transport expenditure which is being incurred either in London or for the benefit of London, we do not believe it is possible to construct a transport budget for London.

Co-ordinating the Provision of Transport Services

15.12 We regard the proper co-ordination of the provision of transport services as a matter of vital importance. It lies at the heart of our concept of what an integrated transport system is. However, we do not believe that this is something which can be imposed from above either by Government or by a strategic transport authority. If a new authority were created, it would have to decide how it proposed to further the goal of securing intermodal interchange, for example.

15.13 One approach would be to proceed by a combination of exhortation and facilitation. That is the approach which the Government is currently pursuing, and which is explained more fully below. We believe that it is a sensible approach, but we do not believe that the creation of a new authority would add anything to the existing machinery

15.14 The alternative approach would be for the strategic authority to secure such interchange itself, with power to overrule operators' decisions on the planning of rail services, the siting of bus stops and the design of Tube stations. This is the approach which proponents of the strategic authority appear to favour. In our view, however, it rests upon a dangerous error. There are in London around 17,000 bus-stops, 269 Tube stations and 893 local stations, coping with around 7 million journeys daily. It is not realistic to envisage a centralised authority trying to take decisions on every aspect of rail, bus and Tube service provision and all the interconnections between them. If it endeavoured to do so, it would spawn a massive bureaucracy, which would become a brake upon progress, rather than a spur to it.

The Government's Approach

15.15 In its approach to transport, both nationally and at the London level, the Government has consistently stressed the importance of having practical decisions taken by those who are closest to the needs of users and to the wishes of local communities. Wherever possible, the Government has sought to privatise transport operations, because it believes that users will get a better service at a lower price from operators whose financial survival depends upon their ability to meet users' needs cost-effectively.

15.16 Similarly, the Government believes that responsibility for designing solutions to local transport problems should rest with the Boroughs and that they, in turn, need to involve local communities and businesses more actively in debating those issues.

A recurrent theme of this document is that transport choices are difficult. There is seldom a perfect solution, which achieves all goals and satisfies all parties. It is therefore important to secure local ownership of solutions to local problems.

15.17 Accordingly, our emphasis is on decentralisation of responsibility and on voluntary co-operation, but with co-ordinating mechanisms available if required.

Voluntary Co-operation

15.18 The principle of voluntary co-operation can best be illustrated by citing a couple of practical examples.

15.19 The London bus priority network (described more fully at paragraph 10.64 above) is being taken forward by the London Boroughs. Individual Boroughs are responsible for the design and implementation of the measures on the roads for which they are responsible. Groups of Boroughs work together to co-ordinate the measures which are being taken in the four quadrants of the Capital and in the central area, reflecting the obvious fact that bus routes tend to straddle Borough boundaries and that there may be little real gain from facilitating bus movements on one side of a Borough boundary, if they then become clogged-up at a bottleneck on the other side. Finally, at the topmost level, the delivery of the Bus priority network is co-ordinated by a London-wide committee of Borough representatives, which meets regularly with the Government Office for London, the Traffic Director, the Highways Agency and London Transport to review progress on the implementation of the network.

15.20 This three-tier structure may appear cumbersome, but it has worked well in practice, and it reflects the fact that there is an important local dimension to the issue. At the London-wide level, the need for a bus priority network is universally accepted and the benefits to the Capital are treated as self-evident. At the local level, however, the introduction of a new stretch of bus-lane may be viewed with some alarm by traders and residents, concerned about the possible impact of the new measures on access to their premises. In some cases, the concerns will be groundless. In other cases, they will be legitimate and will need to be accommodated to the extent consistent with delivery of the primary objective of facilitating bus movement. Either way, the concerns arise at the local level and are best met there.

15.21 We see the bus priority network as an excellent example of an initiative which is being implemented at the local level and co-ordinated, on a voluntary basis, at the London-wide level. The work of the Parking Committee (touched on at paragraph 11.29 above) is another example of this approach. These are models which we would encourage the Boroughs to build upon in addressing other issues, such as the need for a genuinely London-wide approach to night movements of lorries and the exercise of their responsibilities for air quality and for the maintenance of roads and bridges. At a more local level, Boroughs can, in conjunction with operators, actively promote better interchange between modes. Projects such as the Wood Green Transport Interchange and Stratford Regional Station which have both received TPP funding, are good examples of this approach. Working with developers, Boroughs can also promote development which is less reliant on road access.

15.22 Similarly, it is important that London's transport operators talk to one another about their forward plans. There is a difficult balance to be struck here between competition and co-operation. At one level, of course, the operators are in competition with one another for market-share. Such competition is entirely healthy, and works to the benefit of users. The Government has no wish to discourage it, and the regulatory authorities would take a dim view of anything which savoured of an operators' cartel. However, operators also have a shared interest in growing the public transport market within which they all operate. There are issues about interchange facilities, passenger information and new approaches to ticketing which they need to discuss, because failure to co-ordinate would have an adverse impact on all their businesses and on London, too.

15.23 We would expect both bus and train operators to work closely with one another and with London Underground to promote public transport in London. The formation of such links does not require pressure from Government and would not benefit from it. It is, rather, a natural response to the challenges which confront all public transport operators and to the complexity of the London transport scene. So far the rail operators nationally have formed the Association of Train Operating Companies (ATOC). ATOC administers their participation in industry wide schemes, including co-operation with London Transport on Travelcard, through ticketing for journeys that involve crossing

London and the London Concessionary Travel Scheme.

15.24 Last but not least, it is important to foster partnerships which bring together representatives of businesses and local communities in order to reach a clear consensus on what an area's transport needs are and how they can best be met. London Pride has done this at the London-wide level. There are also many successful partnerships at the local level. Stratford Development Partnership, for example, has placed the emphasis on the provision of transport infrastructure and has received assistance with the new bus station in Stratford town centre and improvements to the local road network to improve pedestrian access.

Government Co-ordination

15.25 The Secretary of State for the Environment is also the Minister for London. He chairs EDL(L), which is the Cabinet Committee responsible for co-ordinating all aspects of Government policy on London matters. The Minister for Transport in London, the Minister without Portfolio, and Ministers from the Home Office, Treasury, Office of Public Service and the Departments of Trade and Industry, Health, Education and Employment, Environment, National Heritage and Social Security are also members of the Committee. The main responsibility of EDL(L) is to look at London issues in the round, and to ensure that the different strands of Government policy are properly drawn together. For example, we have stressed in this strategy the important contribution which transport can make towards promoting London's competitive position, but the competitiveness of the Capital is also affected by many other Government policies - on education and training, on land-use planning and housing, on the regulation of business and promotion of trade and so on. It is EDL(L)'s responsibility, supported by the Government Office for London, to ensure that the right policies are being pursued in London and to ensure also that London issues are taken fully into account when national level policy decisions are being taken.

15.26 Like any other organisation, the Government requires the ability to debate new ideas and initiatives in private before canvassing them publicly. The Cabinet Committees provide the fora in which such debates can take place. Accordingly, their deliberations are confidential. The Government does not intend to make an exception to this rule in the case of EDL(L). However, the Government does recognise the need to have a forum, which brings together Ministers and the key London partners, where transport issues of vital importance to the Capital can be debated publicly. To this end, we have established the Transport Working Group and Transport Co-ordination Group.

15.27 The Transport Working Group (TWG) meets twice yearly under the chairmanship of the Minister for Transport in London. The TWG provides a forum in which the main providers of transport infrastructure and services can compare their forward plans and consider how they interact. Its members are;

The Minister for Transport in London (Chairman)

London Transport

London Underground Ltd

London Transport Buses

Q Drive Buses Limited (representing bus operators)

Railtrack plc

British Rail

Office of Passenger Rail Franchising

London Docklands Development Corporation

Highways Agency

BAA plc

London Regional Passengers Committee

London Planning Advisory Committee

Traffic Director for London

Traffic Commissioner

Association of London Government

London First

15.28 The Transport Co-ordination Group (TCG) meets more frequently and is chaired by the Regional Director of the Government Office for London. It has two main purposes. The first is to keep all those who are involved in meeting London's transport needs abreast of developments outside their immediate area of responsibility. To take an obvious example, it is particularly helpful to bus operators to have advance warning of major roadworks. The second is to generate pressure to remove the obstacles which stand in the way of individual transport schemes. For example, a proposal to enhance the frequency of a train service will require OPRAF, the train operators and Railtrack to agree what additional services they can support and the Boroughs to deal with the associated planning applications. There is a real risk that delay in one area could jeopardise the project timetable. TCG provides a forum in which progress on such projects can be checked at regular intervals.

15.29 As well as chairing the TWG and sitting on EDL(L), the Minister for Transport in London has a much broader role to play. He is responsible, under the Secretary of State for Transport, for policy on all aspects of transport in the Capital. In particular, he is responsible for taking a view on the relative priorities of all the competing claims for funds for transport in London. This also entails ensuring, so far as possible, that allocations of transport funds take into account the allocation of funds for transport-related projects from, for example, the SRB Challenge Fund and European Structural Funds. The Government Office for London, which advises Ministers on the allocations of transport and regeneration programmes, has a key role in ensuring decisions on TPP and SRB funds are co-ordinated, and encouraging local authorities to integrate bids for both programmes. GOL also brings together policy development for both transport and planning in London.

The Balance of Responsibilities in Outer London

15.30 While the GLC was in existence, many of the outer London Boroughs resented the GLC's involvement in ones which, quite rightly, they regarded as matters for local decision. As we have stressed, we subscribe to the principle that transport decisions should be made at the lowest practical level. As described above, some London-wide priorities, such as the strategic movement of traffic or the need to promote access to the central business districts, require more central direction. But this is not generally the case in outer London.

15.31 Part of the reason for this is quite simply that parts of outer London differ so greatly. To take an example, Croydon is a major retail and business centre in its own right, quite separate from the central area in many respects. Some areas of outer London, for instance in Bromley, are semi-rural. Some areas are much more closely related in economic terms to inner

and central London, for example predominantly residential areas providing housing for those that work elsewhere. On the retail side, a hierarchy of roles exists, which is illustrated in *Strategic Guidance for London Planning Authorities.*

15.32 These complexities need to be reflected in how transport is planned and managed. The transport picture across outer London is complicated to begin with. Roads in outer London vary from high quality dual carriageways and motorways, to narrow and congested single carriageway roads. Some town centres are bypassed, while others lie directly on the trunk road network. Some areas are well served by a variety of public transport connections while others are relatively poorly served and by radial services only. Several of the town centres in outer London have acute traffic problems leading to problems of air quality as well as congestion. Because of this complexity, and the important role outer London Boroughs have in relation to the economic priorities of their own areas, we believe they should generally be in the lead in establishing priorities. Clearly they must operate with reference to other bodies, and taking proper account of developments where we have established that a London-wide approach, as with the Red Route Network, or a sub-regional approach, as with regeneration programmes, is sensible.

15.33 One of the biggest challenges facing outer London Boroughs is deciding where the balance should lie between seeking to meet demands for car travel or promoting public transport. Whilst the outer London boroughs are currently subject to somewhat lower levels of congestion than central and inner London, there is a steady downward trend in average speeds and, unlike central London, where the system appears to be nearing saturation, there remains considerable scope in outer London for traffic levels to continue rising for some time. The latest average traffic speeds for outer London throughout the day are between 7 and 11 miles per hour faster in outer London than they are in the central area, and between 4 and 7 miles per hour faster than in inner London.

15.34 Some of these problems will be alleviated through central Government action. It has a clear interest in the management and development of the strategic road network; it has an interest in providing for investment in public transport systems; and it has a role in devising strategic planning guidance that is as important for outer London as it is for the central and inner areas. Ensuring local input into strategic traffic programmes, co-ordination between public transport investment and the local scene, and the implementation of planning guidance then falls to Boroughs, either individually or in co-operation.

15.35 The Government is keen to stimulate co-operation between outer London boroughs and other transport providers. This can be achieved through the operation of funding regimes such as City Challenge, TPP, SRB and Capital Challenge if it goes ahead. The success of this approach to date is demonstrated in projects such as;

- the SWELTRAC initiative, which involves a consortium of 10 Boroughs who are working with public transport operators in devising an integrated strategy to restrain demand for car use and promote public transport in south and west London;

- the Wood Green interchange project, promoted by Haringey in conjunction with London Underground and London Transport Buses;

- Stratford Regional Station, involving Newham, the Jubilee Line Extension team and Railtrack,

The structural framework for development set out in the *Thames Gateway Planning Framework and Strategic Guidance for London Planning Authorities* provides a sound basis for such co-operation to continue in the future.

15.36 The Government also welcomes LT's current work on intermediate modes in outer London in which they are exploring potential for improved public transport, from enhanced bus services to light rail. Of course, there will be considerable funding constraints, particularly on light rail schemes, given their high costs. Dedicated bus systems of different types may be a more affordable way forward over the next few years. In any case, as with Croydon Tramlink, the private sector will have to play a considerable role in funding, building and operating any future schemes, which will clearly mean that potential schemes will require a very sound financial and economic case.

Scope for Greater Involvement of Partners

15.37 Of course, co-ordinating committees, important though they are, are not enough on their own to ensure the implementation of this transport strategy. We believe that there is scope for greater involvement of London Partners in the process. Our specific proposals designed to achieve this are as follows;

- we will publish a report in May 1997 and annually thereafter covering progress in achieving the strategy; we are inviting the London Pride Partnership to work with us on the areas this should cover;

- as part of the TPP process, the Government Office for London will seek the views of local government representatives, on the allocation of resources to local transport projects, to gain a clearer idea of London-wide priorities.

- in particular we will continue to work closely with Boroughs on the development of a London-wide bridge maintenance strategy, based on the 'sector approach' to TPP funding; we will consider widening this approach to other areas of working as well, if this seems justified.

15.38 We are happy to consider further ways of involving partners constructively in delivering this strategy.

Conclusion

15.39 With London's economy the size of many small countries, with its multi-faceted economy and pattern of land use, with its complex transport needs reflected in its local regional, national and international connections, we conclude that both managing the existing networks and developing them to meet the needs of London in the 21st century, requires commitment and energy from a wide range of different organisations, working in partnership. For many issues there exist perfectly adequate organisational arrangements which are able to consider the needs of the travelling public, those adversely affected by transport, businesses and other groups. For some of the newer areas, such as air quality management, we are actively considering what the best organisational arrangements should be, building on those which already exist. The publication of this strategy, and importantly the follow-up action to it, will itself provide a focus to take the strategy forward.

Bibliography

London's Action Programme for Transport 1995-2010:- London Pride Partnership; 1995.

Transport in London:- Department of Transport; 1989.

Sub National Population Projections, England, 1993 Based:- Office for National Statistics; HMSO; 1995.

MEPLAN Model for London and the South East (LASER), Scenario Tests for London, Final Report:- Marcial Echenique and Partners; 1995.

London Traffic Monitoring Report:- Department of Transport; HMSO; 1995.

Travel Trends in the London Area: Analyses of the LATS Time Series Database 1971 to 1991: Transport Research Laboratory; 1996.

Managing the Trunk Road Programme:- Department of Transport; HMSO; November 1995.

Competitiveness: Helping Business Win:- CM2463; Department of Trade and Industry; HMSO; 1994.

Competitiveness: Forging Ahead:- CM2867; Department of Trade and Industry; HMSO; 1995.

Healey and Baker: European Real Estate Monitor, Europe's Top Cities:- Healey and Baker; 1995.

Business Relocation: The Case of London and the South East:- Prism Research, University of Liverpool and the Department of the Environment; 1992.

Transport: The Way Forward; Department of Transport; HMSO; 1996.

Sustainable Development: the UK Strategy:- CM2426; Department of the Environment; HMSO; 1994.

Planning Policy Guidance PPG13: Transport:- Department of the Environment and the Department of Transport; HMSO; March 1994.

Strategic Guidance for London Planning Authorities, Consultation Draft:- Government Office for London; March 1995.

Planning Policy Guidance PPG24 - Planning and Noise:- Department of the Environment; 1994.

Neighbour Noise Working Party Recommendations:- Department of the Environment; 1995.

Highways Agency Landscape Strategy for the London Trunk Road Network:- Department of Transport; HMSO; November 1995.

Study of London's Green Corridors:- Countryside Commission; 1995.

Eighteenth Report on Transport and the Environment:- CM2673; Royal Commission on Environmental Pollution; HMSO; October 1994.

1994 Advice on Strategic Planning for London:- ADV26; London Planning Advisory Committee; 1994.

Runway Capacity to Serve the South East, A Report by the Working Group:- Department of Transport; July 1993.

Report of the Heathrow Airport Runway Capacity Enhancement Study:- National Air Traffic Services, International Air Transport Association, British Airports Authority PLC; August 1994.

Up in the Air? Airport Strategy for London:- Association of London Government; 1996.

The London Heliport Study:- Department of Transport; March 1995.

Railtrack Network Management Statement: Developing a Network for Britain's Needs:- Railtrack PLC; December 1995.

Thames Strategy:- Government Office for London; HMSO; May 1995.

Planning Policy Guidance PPG13: A Guide to Better Practice:- Department of the Environment and the Department of Transport; HMSO; October 1995.

Traffic Director for London, Network Plan:- Traffic Director for London; March 1993.

The London Congestion Charging Research Programme - Principal Findings:- MVA Consultants and the Government Office for London; HMSO; July 1995.

Informal Park and Ride Behaviour in London:- Transport Research Laboratory Project Report; Transport Research Laboratory; 1993.

Central London Rail Study:- Department of Transport, Network South East, London Regional Transport and London Underground Ltd; January 1989.

West London Assessment Study, Stage 2 Option Report:- Department of Transport; December 1989.

South Circular Assessment Study Option Report:- Department of Transport; December 1989.

East London Assessment Study:- Department of Transport; December 1989.

South London Assessment Study:- Department of Transport; December 1989.

Regional Planning Guidance RPG9a: Thames Gateway Planning Framework:- Department of the Environment; HMSO; September 1994.

Consultation on River Crossings to the East of Tower Bridge:- Government Office for London; June 1995.

New Ideas for Public Transport in Outer London:- London Transport Planning; June 1995.

Transport Report 1996: The Government's Expenditure Plans, 1996-97 to 1998-99:- CM3206; Department of Transport, Office of the Rail Regulator, Office for Passenger Rail Franchising; HMSO; March 1995.

Transport Statistics for London: 1995:- Department of Transport; HMSO; October 1995.

Travel in London: London Area Transport Survey 1991:- Department of Transport and London Research Centre; HMSO; March 1994.

This Common Inheritance:- CM1200; Department of the Environment HMSO; September 1990.

This Common Inheritance: First Year Report:- CM1655; Department of the Environment; HMSO, 1991.

This Common Inheritance: Second Year Report:- CM2068; Department of the Environment; HMSO, 1992.

This Common Inheritance: Third Year Report:- CM2549; Department of the Environment; HMSO, 1992.

Planning London's Transport:- London Transport; October 1995.

National Travel Survey, 1991-93:- Department of Transport; HMSO; September 1994.

Printed in the United Kingdom for HMSO
Dd 302485 4/96 C25